Indie Horrors!

The Not-To-Be-Missed, The Acceptable, and The Forgettable

HOLLYWOOD DVD

FROM THE SPECIAL FX TEAM WHO CREATED
FROM DUSK TILL DAWN • SPAWN • WISHMASTER

SOMETHING VERY HUNGRY IS ABOUT TO HATCH!

SPIDERS

15

Indie Horrors!

The Not-To-Be-Missed, The Acceptable, and The Forgettable

by Barry Atkinson

Midnight Marquee Press, Inc.
Baltimore, Maryland, USA

Copyright © 2012 Barry Atkinson
Interior layout: Gary J. Svehla
Cover design: Susan Svehla
Copy Editor: Linda J. Walter

Midnight Marquee Press, Inc., Gary J. Svehla and A. Susan Svehla do not assume any responsibility for the accuracy, completeness, topicality or quality of the information in this book. All views expressed or material contained within are the sole responsibility of the author Barry Atkinson.

Without limiting the rights under copyright reserved above, no part of this publication may be reproduced, stored in or introduced into a retrieval system, or transmitted, in any form, or by any means (electronic, mechanical, photocopying, recording or otherwise), without the prior written permission of the copyright owner or the publishers of the book.

ISBN 13: 978-1-936168-28-6
Library of Congress Catalog Card Number 2012938172
Manufactured in the United States of America

First Printing by Midnight Marquee Press, Inc., August 2012

Dedication

Once again, thanks go to my wife,
whose patience while sitting through
*666: The Child, Hybrid, Alien Intruder, The Glow,
Shark Swarm, Total Force, Hydrosphere, The Raven*
and many, many others of their caliber knows no bounds!
And to the island of Crete.
In many ways, this book is a legacy
of my four years spent living there.

I Know Who Killed Me

TABLE OF CONTENTS

Page 8
NEVER HEARD OF IT!

Page 10
HOOKED

Page 12
SIMPLY NOT GOOD ENOUGH

Page 17
235 INDIE HORRORS REVIEWED

Never Heard of It!

Welcome to the wonderful world of the independent, cut-price horror, science fiction and fantasy movie. Movies where most of the aliens are, well, for want of a better word, *Alien* rip-offs; where the leading men and women display all the emotions of cardboard cut-outs; where decent music is more or less non-existent; where direction veers from the truly sublime to the utterly ridiculous; where plots are ruthlessly plagiarized from other, more high-profile productions; where special effects aren't all that special; where the level of gore has to be seen to be believed; where the hero is good-looking but wooden and the heroine a blonde/brunette bimbo; where the dialogue is stilted and shored up with stock phrases; and where the cheapo ethics immortalized by Edward D. Wood, Jr., Jerry Warren and their ilk are still being kept alive and well by courtesy of Nu Image, Asylum, American World Pictures, North American Pictures, RHI Entertainment, UFO, Castel Film Romania, Cinetel Films, PM Entertainment and a host of other small film companies specializing in low-budget fare.

But before we all pronounce sentence, start to sneer, utter hoots of derision and sweep this lot under the carpet, let's pause for a second and take stock of these fascinatingly guilty delights alongside top-rate (but still classed as independent) movies. Movies that were given a limited cinema release but subsequently pulled off the circuits through lack of audience interest. These indie movies *can* be quite entertaining in their own unconventional, quirky fashion, particularly for those of us sick to the back teeth of hackneyed, million-dollar fantasy epics where pomposity rules, where the slogan "This is a Very Important Motion Picture and You Must Watch It" might just as well be emblazoned across posters and in the trailers. Yes, *Campfire Tales*, *High Plains Invaders*, *Reeker* and *Alien Siege* are low-budget fare, but so what? They're fun to watch for what many would

think are all the wrong reasons, but for others all the *right* reasons. As was nearly always the case with '50s and '60s B films, they get down to low-budget moviemaking basics and ideals. These movies are simple variations, if you like, on well-worn genre themes, occasionally coming up trumps (against the odds) with a minor classic. *Alien Lockdown, Croc, Haunted Forest* and *Romasanta: The Werewolf Hunt* are all thoroughly enjoyable, highly commendable exercises in sci-fi thrills, monster mayhem, supernatural-mystery chills and gruesome horror, more than making up for the truly abysmal cinematic techniques displayed in *Alien vs. Hunter, Dracula 3000, Hologram Man* and *Ancient Evil: Scream of the Mummy*. More to the point, this sub-genre has to be of special interest to all buffs *because* of its absolute inaccessibility. British TV, bearing a rather snooty attitude with regard to any product deemed unfamiliar to its audience, containing no big-name actors and obsessed with the celebrity culture (plus, of course, the all-important ratings), would never in a month of Sundays screen something so obscure as *Post Impact* (not even late at night), choosing the better-known (and more mainstream) *Deep Impact* instead. The controlling bodies just aren't adventurous enough and will not take any chances. Majority vs. minority, the latter is the loser. As a result of this blinkered attitude, your average U.K. fantasy aficionado is probably totally unaware that unusual fodder like this exists and he/she is missing out on all the cheapo action. I'm British and lived in Greece while writing the majority of this book, but my brother Dave, residing in England and being a horror/sci-fi buff since the late 1960s, has never, ever come across *Rise of the Gargoyles, Mammoth, Babysitter Wanted, Lake Dead, Deep Freeze, Hoboken Hollow, 30,000 Leagues Under the Sea, Attack of the Sabretooth* or *Rottweiler*.

"Dave, *Mega Shark vs. Giant Octopus* was on MBC2 the other night."

"*Mega Shark vs.* what?"

"*Mega Shark vs. Giant Octopus*. Haven't you ever heard of it?"

"No!"

He wasn't even aware that straight-to-DVD sequels to *Carrie* (*The Rage: Carrie 2*) and *Single White Female* (*Single White Female 2: The Psycho*) existed. Screened mostly on American TV if screened at all, the rest of the world is being deprived of the dubious joys of sitting through these (once in a while) extraordinarily imaginative yet discount fantasy features which, in a way, are far truer to their roots than the latest $100 million fantasy epic playing at the local multiplex, embodying in their chemistry and vision the true spirit of the '50s, the halcyon period for *all* films of a fantastical nature. Hopefully, the selection of movies contained within these pages will bring them to a wider fan base and whet people's appetite for more of the same thing. Therefore, as Martina Ittenbach, one of the inhabitants of the *House of Blood*, might say: "Viewest thou and happieth be!"

Hooked

Yes, American fantasy, horror, science fiction fans may well be familiar with *Dragon, Frankenstein Reborn* and *Alien Siege;* we British are most definitely not. As stated, British television (the various BBC and ITV stations, Channel Four and Channel Five plus those satellite channels available in the United Kingdom) wouldn't be allowed, under the current, still strict censorship laws to screen Asylum's gore-laden *Frankenstein* flick, not even in the wee small hours of the morning. "Mainstream" is the name of their game—independent, non-conformist horror movies don't get a look-see and probably never will. After all, corporate reasoning asks who on Earth would want to sit and watch something like *Boa vs. Python* when 1997's *Anaconda* is up for grabs? The answer is simple—long-standing horror buffs, that's who! So with this in mind, how did I, a British citizen, get to know about the indie horror film industry? Here's how it came to pass.

Moving to Crete in January 2007, the divide in culture between England and Greece came as a severe shock, but none more so than in television presentations and programs. Greek TV is made up of wall-to-wall soap operas, chat shows, second-rate celebrities and game shows, mindless entertainment aimed at the couch potato masses. But sandwiched between this avalanche of dross are the movies (shown uncut), and some surprisingly unfamiliar ones at that.

One evening, a feature called *Lost City Raiders* (due on at 11:30 p.m.) drew my attention, shown on Crete's Mega channel. The title didn't register, rang no bells and couldn't be found in my extensive collection of literature on the cinema. I sat through the initial 20 minutes and, although moderately intrigued, gave up on it, deciding the picture was some kind of cheap made-for-television fodder not worthy of consideration. Four weeks later, on Alpha, *Creature Unknown* (yes, it *was* unknown to this viewer!) made an appearance—the opening 10 minutes of this cheapskate monster offering was all I could put up with before pressing the "off" button on my remote. Catching snippets of *Epoch: Evolution*, *Spiders 2*, *Savage Planet*, *Octopus* and *Shark Attack*, plus the final 15 minutes of *Crimson Force*, didn't really arouse my interest until I had satellite television installed, allowing me access to the five Arabian MBC movie channels, where I quickly noticed that these oddities were being screened regularly (though often very late at night) on MBC2 and MBC Persia, unedited, complete with the blood and guts, the sex, the nudity and the bad language. The ubiquitous *Creature Unknown* manifested itself at one in the morning on MBC2 before I thought, "What the hell. Let's give at least one of these peculiarities a go." Therefore, Nu Image's *Alien Lockdown* (shown as *Creature*) was the first indie that I actually caught in its entirety, followed by *Shark Attack 3: Megalodon* and *Reptilicant*. Then I did what any self-respecting buff would do under the circumstances—checked these offbeat movies out on the internet, when all became more or less clear as to their origins. Now, several months down the line, I was totally hooked! The Arabian channels tend to broadcast three or four indies a week (many, it must be said, repeated), which means I'm now up to speed on such glorious pieces of hokum as *Wyvern*, *Pterodactyl*, *King of the Lost World*, *Deadly Water*, *MosquitoMan*, *Larva*, *Undead*, *War of the Worlds* (Asylum's, not Spielberg's), *Tyrannosaurus Azteca*, *Frankenfish* and *Croc*, not forgetting more teen horror movies than you can shake a stick at. Cheap, tacky, corny, gruesome and totally free of modern-day filmmaking pomposity—that's just how I like 'em! I've always been a sucker for this type of fare (any fan who paid good money over 45 years ago to sit through *Bride of the Monster*, *Killers from Space*, *The Beast of Yucca Flats* and *The Incredible Petrified World* will know what I mean!), so for anybody who has never acquainted themselves with these grade B, and quite often grade Z, thrills of a (sometimes) non-professional type, try sampling a few of the titles contained within these pages. They may well open up a whole new world of fantasy/horror entertainment!

Simply Not Good Enough

Some movies are destined never to make it onto the silver screen, to be shown in their proper environment, a cinema, or, if they *are* released, because of public apathy and failure at the box office, the company decides that enough is enough and hurriedly removes their commodity from circulation. The movie will turn up on DVD months (or even years) later. These curiosities tend to fall into four categories: films so poorly conceived that they are released onto DVD in double-quick time; films made specifically for TV/DVD/video release only; films shown in cinemas for a brief spell, then transferred to DVD; and what I class as "non-films," productions that lack a vital spark, that certain "something" that determines whether or not a paying audience will be satisfied at the end of the afternoon with what they have sat through. Catch, if you can, *A Sound of Thunder*, an expensive disaster (backed by Warner Bros.) of the first order, yet put together with the assistance of one of the planet's biggest film producers. Something somewhere is missing, that vital extra ingredient that binds all the pieces of the jigsaw that go into making a feature film a worthwhile experience. What went wrong? Did the production team view their finished article at the end of the day, turn round to each other and say "Jesus, what a load of crap. Who in their right mind would want to watch this?" No one could *ever* imagine paying to see this motion picture in a cinema. It's simply very weak, uninteresting, inferior product—film-it-by-numbers fare for the teens and young adults.

Equally cheap and cheerful low-grade Ed Wood-type efforts like *King Cobra, Reptilicant, Something Beneath* and *Hybrid*, produced by smaller, independent studios, turn up on American TV but hardly anywhere else, which, in a way, makes it all the more interesting in trying to track them down. Although the majority of the features reviewed in the following pages have never been screened commercially in the United Kingdom, either in the cinema or on television, some have played theatrically in countries like Sweden, Portugal and other European backwaters. Others (*The Dark, Death Tunnel*) have had a brief cinema run before being pulled off the circuits (*including* Britain). Numerous productions (*Catacombs, Frayed*) have been unjustly criticized and inevitably withdrawn from nationwide release on the assumption that they lack mass-audience appeal. Some (*Whisper, Visitors*) have been deemed unfit material for a cinema airing and many are straight-to-DVD fodder. Quite a few (*First Born, The Crows, Ariana's Quest, The Barber, Danika*) are so rare they've hardly been seen at all, and then there are those (*Chronicle of the Raven, Guardians*) that have been honored with a screening at an indie film festival or convention, but nowhere else. Each and every picture, in its own way, whether it is unbelievably tacky (*Savage Planet*), a hidden gem (*Out for Blood*), an undiscovered nugget (*The Hunt*) or has been unfairly panned by the critics (*The Gathering*), is worth a look. Most of them are far more entertaining than their vastly inflated big brothers and will appeal to all devotees of both '50s/'60s fantasy fodder and continental horror cinema. You never know—you could be in for a real surprise! The following assortment of guilty pleasures, schlock, genuine goodies and minor classics, 235 in total, all fall into this unorthodox and quite frankly bizarre category of fantasy filmmaking that would pass by without being noticed. Could be that in years to come, many of these freaky delights will be looked upon as cult viewing for the fantasy connoisseur. But first here's "the canon" for anyone not familiar with these mainly straight-to-DVD flicks. Most of these indie productions share the following characteristics.

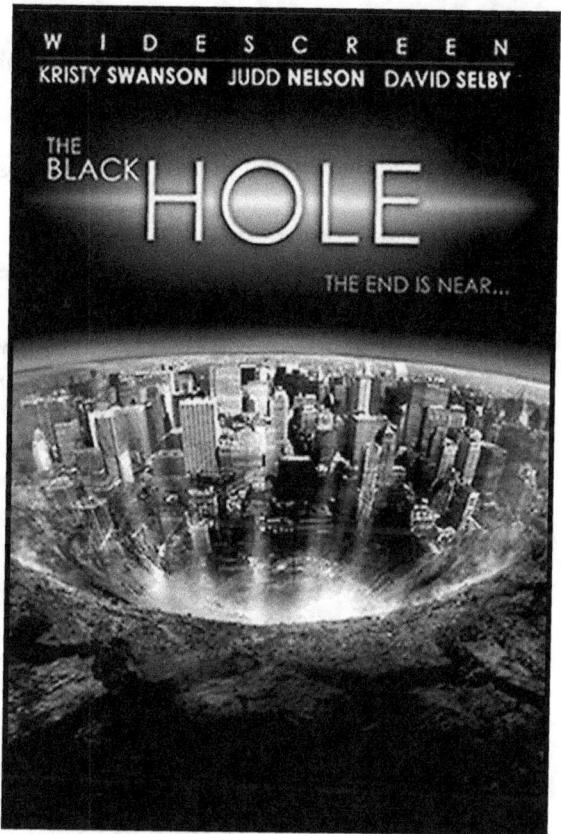

Many films are released with two titles, one specifically for American distribution, and the other for worldwide markets and are international in scope: Canadian, Russian, Czechoslovakian, Romanian, Italian, French and Spanish, among others.

Most leading characters have an ex-wife/husband/girlfriend/boyfriend who just happens to be in on the action.

The paleontologist/anthropologist/marine biologist/doctor is nearly always female, a foil for the all-action male hero.

All science fiction, space movies commence with some lively, half-decent CGI effects that tend to evaporate after 10 minutes, picking up toward the end, leaving a lengthy middle section that can be interminably tedious at times.

Most aliens depicted are bald and resemble humans, some sporting black tattoo-like markings—monster-type aliens tend to smack of cut-price H.R. Giger-type creations.

Screenplays are packed with clichés plundered from hundreds of other fantasy films, with very little originality in the dialogue, which is just as well when you consider the stilted manner in which these lines are delivered, more often than not in very low audio.

Soundtracks, or a musical background, exist, but if you think that you'll get to hear a Hans J. Salter or James Bernard masterwork, you're in for a bitter disappointment. There isn't a single soundtrack among the films reviewed that I would want to listen to over and over again.

Directors tend to concentrate on close-ups and rapid editing to disguise shoddy effects.

You'll see far more gore, viscera, decapitations, dismemberments, disembowelments and plain old blood and guts on display than in your common or garden-variety high-budget cinema release—for instance, *Hoboken Hollow* makes *The Texas Chain Saw Massacre* (both versions) look like a children's tea party, while Universal's *Jaws* pictures pale beside the butchery served up in Nu Image's *Shark Attack* trilogy. And I haven't even mentioned *The Mangler Reborn* or *Jolly Roger: Massacre at Cutter's Cove*!

All aliens/vampires leak green blood.

Those hunted will always stumble across an abandoned, dilapidated house in the woods.

Female nudity is often prominently on display, the busty females all high-class babes!

Directors love plenty of slightly distorted views from the aliens' perspectives, opaque or one-tone color—red or green.

Directorial styles range from *Blair Witch*-inspired camcorder efforts, shaky close-ups, wobbly pans and the odd flash of brilliance. Inconsistency is the name of the game—there are no Jack Arnolds or Edward L. Cahns among *these* filmmakers! Still, many unfamiliar names manage to put on a good show.

All teams or groups facing danger quarrel-argue-disagree with one other. Where's the camaraderie that's supposed to bind these people together?

Many scenes appear showing the cast prowling furtively through corridors and tunnels in close proximity to the monster/alien that is stalking them.

A large number of plots and storylines are unashamedly lifted directly from bigger, more expensive pictures. B versions of A movies, if you like.

Is he dead? Is she dead? Are the children dead? Are they *all* dead? This scenario crops up time and time again, *Danika* and *Long Distance* being superb examples of this style of brain-teasing moviemaking.

The town sheriff is always up against the town mayor whose edict is, "Profits Before Lives," regardless of the killing machine causing havoc in their midst.

There's always a baddie involved who gets his (or her) comeuppance in the final reel, and everyone else in the cast never makes it, except for just two—the hero and heroine.

And in that final reel, those few seconds of screen time, just when you think the protagonist has been finished off, there's the obligatory "no, it *hasn't* been finished off" shot—a waving feeler (*Deep Freeze*), Gary Daniels' green eyes (*Reptilicant*) and Kevin Zegers' room under attack from the "night things" (*Fear* of the Dark); all say, loud and clear, "you thought it was dead, but it ain't!"

By and large, the main leads (male and female) are chosen for their perfectly honed good looks and *not* for their acting ability, which ranges from wooden to passable.

A sprinkling of plots derive inspiration from factual events, or so they say, but take this with a pinch of salt!

Sci-fi disaster movies always have a discredited scientist who returns to save the day.

Budget restraints notwithstanding, audiences get to see some attractive location photography in many of these productions.

Average running time is a respectable 90 minutes—only *Shark Swarm* outstays its welcome at a ridiculous, stamina-sapping 169 minutes.

A trick ending is mandatory.

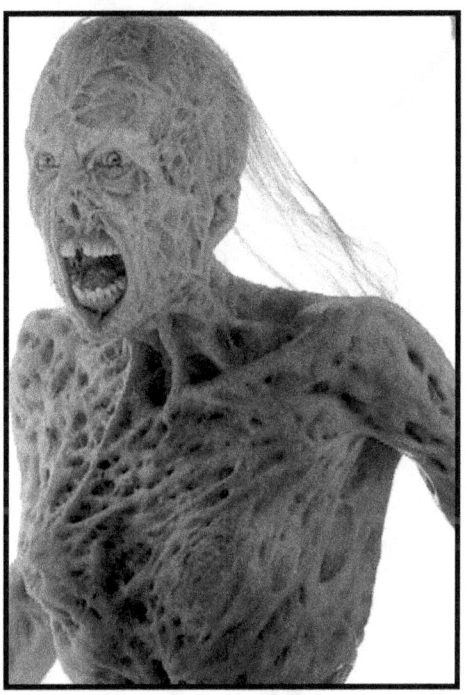

The make-up team creates a great monster from *Darkness Falls.*

Remember, when sitting down after slotting the DVD into your home system, these are movies produced by the likes of Asylum, Nu Image, Sci Fi Pictures and American World Pictures, *not* Columbia, Paramount, 20th Century Fox or Universal. Apart from the odd exception, there are no A-listers flaunting inflated egos on parade. Millions of dollars have *not* been spent on actors, but in a lot of ways, that's an advantage—these movies don't profess to be anything other than what they actually are, so comparisons with fare served up by the majors become a rather pointless exercise, as does needlessly trashing and being overly judgmental. Let's try not to be negative here! Personally, I would rather curl up on the sofa and watch *Deep Core* than the over-trumpeted *The Core* any day of the week. Get these facts sorted out in your head first, don't expect miracles, try not to analyze these productions too much, disengage the brain for 90 minutes and be prepared to enjoy these features just that little bit more!

Film Ratings

Indie Classic	☠☠☠☠☠
Excellent	☠☠☠☠
Good	☠☠☠
Average	☠☠
Poor	☠

235 Indie Horrors Reviewed

Absolute Zero
Front Street Pictures/Marvista Ent. 2006; 86 minutes; Director: Robert Lee; Rating: ☠☠

The Earth's poles are reversed through global warming, leading to a new Ice Age in many parts of the world as temperatures plunge to -273C (-459F).

Absolute Zero is full of so many scientific improbabilities that it's best to turn a deaf ear to what's being said by scientists Jeff Fahey and Bill Dow and concentrate on this piece of sub-*The Day After Tomorrow* whimsy concerning the cataclysmic effects on the Earth's climate due to polarity reversal. The opening sequence blatantly rips off the opening sequence from Roland Emmerich's blockbuster. A research team in Antarctica are almost separated when a deep crevasse opens at their feet, and after a 10,000-year-old body is discovered in an ice cave, paintings on the walls tell of a similar disaster eons in the past, Fahey is up against the objectionable Dow, arguing over the impending big freeze, meeting ex-wife Erika Eleniak and two computer nerds (Fred Ewanuick and Brittney Irvin), thus setting the scene for Miami to be enveloped in raging snow storms and cyclonic winds. Special effects-wise, *Absolute Zero* delivers the goodies in cheapish fashion—shots show an iced-over Miami, blizzards, a berg drifting into the city's

marina, destructive rollercoaster winds, frozen seas and dark cloud masses. But it's a very long time indeed, since we have been subjected to the sight of actors on a sound stage going through the motions in front of a back-projected screen. Dialogue-wise, it's best to take with a hefty pinch of salt the oft-quoted expression made by Fahey and company, "Science is never wrong," because that's certainly the case in this picture! The protracted middle section—Dow trapped in an elevator; Eleniak and daughter Jessica Amlee attempting to rescue the ungrateful, loud-mouthed slob; and Fahey and the computer geeks trying to restore power to the building they are trapped in—sags, the movie picking up toward the climax, a TV broadcast showing the planet to now have a frozen south and tropical north. No happy ending, then! Okay, *Absolute Zero* is no big-bucks presentation, more like a mid-'60s second-feature, but at least it's short and, on its obvious low budget, whiles away the time in adequate fashion.

Alien Abduction
Asylum 2005; 90 minutes; Director: Eric Forsberg; Rating: ☠☠☠☠

Two couples camping in dense woodlands are abducted by hostile aliens and rendered unconscious. When one of the women awakes, she finds herself quarantined in a military hospital with other abductees, all undergoing a disturbing series of tests, examinations and interrogations.

Asylum's nightmarish take on *Invasion of the Body Snatchers* may indeed be low-budget fare, but it's low-budget fare that packs a wallop, some scenes guaranteed to upset the more delicate viewer. What is the real truth that lies

behind the sinister, Spartan establishment where Megan Lee Ethridge's friends have been reduced to a state of semi-idiocy; where parasitic creatures resembling large woodlice erupt from people's bodies and are kept in glass tanks; where human heads are drilled with a strange-looking instrument; where inmates (some disfigured) shuffle around in filthy, neglected rooms like prisoners in an insane asylum; where alien monsters are strapped to beds and where Ethridge is tortured by electric shock treatment? This is what our heroine sets out to unravel as she escapes from her cell via the utility conduits and disguises herself as a nurse. She befriends a male doctor in her quest to solve the facility's secret. Forsberg plants ambiguous clues all over the shop to keep us on our toes—maps pinpointing worldwide UFO sightings, newspaper cuttings concerning Roswell, weird sounds, zombie-like guards and those squirming woodlice—before Ethridge rounds up her fellow campers and attempts to lead them to safety. The conclusion—that she, along with her friends and everybody else in the hospital, are alien replicas cloned from their human counterparts kept in suspended animation in cocoons—comes as a genuine surprise. The final sequence is of the two couples back in the woods where they meet a hiker who informs them that they are the center of intense media speculation surrounding their sudden disappearance—but this is just what the

alien leaders wanted in their plans to take over the world. For a cheapie, *Alien Abduction* contains a pretty good otherworldly score from one Peter Saltzman, but unfortunately, the audio balance throughout fluctuates between half-decent and dreadful, the soundtrack drowning out all dialogue in many scenes. Ethridge, though, is excellent, and we even get to see the lithesome actress strip off for an all-over wash. Her winning performance, together with some moments of sickening torture and not-too-bad alien monsters, go to making this one of Asylum's worthier efforts and a whole lot more riveting than the host of other dull, big-screen variations on Don Siegel's seminal 1956 science fiction thriller.

Alien Intruder

PM Entertainment 1993; 120 minutes; Director: Ricardo Jacques Gale; Rating: ☠

Year 2022. USS Presley is sent into the forbidden "G" sector to determine the fate of USS Honey, whose last message was a distress signal.

In what amounts to nothing more than an overblown episode from the original *Star Trek* series, ship's captain Billy Dee Williams walks through *Alien Intruder* carrying the demeanor of a man suffering from acute depression. You will too after sitting through this monumentally underwhelming slice of space garbage from the PM Entertainment stable of ham-fisted sci-fi actioners, all of which *have* to commence with an extended shoot-out. This movie doesn't buck the trend, with 15 boring minutes of men blasting away at each other, all fighting to win the hand of voluptuous Ariel (Tracy Scoggins), clad in red PVC. Scoggins is, in fact, the product of an alien virus that has entered the Honey's computers, a projected (but very real) hologram that can drive oversexed men mad with her wily come-ons. Williams and four chosen convicts from an outer space Alcatraz head off to find out what happened to the Honey's crew. On Fridays, the cons, to keep them amused and in tow, are allowed to settle down in pods to experience their own virtual reality fantasies, all involving a desirable, compliant woman—The Wild West, a biker gang, surfing and a monochrome *film noir* nightclub. Reaching "G" sector ("No one has ever made it out") after three months and docking with the Honey, Williams and his gang meet up with holographic Scoggins, who soon has the lot of them at each other's throats, crazy with lust and, in the flatly handled climax, looping her arms around startled survivor Maxwell Caulfield after both ships have been blown to bits. The spacecraft are about as amateurish as those featured in *Conquest of Space* way back in 1955, and the acting is strictly-by-numbers. Gale's direction is rudimentary, the storyline juvenile, the soundtrack loud and tuneless and the production marred by fuzzy color. *Alien Intruder*, it has to be said, is one hell of a dull space opera.

Alien Lockdown
aka: **Creature**

Nu Image 2004; 90 minutes; Director: Tim Cox; Rating: ☠☠☠

A meteorite containing a mysterious green rock crashes on Earth in the distant past. Centuries later the rock is discovered in a crater by a team of archaeologists and taken to an isolated laboratory in the Rocky Mountains, where a demented scientist unlocks its DNA code to genetically engineer a violent alien race that is nothing more than an invading fighting machine, hell-bent on destroying the planet.

Cox's *Alien* imitation is a cut above the average and features a pretty good (although not original) monster, created by CGI and animatronics. Geneticist John Savage closes down his mountain research facility and calls on the military for assistance when the creature he has created from the ancient DNA runs out of control. In flies a S.W.A.T. team, headed by beautiful assassin Michelle Goh, who then find themselves on the run from the monster and its face-hugging offspring. The alien hops around the corridors for most of the time like a gigantic mutated reptilian dog, with deadly fangs and claws, occasionally simply sloping off to do its own thing. It's an impressive creation for fodder of this caliber and Cox directs with a fair degree of imagination and suspense. After most of the team members have been slain by the creature and hordes of baby aliens are multiplying like crazy, Goh plants a nuclear device and obliterates the complex and the aliens along with it. Cheaply produced, maybe, but amusing hokum all the same. *Alien Lockdown* is atmospheric in parts and contains good effects work.

Alien Siege

UFO 2005; 91 minutes; Director: Robert Stradd; Rating: ☠☠

The Kolkus, a dying race fatally infected by a lethal virus, attack Earth, requiring the blood of eight million humans to prevent them from becoming extinct.

This run-of-the-mill sci-fi effort starts off in merry fashion as Earth is bombarded by blue rays from a giant orb in space (cue for newsreel footage of natural disasters) and its leaders are then ordered by the Kolkus to provide a "harvest" of humans, 800,000 of which are Americans. If this dictate is ignored, the planet and its inhabitants will be exterminated. The plot revolves around wooden hunk Brad Johnson's efforts to rescue his daughter (Erin Ross) from the mother ship, where she is being held in isolation. The girl has a rare blood anomaly that repairs the virus-racked alien bodies in double-quick time, and the devious ship's commander wants her for himself, planning to take the ship and Ross back to his world through a wormhole in space. As is usual with these thrifty programmers, we get a neat first 10 minutes, a tidy climax and a stodgy filling. Johnson and a team of resistance fighters spend all their time running from the aliens and their fighting craft as he desperately tries to locate his own

amateur-looking ray gun machine that somehow has the capability (looking at the mechanism, which resembles a giant hairdryer) to blast the alien orb from the skies after, of course, he has managed to grab his daughter from their clutches. He succeeds in the end, thus saving the Earth. One or two nice touches on display prevent the mind from wandering. Hundreds of human donors being herded on board a transporter like cattle, their belongings heaped on the camp floor in scenes reminiscent of a Holocaust movie, is most effective. And shots of the fighting craft hunting down the resistance in the woods are executed in reasonable fashion. But, why are the aliens depicted in these cheapos *always* bald (one or two sport hair, but not many)? Can't we have aliens that at least *don't* resemble humans? Quite obviously, the film's budget has been expended on the opening sequence of events, showing the enemy fleet poised above the Earth, and the budget is on display again in the closing few minutes, as Johnson somehow uses his non-flying skills to pilot a small shuttle back to Earth with his daughter, the Kolkus commander and his crew all dead. Carl Weathers crops up as a military man on the side of the freedom fighters. There are a few exciting skirmishes, but overall this is mediocre tosh that just about manages to prevent your eyes from closing over its 91-minute running time.

Alien vs. Alien
aka: **Showdown at Area 51**
Nu Image 2007; 96 minutes; Director: C. Roma; Rating: ☠

   Two warring aliens land near a wildlife refuge. One has arrived to disarm a buried device that has the ability to release a gas that will destroy the Earth; the other is determined to prevent him from carrying out the task, thus paving the way for an alien invasion.
   Most of this cheapo's budget seems to have been spent on the credits sequence, displaying the solar system in all its glory, the fleet of alien ships appearing out of nowhere at the end and two alien crafts battling in a dogfight. Between this, we have the pilots emerging from their ships and spending the

remainder of the film in combat with one another. Each of these humanoid oddballs is decked out in a tacky garb resembling old radiation suits, frogmen's outfits and gas masks, with *Predator*-style weaponry to match. A bunch of dim-witted grunts charge around armed with enough weapons to stock an arsenal, getting slaughtered by these visitors, while a regular guy (Jason London) and his ex search desperately for the "Omega C" weapon, apparently filched from a wrecked alien ship during the 1947 Roswell UFO sightings. Yes, one of those dumb-looking visitors (the nice one) *does* remove his helmet,

but no hideous monster features here, only a shaven-headed male with yellow eyes and face tattoos. The drawn-out climax sees the explosive device located in a chamber deep beneath a rickety barn where it is disabled with a cipher rod after the two aliens have killed off each other. The enemy fleet then departs into outer space. Blonde Gigi Edgley is attractive in a tramp-like fashion as the ex-girlfriend. One or two imaginative moments occur (the underground chamber appears to be half-full of ancient bones and the shots of the massed alien vessels high above the Earth are splendid). C. Roma's bottom-of-the-barrel nonsense is good for a laugh or two, and little else. It's an uninspiring sci-fi clunker of the first order.

Alien vs. Hunter
aka: **AVH: Alien vs. Hunter**
Asylum 2007; 90 minutes; Director: Scott Harper; Rating: ☠

A savage, flesh-eating creature from another world lands in the mountains, soon to be participating in sport between it and an alien big game hunter.

A technically inept sci-fi outing also released under the title *AVH: Alien vs. Hunter*, so don't confuse it with *AVP: Alien vs. Predator*, because if you do, you're in for one helluva shock! Harper's tawdry *Alien/Predator* rip-off represents filmmaking at its most atrocious. Grizzled writer William Katt is jogging along the highway as something falls out of the sky behind him. After he catches a lift from a police officer, the two discover a wrecked spaceship in the woods, the officer savaged to death by a barely glimpsed monster emerging from the craft. After the lively opening 10 minutes, *AVH* crash-dives into a catalogue of bad acting, skew-whiff direction (Harper's camera wobbles and wanders all over the place), slapdash editing, witless dialogue ("Guys, we're in the shit and that totally sucks."), appalling continuity (the same scenes repeated ad infinitum) and lame creature effects. Basically, we have a bunch of characters groping their way through dripping tunnels. Add to this a group of trigger-happy locals trooping through the woods, each being picked off either by the monster (a ferocious H.R. Giger-type alien whose torso is joined onto the body of a large spider—sometimes!) or the hunter, who stomps around in conquistador armor, observing everything through a red-tinted lens. As in *Predator*, he can also appear and disappear at the touch of a button. And like *Alien*, there is one scene that is such a shamefaced steal from Ridley Scott's thriller, where one of the cast is trapped in a tunnel lined with sticky goo, the creature lurking in the shadows (remember Harry Dean Stanton's demise?). If an official of 20th Century Fox ever caught this movie, he or she would be on the telephone to their lawyers for out-and-out plagiarism charges. Katt eventually blows the creature to bits and pieces with a gun filched from the hunter's ship, after most of the cast have been slaughtered. There are a few half-decent flourishes here, including the blood-spattered monster feasting on the entrails of one of its victims; the humans viewed as green, multifaceted images by the alien; and clever photography shot in an orange tint, giving the film a slightly surreal edge. But *AVH*'s failings are legion, and that especially applies to the baffling ending whereby the hunter, after receiving a garbled communication on his ship's radio, removes his helmet to reveal a human face smoking a cigarette. What this is all about, Lord knows. And does anyone actually care? Because, on balance, *Alien vs. Hunter,* as the character in the movie says, sucks!

Alligator 2: The Mutation
Golden Hawk Ent./Group 1 Films 1991; 92 minutes; Director: Jon Hess; Rating: ☠

A crooked Realtor's plans to develop the Regent Park Lakeside resort by ousting the local residents from their homes come unstuck when a voracious chemically enhanced alligator turns up in the town's sewers.

Eleven years on from *Alligator*, we have possibly one of the dreariest sequels ever produced, a 1991 monster movie masquerading as a 1956 one, although even in 1956, bottom-of-the-barrel filmmakers such as Bert I. Gordon could have come up with a more realistic giant 'gator than the model shown here, a large mechanical (and fake-looking) head and tail, together with a few desultory shots of the reptile slowly wading through water. Steve Railsback not only dumps toxic waste into the sewers, he's trampling over all and sundry in order to get his far-from-legal property development project off the ground. The spineless mayor (Bill Daley) is in his pocket, refusing to put a halt to Carnival Day, even though cop Joseph Bologna informs him of the fanged terror gobbling up down-and-outs. Bologna says the monster may now be lurking in the lake, a potential threat to public safety. Dee Wallace-Stone plays Bologna's doctor wife, Brock Peters is the hard-pressed chief of police, Richard Lynch the leader of a gang of five alligator hunters and Holly Gagnier is the mayor's daughter. It's a reasonable cast simply playing out the tired plot to its predictable conclusion—Railsback topples into the lake and is eaten and the alligator, having swallowed a quantity of dynamite, is blown to bits without a single ounce of tension, suspense, excitement or even gore-spattered effects to get the juices flowing. Hell, this lame effort makes RHI's *Croc* appear to be an Oscar nominee by comparison. And that cheesy ending, with everybody clapping as Bologna and his partner emerge victorious from the sewers, the saurian scattered to the four winds, makes 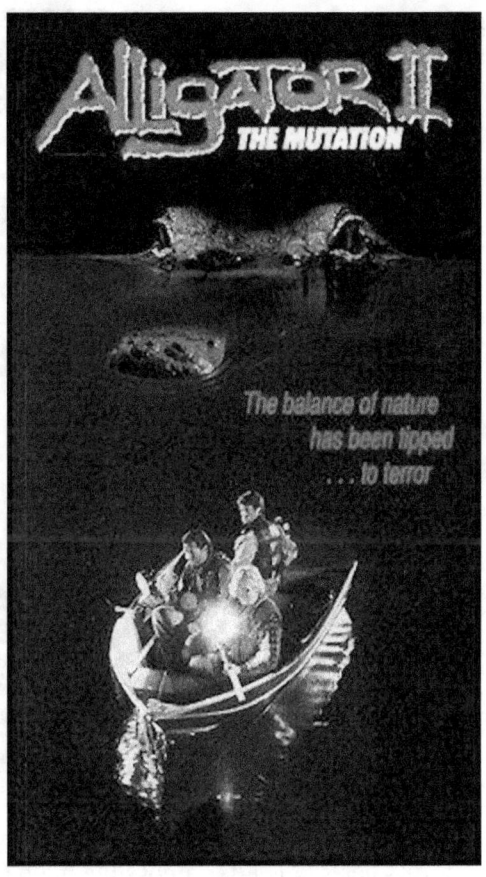 for cringe-worthy viewing in the extreme. A film to give all giant alligator/crocodile movies a bad name!

An Erotic Werewolf in London
Seduction Films/E.I. Independent Cinema 2006; 69 minutes; Director: William Hellfire; Rating: ☠☠☠

A lesbian lycanthrope travels to London to seek out the necessary sexual thrills that will arouse her into becoming a werewolf during the full moon.

Erotic lesbianism isn't exactly new to the horror genre. Hammer gave it a go in *Lust for a Vampire* (1970), while the continentals liberally sprinkled lesbian scenes throughout their 1960s/1970s pictures, giving the British censor an almighty headache in the process. Then we had Jesus Franco's explicit *Vampyros Lesbos* (1971), a low-budget effort that had vampiress Susan Korda sucking the life out of her victims, and *not* from their necks! But these were vampires. What about werewolves? Well, werewolves aren't exactly sexy unless you produce a softcore (verging on hardcore) flick featuring nubile porn princess Misty Mundae and her scrumptious pals writhing pleasurably all over one another, their new

friend, Anoushka, a werewolf who inflicts Mundae with lycanthropy after a bout of steamy (eight minutes long) lovemaking. There's very little cinematic prowess on offer here, but that's not the aim. The aim is to titillate and, in this respect, *An Erotic Werewolf in London* succeeds in spades. In between the groping, the panting and the orgasmic lust (the opening sex scene with Ruby LaRocca in a gay bar lasts 12 minutes; Mundae is seduced by two randy female nurses), reporter Zoe Moonshine is ordered by her boss, editor John Link (this actor should visit a dentist—urgently!), to write an article about the growing number of werewolf attacks in London. So the girl interviews blonde, slinky Anoushka who informs her she is after a possible mate (Linda Murray is the target), as well as all the succulent female flesh she can sink her teeth into. There are three transformation scenes, if you can call them that—Anoushka (twice) and, at the end, Mundae. They both sprout fangs, tuft hair and long black fingernails, growling like bitches in heat (which, judging by their performances, they are!), but you'll be so engrossed by the amount of full-frontal goodies on show that you probably won't even notice them. This is the kind of prohibited movie that the dirty raincoat brigade could only catch in Britain's art-house cinemas during the 1960s. Hellfire's salacious morsel will ensure that you'll never need to take those Viagra tablets again—and it's best not to read too much significance into the film's running time!

Anacondas: The Hunt for the Blood Orchid
Middle Fork Productions 2004; 97 minutes; Director: Dwight H. Little; Rating: ☠☠

On behalf of a pharmaceutical company, a scientific team travels to the jungles of Borneo to collect a species of rare orchid with life-enhancing properties, but the orchid only flowers once in seven years. Unfortunately for them, the trip coincides with the anacondas' mating season and the giant reptiles are in a frisky mood!

A belated, medium-budget sequel to 1997's *Anaconda* (which didn't get a decent cinema run in Britain), Little's no-brainer is stocked full of unappealing characters and seen-it-all-before situations. It features very few scenes of giant snake action, contains a low gore count, suffers from an incredibly banal script and is hampered by a plot that could have been written on the back of a postage stamp in 60 seconds. A team of doctors (three guys, two gals) hire a rickety boat from beefcake Johnny Messner, motor up the river, tumble over a waterfall, escape from 20-foot snakes that wolf down various cast members, and await another battered old launch that comes to their rescue but falls foul of a huge reptile. Baddie Matthew Marsden locates the precious red blooms at the expense of a few lives, only to be bitten by a poisonous spider, toppling into a breeding pit full of writhing anacondas as just reward for his misdeeds. Oh, I nearly forgot to mention Messner's pet monkey, the true star of this lowbrow presentation. Salli Richardson-Whitfield does a bad impersonation of Jennifer Lopez from the original film. KaDee Strickland plays the token blonde babe.  Cowardly Eugene Boyd shrieks incessantly if so much as a leaf flutters behind his back. The steaming, rain-drenched jungle settings save the movie from being a one-star bummer; oddly, the film has the look and feel of 1995's *Congo*, itself a hyped-up box-office flop, an artificial horror adventure in all aspects. Independent companies Asylum or Nu Image would have had a field-day with this material and come up with a better job—give me *Boa vs. Python* any time!

Ancient Evil: Scream of the Mummy
Rapid Heart Pictures 1999; 86 minutes; Director: David DeCoteau; Rating: ☠

An ancient Aztec mummy is revived in a museum and goes on a rampage, assisted by a deranged student worshipper.

This is a stinker of epic proportions that can be summed up in two words—indescribably dreadful. What a flimsy excuse for a story! Five archaeology students and their teacher fall prey to an Aztec mummy that is resurrected by a crazed sixth student. The overweight, shambling, bandaged figure with the face of a car-crash victim disposes of the teacher and three of her students with

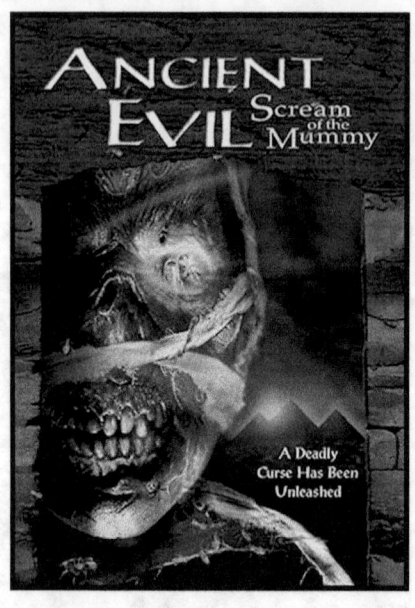

a curved dagger, before killing acolyte Trent Latta, ridiculously kitted out in a tatty Aztec costume and expiring with a gurgle after a tussle with Jeff Peterson. Filmed at deadening pace in four rooms and a verandah area, employing incessant flashing blue lights of the pantomime variety to signify lightning and over-using the tilted camera angles designed (unsuccessfully) to drum up some tension, this one-dimensional disaster must surely rank as a contender for the worst horror movie (and certainly the worst *Mummy* movie) ever made. Acting, direction and script plumb new depths in awfulness, making the likes of *Pharaoh's Curse* (1956) and *The Mummy's Shroud* (1966) seem like masterpieces by comparison. If there *is* such a thing as a "Horror Hall of Shame," then DeCoteau's abysmal concoction should be sitting right there at the top of the pile.

Ariana's Quest
aka: **Sins of the Realm**
North American Pictures 2002; 94 minutes; Director: Lloyd A. Simandl; Rating: ☠ (or ☠☠☠☠☠)

In medieval times, the deposed queen of the Kingdom of Andora journeys to the end of the world to seek out a magical sword that will restore her to the throne.

Rarely seen outside of Europe, Simandl's Czechoslovakian/Canadian collaboration reaches unimaginable heights in silliness, campiness and kitsch. The dialogue is straight out of the pages of *The Black Shield of Falworth* (1954), the castle sets the kind you would see at a school play, the acting amateurishly hammy and the direction not far short of Jerry Warren's legendary clunkers of the 1950s. It's got one-star rating written all over it. But wait—surely it must warrant five stars because *Ariana's Quest* is so obscure, such a curiosity, so awful in parts that it's the very *embodiment* of the indie movie, almost a classic of bad taste in every department. Rena Mero plays Ariana—loose blouse, plunging cleavage, skin-tight pants, knee-length boots, blonde rinse, headband and pronounced American accent. This woman looks as though she has just emerged from a Los Angeles beauty parlor. When Mero's father dies, she is crowned queen but the slobbering Predrag Bjelic arrives from a rival kingdom, demanding her hand in marriage and an heir. Aided by a female thief (Eva

Aichmajerova), PVC-clad Mero escapes from his vile embrace and is pursued by PVC-clad assassin Daniela Krhutova who, after a promise of freedom from slavery, joins forces with the two women in their search for the sword, which is hidden in a remote cave. Meanwhile, Bjelic's scheming sister (Katerina Brozova, also attired in PVC) poisons Bjelic. "The King is dead. Long live the Queen," she shouts triumphantly through surgically enhanced lips (this phrase is repeated three times overall). Krhutova (the spitting image of Patricia Laffan in *Devil Girl from Mars*) is killed in a skirmish before the other two women reach the cave, cross a river of molten lava and confront the new queen of Andora in a cardboard-looking cavern. The priceless conclusion to this outlandish piece of tat has Mero retrieving the sword from the sacred stone and Brozova

perishing when the roof caves in. The ex-queen and her light-fingered pal emerge from a well into a vast Egyptian temple. Krhutova's sensuous spirit appears in a blue Egyptian dress, looking like Liz Taylor's Cleopatra, guiding the couple on the road to a flaming red dawn with the promise of a new future. Umpteen minutes devoted to theatrical swordplay produce not one single drop of blood. The blaring, chanting music (accent on crashing cymbals) grates on the nerves after the first quarter of an hour, and Mero's ample bosom rises and falls every time she moves, threatening to spill out of her skimpy costumes. Thought-provoking this picture is *not*! But what it *will* do is put a smile on your face—after all, 94 minutes doesn't come any more ludicrous than Simandl's Czech-ploitation fantasy feature. And the female leads, dumb though they may be, are all mouth-wateringly ravishing!

Asylum
Hyde Park Pictures 2008; 93 minutes; Director: David R. Ellis; Rating: ☠☠

Six students explore a forbidden wing in their college, which was formerly an asylum presided over by a mad surgeon who specialized in torturing neurotic teenagers.

There have been almost a score of horror films released under the *Asylum* banner, but unfortunately, this isn't one of the better ones. Ellis' fluid camerawork in the opening sequences, tracking Sarah Roemer on her first day at

college, will lull you into a false sense of security. Are we to finally experience a teen horror movie with a bit more wit and intelligence than most? The answer, regrettably, is no. Roemer teams up with ex-druggie Jake Muxworthy and four other youngsters, all nursing disturbed backgrounds. We encounter computer whiz kid Cody Kasch (abused by his drunken mother), preening hunk Travis Van Winkle (fed on junk food by his demented mother), Latino doll Carolina Garcia (abused by her father) and blonde bimbo Ellen Holman (abused by her parents). Janitor Joe Inscoe knows all about the old Burke asylum—he was an inmate in the place when only nine years old. Roemer herself saw her mentally ill father shoot himself dead when she was eight, her brother committing the same act years later. Does insanity run in her family? Breaking into the coded numbers of a locking system (via Kasch's computer) and entering the catwalk that connects the reputedly haunted dorm to the asylum, an asylum abandoned in 1939 after doctor Mark Rolston was murdered by his patients for carrying out one lobotomy too many, the group explores the dark, grim hospital wards and spooky, empty corridors, completely unaware that Rolston's withered-featured phantom is lurking in the shadows. They are then, one by one, cornered by the doctor who shows each victim a brief, traumatic vision from their past lives ("Give me your pain and suffering"), before plunging a metal spike into each of their eyes (Garcia gets to be trepanned). Roemer and Muxworthy are the surviving couple that escapes into the woods, followed by Rolston. Roemer shoves a metal spike through *his* head and he disintegrates in clouds of black smoke, the ectoplasmic incarnations of his former patients gathering in the light to rejoice in their tormentor's vanquishment, celebrating good triumphing over evil. Although well-paced and smartly edited, *Asylum* is cliché-ridden teen horror fare and even die-hards must now be hardened to the kind of atrocities on show here, which admittedly are bloodily executed but become wearisome after a while. Rolston acts like a third-rate Freddy Krueger, exuding not an ounce of menace, and the teens, although marginally less obnoxious than normal, are still profanity-spouting teens, whichever way you look at it. This is okay fodder for a mid-1980s audience, perhaps, but for 2008, kids on the run in derelict asylums have worn a bit thin.

Attack of the Sabretooth
Sci Fi Pictures/Film Brokers Intl. 2005; 90 minutes; Director: George Miller; Rating: ☠☠☠

On the Fijian island of Valalola, a tycoon is attempting to interest investors in a theme park that features, as its main attraction, two sabretooth tigers of the species Smilodon, cloned from fossilized DNA.

First, here's the kitsch ending. Owner Nicholas Bell of the Valalola Island resort flees from a one-ton sabretooth with deformed hindquarters, the monster slamming against the door that Bell has quickly shut behind him. The vibrations cause one of the gold-painted fangs of a huge model Smilodon on the building's roof to work loose and plummet to Earth, straight through the tycoon's open mouth, spearing him to the ground. Miller must have been so taken with this scene that he shows it from different angles for around 15 seconds, his camera lingering over the grotesque, outstretched corpse. But the rest of this chirpy *Jurassic Park* rip-off is just as way-out, not to mention gruesome. White-suited Bell is hosting a swish party to persuade wealthy investors to back his venture, a "Primal Park containing genetic miracles, a unique zoo," promising them untold riches as, according to him, the project is a sure-fire winner. However, several things happen to put a spoke in Bell's high-flying works. His despised brother-in-law (Robert Carradine) arrives on the scene, bimbo on arm, sneering at Bell's preposterous ideas. Five teens turn up on a scavenger hunt, breaking into the restricted half-constructed site and cutting off the power. And in the opening few minutes, a security guard loses his arm, and his insides, to a monstrous beast. After 30 minutes, chaos reigns—the security system is down and two big cats and a massive, deformed specimen embark

on a rampage (they've been bred as bulimic, preferring to kill for the pleasure rather than appetite), nipping off heads, gorging on entrails and severing limbs. Gore-wise, *Attack of the Sabretooth*'s quota hits the high spots. Blonde Amanda Stephens is decapitated and torn asunder. Teen honcho Billy Aaron Brown loses his head when a predator in the roof plucks it off, the headless body dropping to the floor. Carradine meets the same fate in the outside compound, *his* headless body tottering after his girlfriend. Blood welling from beneath a door forms a lake in the corridor, and a surfeit of severed arms and legs appear. Bell frantically tries to assure all in attendance that nothing is amiss, but behind the scenes, everything *is* amiss! As in Spielberg's dinosaur movie, you have the lab full of fetuses and incubators, the prehistoric park, the disapproving female (Stacy Haiduk), the breakdown in the computer system, the rough-diamond handyman (Brian Wimmer) and, instead of CGI 'raptors, CGI Smilodons stalk their prey (outlined in glowing red) in the confines of the complex. Granted, the acting is ham-fisted at times, the dialogue occasionally crass ("People could get eaten!"), but all in all, this isn't too bad a monster-on-the-loose/gore-fest. It's far better, in fact, than IFG's *Sabretooth*. The giant furry cats look realistic (particularly the misshapen one), and visually, the brightly photographed lush tropical locations are a sight to behold.

The Attic
New Films Intl. 2007; 88 minutes; Director: Mary Lambert; Rating: ☠☠

After moving into her new family home, a young woman is tormented by what appears to be the evil spirit of her long-dead twin sister.

It used to be the maxim that ghost stories in movies had a beginning, a middle and an end, with every plot thread making complete sense, everything tied up by the climax to the satisfaction of all. Not any more. Mary Lambert's supernatural offering (she directed 1989's *Pet Sematary*, not one of the better adaptations of a Stephen King novel), shot digitally by the look of it, leaves all kinds of plot threads hanging in mid-air, meaning the viewer will come away frustrated and not a little annoyed because buried among the twisty storyline is the potential for a nifty little shocker. Elisabeth Moss stars as the distressed youngster, seeing a sickly looking girl uncannily resembling herself in the attic mirror and then again out in the leafy garden. When said spirit forces her to take a tumble out of the attic, Moss embarks on a relationship with hunky paramedic-cum-detective Jason Lewis and enlists his aid in trying to unravel the secret behind the mysterious figure and blue Wiccan symbols appearing on the attic walls. As always, her parents (John Savage and Catherine Mary Stewart), her simpleton brother (Tom Malloy) and psychoanalyst Thomas Jay Ryan refuse to believe her fanciful tales, and we are left to ponder whether the neurotic Moss, withdrawing into a shell, refusing to go out or eat and spending days writing in her diary, is a mental case who is imagining it all. Slashing her brother's throat when the spirit communicates through his lips—"You will never leave this house. This house is part of your soul"—Moss discovers that she *did* have a twin called Beth who was born brain-damaged, dying 12 days after the birth. In a frenetic shambles of a climax, she "kills" the twin (who promptly vanishes), shoots her parents (blaming them for the death of the non-existent Beth) and blows her brains out after learning that there was *no* twin and (more importantly) *no* paramedic/cop (Lewis). In the last few minutes, a new family takes up residence in the house, Lewis is now an estate agent, telling the family's teenage girl (who is looking nervously around the attic) that there is nothing in the house to be afraid of—apart

from him, obviously! No doubt this end scene is meant to tie in with the pre-credits sequence of another teenager done to death by *her* phantom look-alike. So now we have Moss' journal. Was she enacting events that she made up, the product of a fevered mind? We have Lewis. Does he exist and is he somehow connected to the Wiccan symbols, a demon of sorts preying on young women? We have Carl Middleton as an expert in the occult, brought in by Lewis. What has he got to do with any of this? We have Moss' parents. Did they practice witchcraft and did the father harbor unwholesome feelings for his daughter? We have the police. Under what circumstances did a woman die here 30 years previously? By cramming too many eggs into one basket, the potential for a straightforward spooky spine-chiller has been frittered away, presenting a mixed-up brew that has its jumpy moments but not enough cohesion to warrant several viewings (and, as we buffs know, a decent thriller warrants *many* viewings!). Modern-day horror directors please note—less is more!

The Baby's Room
aka: **Peliculas Para No Dormir** and **La Habitacion Del Nino**
Filmax Intl./Telecinco 2006; 77 minutes; Director: Alex de la Iglesia; Rating: ☠☠☠

A couple and their seven-month-old son move into an old house. After settling in for the night, the husband first hears strange laughing noises coming from the child's room. Afterwards he sees a malevolent figure dressed in black hovering over the child's cot on a baby monitor, but when he enters the room, no one is there.

One of the features making up the *6 Films to Keep You Awake* series produced for Spanish television, this simplistic shocker just goes to demonstrate that producers don't need millions of dollars and big-name stars to come up with a supernatural offering that tingles the spine, as *The Baby's Room* certainly does. Javier Gutiérrez and Leonor Watling play the squabbling couple setting up home in a dilapidated building that has seen better days and is shunned by the local residents. When Gutiérrez hears disquieting sounds emanating from the baby's room, he sets up an infrared monitor to find out the cause and, the next night, spots a figure sitting by the crib, staring at the infant with evil intent. The director uses this spooky manifestation as the catalyst for the subsequent deterioration in the couple's shaky marriage. Watling, convinced that her husband is having some form of nervous breakdown because she doesn't see the apparition, moves out with her child as she thinks the tot is at risk. Meanwhile, Gutiérrez, his feverish state of mind affecting his job on a newspaper, sets up a bank of eight monitors that show the house as it *used* to be (hidden rooms behind the wallpaper). Alarming events unfold involving the savage death of a baby and woman at the hands of her insane husband that only the infrared cameras are able to reveal. Marcia Asquerino appears as the gray-haired resident of a home for the aged, warning Gutiérrez that the house harbors a dark, tragic history, and the tangled resolution (or obligatory twist in the tail) will have audiences reaching for the rewind button. Watling is carted off in an ambulance after a fight with her husband, but the man left holding the child may *not* be Gutiérrez. He's trapped inside the place as shown on a monitor screen, the psycho in black having seemingly taken over his role. Putting aside for a moment the woeful dubbing, this overacted continental chiller is of the type that many privately owned British cinemas were quite happy to present to the horror loving public back in the 1960s. Okay, it *looks* that dated, but over 77 rapid-paced minutes, the movie delivers a satisfying number of goose-bumps, far more so than many more costlier efforts.

Babysitter Wanted
Big Screen Entertainment 2008; 83 minutes; Directors: Jonas Barnes and Michael Manasseri; Rating: ☠☠☠

A college student takes up a part-time job of babysitting for a couple's five-year-old son on their rural farmstead, but she finds herself in danger from a killer on the prowl.

A serviceable, low-budget thriller that begins in true carve-'em-up style. A woman, strapped to a bench, marks drawn on her body where a butcher will dismember her—and then, halfway through, the film changes tack, becoming a supernatural/slasher outing. Sarah Thompson stars as the student who agrees to look after young Kai Caster on Friday nights while his parents (Bruce Thomas and Kristen Dalton) are attending local farmers' gatherings. But the girl seems to be under surveillance from the moment she arrives at the farm and Caster himself is an oddity, eating diced raw meat from the fridge (his mother states that he is on a special diet), not uttering a single word except "hungry" and refusing to take off his cowboy hat. Something, obviously, is not quite right with the lad! The movie successfully raises the jumpiness factor by subjecting Thompson (who is great in the role) to the old standbys: the house being watched, lights going off, windows banging, a shadowy figure lurking outside, the boy disappearing, someone constantly telephoning and the door handle rattling. And what is that bizarre arrangement of skulls and candles doing in an alcove? They're connected with the creepy toddler. It transpires that this little devil is the son of Satan, requiring virgin female flesh to feast on, his omnipresent cowboy hat hiding a pair of horns. The boy's father is the murderer and Thompson's stalker, turning out to be a priest determined to exterminate the kid. The final 20 minutes is graphic gore fare. The father butchers one drugged girl in front of Thompson and targets her as the next victim. Thompson escapes after a series of frenzied, bloody head-to-heads involving knives, an ax, meat hooks and guns in which both parents die horribly. The end sees Thompson and boyfriend Matt Dallas retrieving the priest's silver sacrificial dagger from the farm/slaughterhouse and going after the fiendish Caster, who is still out there somewhere with a new parent. The religious motif hinted at early in the picture (Thompson and her mother are both deeply religious Catholics, as is Dallas) is never fully realized, although it loosely ties in with the devil element. In some ways this is a more convincing "satanic brat" feature than the recent *Omen* movie and Thompson virtually carries the action on her own, a one-girl show that doesn't resort to the usual screeching teenage histrionics for a change.

The Barber
Prophecy Entertainment 2002; 94 minutes; Director: Michael Bafaro; Rating: ☠☠

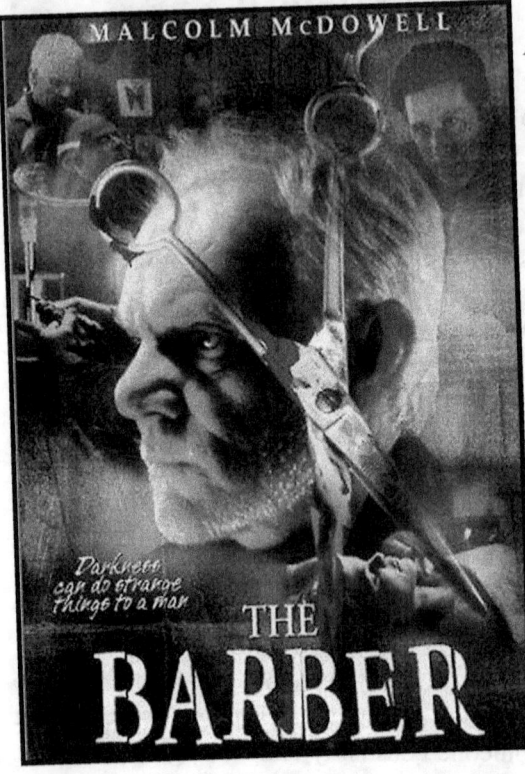

A barber working in the small Alaskan town of Ravelstok is, unbeknown to the residents, the notorious Green River serial killer.

Journeyman actor Malcolm McDowell turned up to star as a cunning psychopath in a little-known Canadian "fruitcake in our midst" drama, adding much-needed gravitas and acting meaning to a mundane production shot in muddy color, mostly at night. When a local prostitute's frozen corpse is found buried in the snow, suspicion concerning her death falls on the local sheriff (Jeremy Ratchford). The FBI send in agent Garwin Sanford to investigate. The wily McDowell (who narrates the story) is by all counts a bit of a ladies' man, despite his age, and carries on committing one cold-blooded murder after another, right under the noses of the law and the redneck community. McDowell hitches a ride out of town at the end, aided by an unsuspecting Sanford, after McDowell has done away with the pathologist, who determined he was the maniac using fingerprint matches. Not really inventive in plot, overly talkative, slow moving and sabotaged to a certain extent by wooden performances (apart from McDowell), *The Barber* strives to be slightly less conventional than other psycho-killer flicks and partly succeeds, but only through the efforts of the always-watchable *Clockwork Orange* star.

Bats
Destination Films 1999; 91 minutes; Director: Louis Morneau; Rating: ☠

African fruit bats genetically engineered by a secret government research laboratory to become killing machines cause havoc in a Texas town.

Bats never made it onto the U.K.'s cinema circuits and it's not hard to understand why. Badly directed (a predominance of close-ups followed by hyperactive camerawork in the bats-against-man sequences), poorly written and stocked with cardboard characters (tomboy doctor/bat expert Dina Meyer, hip black dude and electronics whiz-kid Leon, hick sheriff Lou Diamond Phillips and dastardly mad scientist Bob Gunton), this movie only goes to prove that while bats on their own *can* be scary (the bat as a plot device to induce terror is as old as cinema itself), in a group of thousands, they're no more menacing than a swarm of bees. The plot's over and done with in 10 minutes. Ravaged corpses are discovered in Texas, Meyer deducing the winged mammals to be the culprits. Gunton admits to producing an intelligent, aggressive strain of bat infected with a virus, while Phillips makes eyes at Meyer. The alarming news arises that the flying devils are

capable of conquering America in only six months. The scene is set for panic, pandemonium and evacuation. The story and cast are jettisoned in favor of massed attacks on the populace, people dying, cars crashing and going up in flames, one absurd situation following another (Meyer in a bowling alley ticket booth, fending off the creatures, is a hoot). The final sequence occurs inside a vast mine, where Meyer and company reconnect a crippled cooling machine in a large cavern and then seal the workings with explosives, thus imprisoning the bats. The direction here is flatly handled considering the possibilities for some suspense in this setting. What we have is an uninspiring finale to an uninspiring picture. Granted, the bats' features are grotesquely repellent, a few moments of gore transpire to liven things up (Gunton has his throat ripped out by one of his creations), but the cast looks uncomfortable (especially Phillips) and *Bats* is turgid, nondescript horror for the undiscriminating punter.

The Beast of Bray Road
Asylum 2005; 85 minutes; Director: Leigh Scott; Rating: ☠☠☠☠☠
 The townsfolk of a small rural community in Walworth County, Wisconsin are menaced by a savage creature that, legend has it, was observed as far back as the early 1800s by settlers.

Based on actual accounts of werewolf sightings in the area, *The Beast of Bray Road* is one hell of a horror movie from Asylum, directed with real zest and a feel for the genre by Leigh (*Frankenstein Reborn*) Scott. Based upon these two shows (which would have made a tremendous double-bill in the days when double-bills existed), the man should immediately be put in charge of a major motion picture, but wait a minute! Would one of the big studios *dare* show a werewolf ripping off a girl's leg and chewing on it like a dog with a bone in front of her before she expires in agony, or another female hauled into a tree, the bottom half of her body falling to the ground, followed by entrails and viscera? Probably not, but these scenes of gratuitous blood and guts are part and parcel of the indie scene and Asylum in particular. Another essential element is the scantily dressed bimbos inhabiting these redneck towns, all too willing to strip off without a moment's hesitation for a raunchy sex scene, despite a monster lurking in the vicinity. And this shocker is packed with them. Sheriff Jeff Denton plays the officer up against what he first thinks is a psychotic killer, but blood samples and hair taken from crime scenes show a bewildering mix of human and wolf DNA, thus strengthening the theories of Thomas Downey, a crypto zoologist, who reckons there could be a werewolf, or even Bigfoot himself, prowling the woods, particularly when he discovers unusual teeth marks on a victim's leg bone. A trail of slaughter (heads ripped off, faces slashed, chests clawed open and entrails feasted upon) leads to the hard-to-swallow conclusion (the film's only minus point) that Sarah Lieving, the owner of Kelly's Bar, is the lycanthrope, the girl's eyes changing to green, her fangs bared, as she attacks Denton before being burned alive and dispatched with a volley of silver bullets. Scott orchestrates the gruesome set pieces to perfection (people grabbed in cars; a hairy arm crashing through a doorway; a shambling figure seen out-of-focus) and the beast itself, a cross between a werewolf and a shaggy Yeti, is a refreshing alternative to other movie lycanthropes, although there isn't a single full transformation in the picture. Not that this matters, but *The Beast of Bray Road* is top-notch wolf man fodder and wouldn't look out of place as a feature on the main circuits. It's that good.

The Black Hole
Nu Image 2006; 90 minutes; Director: Tibor Takacs; Rating: ☠☠

At the Midwestern Quantum Research Facility in St. Louis, a radiation leak creates a black hole deep under the laboratory, which threatens to destroy the world.

Not only do we have a revolving black hole but, as a bonus, its bastard offspring, an electrical entity that feeds off power lines, reducing humans to disintegrating skeletons, as it travels around the city with physicists Judd Nelson and Kristy Swanson in hot pursuit. I'm all for movies getting straight into the action, but in the case of *The Black Hole,* there is absolutely no preamble whatsoever, leaving the audience to pick up the plot pieces as Nelson, Swanson, General David Selby and others spout lines of incomprehensible balderdash ("there's an anomaly energy signature"), while the facility crumbles around their ears. Tremors occur, the black hole grows ever larger and a spindly and silvery man-shaped monster, emitting bolts of electricity, smashes through the complex, fixing itself to the nearest pylon. Mister President wants to nuke the black hole but Nelson thinks it best to lure the creature to the expanding mass, which is decimating the city as the two are connected, feeding off each other's energy fields. He succeeds in the end by driving a van, with the thing perched on top, straight at the advancing black hole. Bang! Creature and black hole collide, there's a gigantic blue explosion and it's all over. For such a low-budget sci-fi enterprise, the special effects, mostly seen as television broadcasts of the catastrophe, work well. Buildings topple, the St. Louis Gateway Arch collapses and the entity occasionally reveals eyes and limbs as it creeps along high-voltage cables, searching for power transformers. It wipes out a squad of soldiers in a manner similar to the Id monster in *Forbidden Planet*. What *doesn't* work well is the acting. It's dreadful throughout. Judd mutters his lines to himself, his hair standing on end as though he's received an electric shock from the entity, while Swanson runs around, mouth agape, giving the impression she has no idea what's going on. Naturally, Judd, as well as romancing blonde Swanson, has an ex-wife to contend with (blonde Jennifer Quakenbush), which brings us to another cinematic conundrum. How is it that all these nerdy fellers can attract good-looking women? Putting these irritants aside (and the picture *does* have a rushed, disjointed feel to it), *The Black Hole* is far more engaging than Disney's 1979 movie

of the same name. At least it boasts an unconventional monster, a classic example of the visual triumphing over the cerebral.

Blackwoods
Tanus Films 2002; 88 minutes; Director: Uwe Boll; Rating: ☠☠

A young man has recurring visions of a car crash in which a woman has been killed. Could his current girlfriend be the reincarnation of that woman?

A muddled although mildly compelling semi-supernatural offering along the well-worn lines of—"Is this guy dreaming or is he dead?" Patrick Muldoon plays the man whose girl (Keegan Connor Tracy) disappears while on an outing to meet her folks. When he finally locates her, shacked up in the forest with her hillbilly family in a dilapidated house, he is accused of murder, given a mock trial and chased into the woods in the style of a *Most Dangerous Game* manhunt, the deranged family armed to the teeth. We see a series of puzzling flashbacks relating to the accident and the girl, indications that *something* is amiss as nobody else in Muldoon's presence (apart from the family) has seen him in the company of this mysterious female. What was the reason behind Muldoon spending three years in a psychiatric hospital nursing his guilt over the accident? Why didn't the waitress serving the couple drinks at a diner see the girl? Why can't the porno-loving geek in the motel where the couple stopped recollect the girl ever staying there? Did the family have two daughters, or only one? Was Muldoon acting out a charade with an invisible companion in an effort to ease his self-reproach? The equally perplexing conclusion—Muldoon eliminates two of the hillbillies, then appears to be running from nobody, *then* stabs himself and vanishes into thin air as the local sheriff spots him—hints that he may have been a ghost, painfully reliving past events, a continuous guilt trip for the soul. "You can't escape your past, no matter how you try" and "Things have a way of coming back—some folks might call it a haunting" intones the sheriff at the end, as Muldoon wanders like a lost spirit through the woods, a clue perhaps to solving, or even understanding, this baffling piece of waffle that would have been a whole lot more passable if produced on a bigger budget with better stars.

Blame
aka: **Peliculas Para No Dormir: La Culpa**
Filmax Intl./Telecinco 2006; 75 minutes; Director: Narciso Ibanez Serrador; Rating: ☠☠☠

A gynecologist employs an unmarried mother as nurse at her clinic, the woman's appearance triggering off a series of savage murders.

The third entrant in a series of horror features produced for Spanish television under the title *6 Films to Keep You Awake*, *Blame* becomes a little too wrapped up in its Freudian connotations to appease the fan who prefers his fodder served straightforward. But for those who lap up thoughtful, psychological continental horror, there's much to relish in its pared-to-the-bone running time. Unmarried mother Montse Mostaza takes up her new post at Nieve de Medina's rambling clinic with seven-year-old daughter Alejandra Lorenzo in tow. From the start, Brazilian director Serrador craftily delivers disquieting hints that not all is as it seems. Somebody (or something) raps on an interconnecting (and firmly locked) door to the adjoining building; de Medina displays undisguised lesbian feelings toward Mostaza; the doctor practically bamboozles young, unmarried women into having abortions; Cristina, a friend of de Medina, has mysteriously disappeared (is she the victim at the very beginning whose blood-spattered corpse, wrapped in a green hospital gown, is dragged across a floor?); when Mostaza herself becomes pregnant and her boss gleefully performs the abortion, the fetus goes missing; and why have several girls left the clinic suddenly over the previous three years? As one girl is brutally slain, her body

fed to a furnace, we are left wondering whether de Medina has lost her mind, taking her moralistic stance one step too far. This moralistic tone seems to be the movie's foundation, which is that those who conceive outside the sanctity of marriage should be made to feel guilty and suffer the consequences, no matter what. But when the doctor herself has her throat cut, it appears that Mostaza is the mad one, curling up in the fetal position beside a rocking crib with her daughter in a cobwebby attic after she has shoved de Medina's corpse into the flames. *Blame* leaves a lot of questions unanswered and loose plot-ends untied, but perhaps that's the purpose, as so often was the case in continental horror cinema's golden age, 1957 to 1970. All in all, *Blame* is a macabre gem of the minor variety.

BloodMonkey
RHI Entertainment/Thai Occidental 2006; 90 minutes; Director: Robert Young; Rating: ☠☠☠

Eye of the Beast
RHI Ent./Paquin/Peace Arch 2007; 90 minutes; Director: Gary Yates; Rating: ☠☠

Grizzly Rage
RHI Ent./Paquin/Peace Arch 2007; 86 minutes; Director: David DeCoteau; Rating: ☠☠

The Hive
RHI Ent./Thai Occidental 2008; 90 minutes; Director: Peter McManus; Rating: ☠☠☠

In the Spider's Web
RHI Ent./Thai Occidental 2007; 90 minutes; Director: Terry Winsor; Rating: ☠☠

Maneater
RHI Ent./Paquin/Peace Arch 2006; 90 minutes; Director: Gary Yates; Rating: ☠☠☠☠

Six titles from Maneater's series of "animals against man" genre movies, where the accent is on lashings of body spillage rather than plot or characterization, appealing to the gore-end of the market. Although produced by RHI, all six are markedly different, brightly lit cinematography combined with fine location work really the only common link. First let's examine *BloodMonkey*, a nice little movie, but where's the monkey? The final few seconds show the beast in all its ferocious glory, but it's annoyingly missing from the preceding action. F. Murray Abraham plays a scientific zealot luring six grad anthology students into an unexplored valley (no cell phones allowed!) in the African mountains, unsuspecting bait for a rare species of super-intelligent, human-hating simian. Assisted by unscrupulous huntress Prapimporn Karnchanda, they descend into the valley, and by the movie's close, all  eight have been slaughtered. We have the numb-brained jock (Matt Reeves), the goofy obsessive enthusiast (Sebastian Armesto), the blonde cracker (Laura Aikman) and the hero (Matt Ryan) among the team, all up against the snarling Abraham and the huge killer chimp. Surprisingly, the gore quota is almost restrained and much, much more should have been made of that murderous fanged creature quickly glimpsed at the end. Attractively rugged Thai scenery makes amends for a disappointing picture.

Eye of the Beast concerns a giant squid concealing itself in the depths of a Canadian lake, leading to depletion of local fish stocks and a sucker-indented torso washed up on the shores of Fells Island. Fishermen blame the indigenous Indians, so fishery department law officer Alexandra Castillo has her work cut out in trying to keep the peace between the two quarreling factions, fully aware that a colossal squid is the main culprit. As a child, she saw the monster carry off her father. James Van Der Beek from the National Oceanographic Research Agency turns up to investigate the mystery, culminating in a showdown with the sea monster when two boats set out to hunt it down. Castillo hurls an electrified dart into the squid's enormous eye after one launch, while most of the cast have fallen prey to those rubbery tentacles. The script is so-so (although are *all* females living on these remote Canadian islands obsessed with sex and finding a mate?), the performances satisfactory, but far less satisfactory are the partial shots of the monster. This is an adversary we should have seen a lot more of, to relieve the tedium if nothing else. If you're a fan of '50s B and Z creature-features, this is right up your street.

Five minutes into *Grizzly Rage* and you'll be praying that said grizzly bear will suddenly appear out of the blue and wipe the four geeky main players off the face of the planet and have done with it. But no, the creature doesn't do us that favor. Besides, there isn't a great deal of the raging grizzly in evidence throughout the entire 86 minutes. Tyler Hoechlin, Graham Kosakoski, Brody Harms and Kate Todd drive off at breakneck speed (to the sound, naturally, of rock music) on vacation, illegally enter a nature reserve, run over and kill a bear cub and then find themselves targeted by the enraged mother. "If that's a grizzly cub, there's a real pissed-off mama grizzly real close," says one of the dudes before Harms is slashed to death and the vehicle gets stuck in a quarry, cutting off their escape route. Kosakoski, footing it to the freeway, stumbles across an old house containing bear traps, gets clawed to pieces and dies, leaving Hoechlin and Todd to commiserate in each other's arms. But the final few moments hint that the grizzly has claimed them as well. Considering the protagonist is one of the most powerful beasts on Earth, *Grizzly Rage* is *very* low on the gore/body part count—hell, not one single person has his/her head ripped off! DeCoteau's direction is more animated than his leaden job on *Ancient Evil: Scream of the Mummy* and he attempts to substitute bloody mayhem with suspense. But the movie lacks gruesome action and, although competently made, is a tad on the boring side.

Millions of inexplicably intelligent ants are on the march in South East Asia in *The Hive*, a modern take on 1954's *The Naked Jungle,* but fortified with horror overtones. Diving straight into the explosive action after a grisly opening scene of a mother and her baby stripped to the bone (fortunately, we are spared the sight of the baby's demise), heavily armed grunts employed by Thorax Industries wade into the insect hordes, blasting them to oblivion using electrically charged super-guns. But this specific species of ant possesses an uncanny intelligence. Tom Wopat and Kal Weber spot them in a clearing forming tentacles that have the ability to see. When 200 million ants are discovered on another island, Weber and doctor girlfriend Elizabeth Healy visit their lair and are informed by an ant-like computer that the insects just want to be left in peace and keep the island for themselves. Shot in Thailand, *The Hive* is great entertainment in the rousing first hour and then goes curiously flat, as though all concerned had run out of inspiration and funds. It picks up in the climax when Wopat, a bomb strapped to his chest, blows the colony to kingdom come as the insects in the millions form one huge ant with an attitude problem. The premise that the ants were of alien origin, unveiled by the authorities in the closing minutes, is frankly nonsensical, even though an ant-shaped ball of blue light has been seen zooming skywards to the heavens. Also, various theories put forth regarding communication between different insect species all peter out into dead-ends. However, the effects depicting the swarming ants causing death and destruction are fairly accomplished, the Thai locations picturesque and as second-rate thrillers go, *The Hive* is one of the better of the "straight-to-DVD" sub-genre creature features.

In the Spider's Web is just plain daft, another group of students at the mercy of grizzled Lance Henriksen, a struck-off doctor living with the natives in the Indian jungle, paralyzing victims with spider's venom and selling their organs on the black market. Emma Catherwood runs around in hot pants, continually falling into giant webs that resemble lace curtains, while Lisa Livingstone spends almost the entire 90 minutes screaming her head off. This, combined with Cian Barry's incessant shouting, will have audiences reaching for earplugs. Henriksen's brother wanders here, there and everywhere, his head covered in a webbed hood. After the hood is removed, he resembles Vincent Price in *House of Wax*. One or two grisly moments (cocooned bodies covered in seething masses of spiders, Henriksen removing body parts), a splendidly cavernous domain (home to the arachnids) and picturesque Thai location photography lift this mishmash of varying ideas out of a rut. But in all honesty, die-hards will nod their heads wisely, knowing full well that Jack Arnold's 1955 classic, *Tarantula* is *the* one and only spider movie worth a light—all others are simply pretenders to the throne.

Lastly, we have *Maneater*. Hey, a horror movie with heart! A 600-pound Bengal tiger is loose in the woodlands of Taruga County. Sheriff Gary Busey, eccentric English big game hunter Ian D. Clark and a team of National Guard soldiers are trying their damnedest to kill the supreme hunting machine during the town's Corn and Apple Festival. Young Ty Wood somehow has an almost supernatural affinity with the beast. In addition, lived-in-the-face Busey has a tetchy mayor to contend with ("This tiger mustn't interfere with the festival" subplot), as well as snooping news reporters descending on his doorstep in droves. A high gore quota (half-eaten arms, legs and torsos and no lack of bloody pools), an intelligent screenplay, believable performances, a degree of edgy tension and crystal-clear photography all play a part in making *Maneater* an unexpected

delight. The movie cuts down on the clichés and produces a "savage animal" flick with depth, even though the climax feels a mite hasty in conception. A fusion of *Jaws* on land and human drama, expertly pieced together by director Yates, will satisfy those who prefer their horror to be more well-rounded than usual, at the same time appeasing the bloodlust in us all!

Boa vs. Python

UFO/Blaze Productions 2004; 92 minutes; Director: David Flores; Rating: ☠☠☠

When an 80-foot python escapes from a truck transporting it to a game reserve, the FBI decides to unleash a similar-sized boa constrictor, implanted with tracking sensor devices, in the hope that it will kill the reptilian predator.

Chock-a-block with perfectly-honed babes and testosterone-charged males mouthing one clichéd line after another, *Boa vs. Python* would have been much better if treated with a bit more seriousness. As it is, the cheesy approach works against it. Macho-man Adam Kendrick, busty girlfriend Angel Boris Reed and five wealthy big game hunters decide to enter tunnels under a vast water treatment plant in Philadelphia to kill the giant python, after the creature has broken out of its container, unaware that FBI agent Kirk B.R. Woller, doctor David Hewlett and scientist Jaimie Bergman have taken a colossal queen boa from Hewlett's snake reserve and let it loose in those selfsame tunnels. This is the catalyst for everyone except Hewlett and Bergman to get swallowed alive (including most of the military), as both reptiles attack not only their human hunters but also each other. With dialogue like, "Die, you slithering piece of shit," Reed exposing her ample breasts full-on to camera, and a near-the knuckle scene in which a courting couple are gobbled up, the girl experiencing a *When Harry Met Sally*-type orgasm as the python slides between her skirt, it's nigh on impossible to treat this movie as nothing less than pure schlock. The glossy CGI snakes are acceptably monstrous, particularly in the final sequence where the python bursts into a lap-dancing club (cue for yet more luscious female bodies), targeting the DJ as its next meal, and the climax whereby a subway train decapitates the python and the boa's electrocuted when Hewlett corrupts one of the sensors in its body. It's just a pity that the profanity-strewn script (hard to believe that this was only rated "15" in Britain) and hammy acting is to the film's detriment, although Flores does direct with a fair degree of pace to keep things moving.

The Bone Snatcher

First Look Media 2003; 90 minutes; Director: Jason Wulfsohn; Rating: ☠☠

Prospectors mining for diamonds in Africa's Namib Desert disturb a creature known by the local tribes as the Sandmother, which emerges from its dome-like nest and devours the flesh from humans, utilizing their bones to move around.

The one thing this South African creature-feature has going for it is the pristine desert locations, crisply photographed in bleached-out colors to fully capture the heat and the glare. Otherwise, it's the standard "what's-out-there-on-the-loose?" chain of events that ultimately offers nothing new in this well-trodden area. Scott Bairstow arrives at Eland Mines to carry out geological work but finds himself transported in a lorry full of roughnecks (including good-looker geologist Rachel Shelley) over the wastes in search of three missing miners, whose mutilated corpses are eventually discovered miles from anywhere. The group then find themselves prey to the monster, a creation formed from an amorphous mass of ants bound together in animal structure by the bones they ingest. When shot at, this oozing mass collapses like a deck of cards and re-forms. Once

you realize what this thing actually is, it's not too difficult to lose interest in the remaining 40-odd minutes as the humans are whittled down to three survivors, hounded by the creature in abandoned mine workings where Bairstow plunges a knife into its separate brain. The Sandmother grabs the other male and they fall into a shaft, a tube of nitroglycerine putting paid to the monster. The final scene sees Shelley driving away with the queen ant's brain in a wooden box, after giving Bairstow the brush-off. The oft-used perspective shot from the creature's viewpoint is presented in infrared to good effect and there are a few grisly moments, but overall, *The Bone Snatcher*, despite that splendid desert scenery, is copycat horror fodder filmed in novel surroundings, nothing more and nothing less.

Boy Eats Girl

Odyssey Entertainment/Lunar Films 2005; 80 minutes; Director: Stephen Bradley; Rating: 💀💀

Heartbroken when he spots his girlfriend with another boy, a teenager accidentally hangs himself but is brought back to life as a zombie that craves human flesh.

If you are age 20 or over and a not big fan of *Shaun of the Dead, 28 Days Later* and others of their type, read no further; *Boy Eats Girl* will most certainly *not* be your cup of tea. This British (Irish, to be more specific) teenage zombie flick commences in spooky fashion, the pre-credits sequence depicting a woman discovering a hidden crypt behind a church wall, the chamber decked out in bones and candles, containing an ancient book detailing voodoo rites and other forms of sorcery. Then—blam!—in kicks the teenage rock music

and we're on a different tack altogether. David Leon is a lovelorn college kid on the verge of proposing to Samantha Mumba. When he espies her sitting in a car with the local Romeo (she was only hitching a lift), Leon slopes off to his bedroom, downs a whole bottle of whisky and ties a noose around his neck. As he is standing on a stool, debating whether or not to commit suicide, Mum barges in, knocks away the stool and the poor sap dies. But Mum has filched the book on the black arts from the church and resurrects her son as one of the living dead, impervious to pain and possessing superhuman strength. Puzzled by his abnormal condition, the youth wanders over to the school disco. During a fight with bully Mark Huberman, he savagely sinks his teeth into the guy's face. The result? Huberman is now a zombie himself and, in the blink of an eye, most of the other kids are as well! From this point on, all plot development is hastily discarded and the movie plunges into farce as the town is overrun by gangs of bloodstained students on the hunt for raw meat. Leon, the original perpetrator, keeps his zombie tendencies in check until the final reel when Mumba carves up the zombie masses in a thresher machine. Leon, bitten by a magical snake taken from the church crypt, recovers as his normal, pre-zombie self. Some cute ensemble playing from the young cast, especially Tadhg Murphy as the dopey Digs and Sara James the brazen tart Cheryl, shine. And a gloriously over-the-top climax (mangled arms and legs, fountains of blood and guts, beheadings, limbless torsos, chewed up entrails) cannot atone for the serio-comic approach that will turn most older cinema-goers off. This is definitely for those on a lads' night out with a few beers in hand, but it's a very long way off from *White Zombie*, *I Walked with a Zombie* and even '50s schlock classics like *The Dead One* and *The Four Skulls of Jonathan Drake* (and let's not forget Hammer's splendid *The Plague of the Zombies*). Oh for the days when solid, cinematic expertise was bestowed on pictures such as this.

The Breed

First Look Pictures/ApolloProMovie 2006; 87 minutes; Director: Nicholas Mastandrea; Rating: ☠☠

Five teenagers go on vacation and stay at a log cabin situated on an island, which, unbeknown to them, is home to a pack of ravenous, rabid dogs.

Do canines, however vicious, constitute good horror cinema? Better than bees or bats, perhaps, but they're not *that* much better. So what we have here is a very commonplace scenario featuring three guys and two gals up against a score or more of snarling, genetically enhanced Alsatians that have broken out of an island compound, roaming and killing at will. Can the imperiled teenagers outsmart these dogs and get off the island?

With Wes Craven as executive producer, audiences can expect a fair amount of savage gore and they get it, although not by the bucket-load. Suspense is the name of the game—who's first to get chomped up, and who will make it? After an interminable opening 15 minutes showing the youngsters drinking, flirting and generally fooling around, blonde Taryn Manning is the first to be bitten, undergoing disturbing changes in personality as the rabies worm their way into her system. Hill Harper follows her, ripped to pieces in the cabin's cellar. Although the director expertly orchestrates the attacks to gain maximum effect from those slavering, drooling jaws, by the time brothers Oliver Hudson and Eric Lively, plus Michelle Rodriguez, sail away in a boat, a certain amount of boredom may have set in with older hands or anyone not overly excited by yet one more teen horror movie. It's competently put together, the young cast are okay, but it doesn't exactly break new ground and those infected dogs simply aren't frightening enough to get the pulses racing.

Campfire Tales

Vault 1997; 88 minutes; Directors: Martin Kunert, David Semel and Matt Cooper; Rating: ☠☠☠☠

After their car spins off the road at night, four teenagers sit it out in the woods, and to while away the time, they tell one another three ghost stories. This

is a first-class minor horror picture containing a savage twist in the tail. Story one, "The Honeymoon," tells of a young couple in their camper on their honeymoon being menaced by murderous (although barely seen) monsters in the woods. The second story, "People Can Lick Too," concerns a young girl on the eve of her 12th birthday who informs her Internet friend Jessica that she is home alone that night. Unfortunately, "Jessica" is a child-killer and proceeds to stalk the girl in her own house. Story three, "The Locket," is the best structured and most startling of all the tales. A biker stops at a lonely house after his machine develops problems and he gets caught up in a terrible tragedy, as the mute girl who resides there is terrorized by her father, a redneck psycho who has murdered repeatedly, died and now has returned to the scene of his crimes in a ghostly time loop. Rescuing the girl, the biker sits with the young girl in a park. He removes her necklace and her decapitated head falls off. At the conclusion of the three tales, Jay R. Ferguson inexplicably finds himself alone, but suddenly paramedics are resuscitating him. His three friends died in the crash and all those around him—the police, the doctors, the witnesses—are characters from the earlier stories and this dawns on him as he expires. The connecting story, "The Hook," (shot in monochrome at the very beginning and end) is less involving, simply a plot device to link up the climax to the opening crash; nevertheless, this is a fine anthology of modern horror tales in the style of *Black Sabbath* and others from the 1960s, containing pleasing performances from the young cast, imaginative direction and a fairly sensible script.

Catacombs
Twisted Pictures 2007; 100 minutes; Directors: Tomm Coker and David Elliot; Rating: ☠☠☠☠

Following a rave party in the infamous Parisian catacombs, a young American woman becomes lost in the maze of ancient passages, trailed by a legendary masked madman.

Lithesome Shannyn Sossamon flies to Paris, meets up with bitchy sister Alecia Moore and doesn't even have time to unpack her suitcase before she's whisked off to a rave in the gloomy vaulted galleries covering a 300-mile area.

These vaulted galleries are home to over seven million skeletal bodies interred centuries ago when the city ran out of burial space. On pills for her nerves, she is plied with absinthe and told of an insane creature raised by the mythical Cult of the Black Virgin that still inhabits the labyrinth. Minutes later, her sister is savagely murdered and Sossamon finds herself on the run from the growling, homicidal maniac. Given a very limited release in the United Kingdom, *Catacombs* is intensely claustrophobic, which isn't surprising given the setting. Sossamon blunders around in the all-enveloping darkness with a failing torch, stumbling in terror up one blind alley after another, running down bone-lined passages, fleeing from rats in a conduit, coming up against barred gates, negotiating strange rooms cluttered with junk and meeting a fellow lost (but sinister) soul (Emil Hostina), who is also desperate for a way out. The final coda is a belter. Sossamon has been the victim of a prank, undergoing a perverted initiation ceremony to prove her "worth" in the eyes of her spiteful sister. Everything has been a set-up. But her revenge is sweet. Unhinged by her ordeal and goaded by the hateful Moore, she shows not the slightest bit of sisterly love by slaying her and her friends with a pickax. The opening sequence during the rave, with its strobe light effects and pounding death metal music, might put some fans off, and a lot of the movie's footage is almost entirely pitch-black, but really, this is a one-woman show. Sossamon is tremendous in the part, and the ghoulish catacombs locations are quite unique, redolent of death and decay. They lend the production a malignant atmosphere all its own.

The Cave
Screen Gems/Cinerenta 2005; 97 minutes; Director: Bruce Hunt; Rating: ☠☠

Exploring a vast system of caves in Romania, a team of professional cave divers is stalked by flying, carnivorous monsters.

The Cave kicks off in terrific fashion. An avalanche of rock beneath an ancient church in the Carpathian Mountains in the 1970s traps a gang of adventurers as they hunt for a fortune in lost treasure and perish from an unseen

force. Thirty years later, Cole Hauser and a team of in-fighting divers enter the same cave network and, three miles from the entrance, are picked off by weird, people-eating creatures that lurk in the shadows. After that impressive opening sequence, it really is a case of who makes it out unscathed and who doesn't, and the real shame of this picture lies in the fact that despite some spectacular underground sets (the lighting and photography are exceptional) and moments of claustrophobic tension, we simply don't see enough of the beasties to satisfy our appetite. This is a major fault with many of today's CGI monster movies, something audiences couldn't level at the creature-features of the '50s and '60s, when *every* little detail was on display. A peek at a claw here, a quick shot of a head there—it just isn't acceptable. The obligatory trick ending—Hauser and two others escape after the team have been depleted, but he is savaged by one of the things and may be infected by a parasite—doesn't make up for *The Cave*'s shortcomings. If more had been made of the dragon-like flesh-eaters, this would have been a respectable addition to the modern-day "subterranean" horror film (as was the similar *The Descent*). As it stands, the movie cheats on its audience and pretty much fails to deliver the required monster thrills and spills.

The Cavern
aka: **WithIn**
Dead Crow Productions 2005; 95 minutes; Director: Olatunde Osunsanmi; Rating: ☠☠

Eight cavers explore an unknown caving system in Kazakhstan's Kyle Desert and are picked off by a savage creature that lurks in the dust-filled labyrinth.

The Descent revisited, but whereas Neil Marshall's 2005 horror outing was expertly crafted to produce the maximum in subterranean shocks, *The Cavern* is ineptly handled from the moment the six guys and two girls enter the cave, climb down a shaft and become cut off from the outside world when their lifeline is severed, along with the caver waiting to haul them out. The group leader (Mustafa Shakir) nurses a dark secret. On an expedition to a system in Peru, his partner died in a flooded passage. Did he let go of her hand on purpose, knowing that she was carrying on an affair with his best pal? But this particular plot thread (stolen from Marshall's movie) is never given its head, as the team blunders through narrow tunnels and water-filled galleries, shadowed by a presence bent on slaughtering them one by one. Anybody who has ventured deep into Earth's natural underworld will readily acknowledge that the director has fully captured the humid, claustrophobic atmosphere peculiar to confined spaces to a tee. But from very early on, *The Cavern* descends into farce as the panicking explorers shout and yell hysterically, rendering the dialogue for the most part totally inaudible. The monster (if it *is* a monster) is hardly seen (a hairy shape with skull-like features), and the continual flashing and bobbing of the lighted helmets is certainly not suitable for those prone to seizures. And it's all very well and good being forced to stare at a pitch-black screen while one girl shrieks and sobs, but one needs to know just what the hell is taking place. The creature turns out to be a badly scarred, demented Russian who, as a young boy, wandered into the system in 1980 and never emerged. Cornering the two surviving women (who have just gorged themselves on a decaying corpse, realized it and thrown up), the crazed cave dweller takes out his pent-up sexual frustrations on one of them, leaping on her in a mad frenzy of rape, and the picture suddenly ends as she screams in terror. There are buckets of gore and mutilations, but it is nigh on

impossible to figure out who is who and what's happening, due to the feverish directorial method utilized. For the ultimate in "cave horror" flicks, stick to Marshall's brilliant *The Descent,* which remains the pick of the pack.

Cerberus
Sci Fi Pictures/Cinetel Films 2005; 92 minutes; Director: John Terlesky; Rating: ☠☠☠

A crime syndicate steals Attila the Hun's priceless breastplate from a Bucharest museum and abducts the debt-ridden brother of an antiquities historian, thereby forcing the historian into traveling from New York to Romania to pay a ransom for his release. The real motive, however, behind the expert's required presence lies in the inscription on the artifact—whoever deciphers it will dis-

cover the Sword of Mars, said to be forged by the Devil and rendering those who possess it invincible.

More of an *Indiana Jones*-type fantasy adventure than a horror movie, *Cerberus* is a fast-moving frolic, basically a heroes vs. villains matinee number stretched out to 92 minutes and featuring, as the title monster, a giant three-headed, snake-tailed canine that is the guardian both of the sword and Hades, and a worthy adversary to boot. Legend has it that the mad conqueror signed a pact with Satan in order to defeat his enemies with the sword, so it stands to reason that when despicable Greg Evigan lays his hands on it after doctor Emmanuelle Vaugier, Sebastian Spence and their two assistants have done all the donkey work—scaling the walls of a 13th-century fortress known as the Citadel, clambering down gloomy passageways, discovering Attila's burial chamber and locating the fabled sword next to the Hun's skeleton—he entombs the team within the walls, leaving them to deal with the resurrected hound from hell. Arriving at a nearby village, Evigan then shoots or hacks to death his partners (plus a few villagers) and double-crosses boss Garret Sato, all the while impervious to bullets because of the sword's unholy powers. By the time Vaugier, her wimpy brother (Brent Florence) and action-man Spence have emerged from an underground tunnel constructed beneath Attila's tomb, the monster-dog has been on the prowl in and around the village, ripping off heads and legs, strangling another with its tail and cornering Evigan in the street, tearing him apart. Spence finally hurls Attila's sword at the dog, which vanishes into a fiery pit, along with the weapon. Perhaps a little too gruesome for the kids in some places, this enjoyable little movie has pace, excellent sets (especially in the crumbling fortress) and a striking CGI monster. But it is mucked up in one department—Vaugier's vocal delivery. Clear enunciation appears to be on the wane in modern-day cinema and the actress's nasal whine renders a good 80% of her speech totally inaudible. She's by no means the only guilty party among today's breed of actors, but this trait often spoils a good picture as it does here, preventing *Cerberus* from getting (in my opinion) a four-star rating.

Children of Wax
aka: The Killing Grounds
Nu Image 2007; 102 minutes; Director: Ivan Nichev; Rating: ☠☠

In Berlin, against a background of violent gang warfare, a serial killer is on the prowl, murdering children and dumping their wax-coated, masked bodies around the city.

A very odd marriage between hardcore violence and continental horror cinema from the 1960s, with shades of Fritz Lang's *M* (1931) tossed into the mix. Shot in Bulgaria, the Turkish community is not only under threat from the Skinheads, a bunch of shaven-headed German thugs sporting tattoos and metal teeth (one has a glowing false eye), but also from a mysterious child-killer. The fiend is kidnapping Turkish under-12-year-olds at the rate of one a week, breaking their necks, coating the bodies in wax, painting their nails and placing a mask over their faces. He leaves the corpses in rubbish bins and on waste grounds. Armand Assante plays the Turkish police chief trying to keep the peace between the rival gangs and hunt the killer down. The link for the two stories is that the Turks think the Germans are responsible for the murders, while all the time it is creepy Udo Kier. Watching *Children of Wax* is like being subjected to two different films running side-by-side. Stark, on-the-streets photography depicting the bloody skirmishes as the gangs clash co-exists with

the continental-style film craft displayed in the scenes of Kier fondling the corpses of his young victims in a room full of dolls (how the Italian, Spanish and French directors love those dolls and masks). Kier is shot dead in the final seconds after almost doing away with Assante's wife and young son, and the two rival gangs more or less make up with one another. Horror buffs would agree that the movie would have been far better if it had concentrated more fully on the child-killer angle and not on the gangs' disagreements. Hidden among all the fights and dramatics is a classy, traditional psycho thriller just waiting to have its head but not being allowed to do so.

The Choke
aka: Ax
North by Northwest Entertainment 2006; 90 minutes; Director: Juan A. Mas; Rating: ☠ (or ☠☠)

Locked inside a nightclub, members and associates of punk rock group The Choke become victims of an ax-wielding killer.

A cast of seven teens finds themselves shut inside the world's biggest (and emptiest) nightclub (filming took place in an abandoned bread factory) with barred exits, on the run from a maniacal killer. Whittling the cast down to two, Bee Simonds turns out to be the guilty party (not the Bible-spouting vagrant seen lurking in the background), obsessed with the band's lead singer (Sean Cook) and insanely jealous of anyone who gets close to him. Last seen driving the band's van down a highway, smirking Simonds is undoubtedly free to carry out more murders as the fancy takes her. What we have here is bog-standard teen slasher slice 'em and dice 'em fodder, suitable for under-20s only. Anyone older will find this moderately gory picture about as appetizing as a bowl of cold cabbage soup. But viewed dispassionately and casting aside any prejudices more mature fans may harbor against the teen horror scene, is *The Choke* any good as a movie per se? Well, director Mas stages the slayings with competence, assisted by glossy color photography, the young cast verges from the odious (club owner Andrew Parker) to stupid (drummer Tom Olson) to intelligent (rockumentary filmmaker Sam Prudhomme) to spaced-out (Goth bass player Brooke Bailey). The punky soundtrack fits in with the musical setting. On the downside, the script leaves a lot to be desired ("We're all gonna die." "We need to get the f—k outta here!"), and the plot is as thin as rice paper. But then, the paying audience for fare of this type doesn't expect intricacies and Shakespearean prose anyway. Within the bounds of this particular genre, *The Choke* is two-star, adequate, mildly agreeable fare. For non-aficionados, it's one-star claptrap.

Chronicle of the Raven
aka: **Jennifer's Shadow**
Hybrid Pictures 2004; 96 minutes; Directors: Daniel de la Vega and Pablo Parés; Rating: ☠☠☠

A young woman travels from Los Angeles to Argentina to attend the funeral of her sister, who has died from a mysterious hereditary disease.

An unfamiliar Argentine excursion into the world of Gothic cinema, featuring Gina Philips as the woman at loggerheads with her intimidating grandmother (Faye Dunaway) over the reasons surrounding her sister's inexplicable demise and the sale of the family house (which Dunaway opposes). She's also trying to find out why Aunt Emma (an emaciated Hilda Bernard) is bedridden, afraid of something lurking in the attic. We're in Poe territory here. A raven is slotted into the scenario at frequent intervals, pecking at raw, bleeding flesh, as well as a *House of Usher*-type family curse. The movie has the look and careful pacing of one of Roger Corman's early 1960s Poe flicks, augmented by Micha Liberman's atmospheric, sparse string quartet score and dark, inky cinematography. But does this densely plotted film work as a solid slice of Gothic horror? Well, Philips is effective in the role of the narcissistic American suffering from troublesome, violent dreams, her body losing organs (although she still survives).

She enlists the aid of an ex-medic (Duilio Marzio) to solve the house's arcane secret, while Dunaway, 40 years on from *Bonnie and Clyde*, has lost her kittenish radiance, content to act like a malicious, campy diva, a foil to Philips' damsel in distress. The explanation behind the deaths of her parents, sister and, midway through the movie, her aunt, is obscure to say the least. It all stems from a tome called *The Malam Rites: Rituals and Spells*, telling of ancient gods that fed off the dreams of the living, devouring organs when the victims are in a state of catalepsy. Dunaway is the villainess of the piece, ensuring that whatever she worships in that gloomy attic is supplied with flesh to feed on, even if that flesh belongs to her own family, in order that she may live forever. Philips ends up interred alive, leaving us to wonder whether boyfriend Nicolas Pauls was in cahoots with Dunaway, as both slam the lid shut on Philips' coffin. It's all a bit tortuous and unclear (these gods apparently abhor cemeteries—no live flesh there!) but the picture is attractively presented and, as mentioned, has a distinct 1960s continental sheen that raises the production a few notches above the average.

Chrysalis
Gaumont/TFI Films 2007; 94 minutes; Director: Julien Leclerq; Rating: ☠☠

A covert government body has created a machine that can transfer people's memories onto a computer card, thereby manipulating them by changing the digital images to suit their own purposes.

Filmed in steel-grays and muted blues, the French-produced *Chrysalis* is about as devoid of color as the cinematography itself, a soulless exercise in sci-fi *film noir* that will be of interest to all those who enjoyed *Blade Runner*, *Minority Report*, *Equilibrium*, *Gattaca* and their ilk, but not to anyone else. Does the future (in this case Paris, 2025) have to be *quite* so bleak and depressing as depicted here? Craggy Albert Dupontel is an embittered cop on the trail of both his wife's murderers and whoever is killing young women in the city, the corpses displaying odd scratch marks over and under the eyelids. Saddled with chatty new partner Marie Guillard, Dupontel opens a can of worms when he slowly unravels the clandestine goings-on at a high-profile clinic supposedly dealing in plastic surgery. Marthe Keller plays the chief doctor meddling with the brain's memory banks (including her daughter's), the so-named "Chrysalis Project" stolen by the criminal head of an organization who wishes to gain control of these cards and rearrange them by implanting in the donors his own villainous thoughts, thus forcing them to bend to his will. After the non-verbal Dupontel has had a large part of his memory swiped, he defeats the mastermind (Alain Figlarz) in a bone-crunching fistfight and finds out that counter-intelligence is behind the plot to steal the device. The last seconds see him wandering off with Keller's daughter (Melanie Thierry), both with damaged minds, finding solace in each other, while Guillard threatens to expose all and sundry to the press. This movie is too downbeat and hard going by far. Yes, filmmakers can commence with a five-minute opening gun battle and throw in two bloody arm-to-arm clashes, but these scenes are only included to gratify the video arcade fanatics and, ironically, highlight just how drab the remainder of the picture is. Dupontel is the best thing in it, his gaunt, lined features mirroring his inner pain. But as for the stark, utilitarian sets, scientific bunk, a Disney-type holographic operation and the emotionless acting to match the austere ambience, audiences will need a dose of happy pills after being subjected to Leclerq's fatalistic offering.

Contamination
Rodina Film Company/RGI Productions 2008; 90 minutes; Director: Rodion Nahapetov; Rating: ☠☠

The megalomaniac head of a psychiatric clinic infuses his patients with treated blood, manipulating their DNA to produce mindless assassins.

2008? More like 1968 in this bizarre U.S./Russian thriller that unsuccessfully fuses political assassinations and intrigue with *Frankenstein*-type lab sequences, giving it the appearance of a continental "mad doctor" movie of the late 1960s. The lousy dubbing (common in that particular decade) completes the picture. The director himself plays a schoolteacher, an innocent suspect caught up in a political assassination. Freed from prison on a false plea of insanity, he is whisked off to Eric Roberts' clinic near Moscow and treated for schizophrenia, even though he is as sane as the next person. Roberts is in cahoots with leading figures of authority that are supplying his clinic with unwilling volunteers in return for cash. Daughter Xenia Buravsky smells a rat and uncovers—with the help of her new husband (Ilya Blednyi), a girlfriend and a congressman—the clinic's dark secret. Roberts is transfusing his loony patients with contaminated blood, altering their personalities to form a band of "political psychos" who are used as tools to murder well-known figures and then are eliminated themselves, leaving no clues as to the identity of the killers. Commencing in fine fettle, *Contamination* deteriorates after an hour and loses focus, entering into a series of blundering sketches as Roberts abducts Buravsky with the aim of mixing her blood with her father's, leading to the laboratory sequences in the basement (the best bits in the film) where audiences half expect to see Peter Cushing (or Wolfgang Preiss) wander in on set. As one would expect, father and daughter escape from the dungeon-like basement area via the conduits, the crooked cop (Roberts' confederate) receives a face full of acid, and the perma-tanned psychiatrist ends up a semi-comatose patient in his own clinic after the subjects of his experiments have turned on him (*The Black Sleep, Creature with the Atom Brain*—those 1950s source references are all present). Karen Black, unaccountably given star billing, is onscreen for around five minutes, her role (that of a loud-mouthed American tourist, charging about in a combat jacket) completely superfluous, and Roberts will *not* be entering the Horror Hall of Fame as one of the screen's maddest of mad doctors, as oily as his performance is. For the real McCoy, tune in to the continental horror cinema of the 1960s and you'll then see why *Contamination* is but a poor counterfeit copy of this much-revered genre.

The Covenant: Brotherhood of Evil
aka: **Canes**
Insight Film Studios/Fries Film Group 2006; 90 minutes; Director: Michael Bafaro; Rating: ☠☠☠

A PR executive blinded in an assault sells his soul to a satanic cult in order to regain his sight.

"What would you give to have your sight back?" Well, in Edward Furlong's case, it means eliminating all those who stand in the way of his quest to reach the top of the corporate ladder, including the company vice-president and finally his own wife, Chandra West. Furlong is a PR high-flyer who loses out in a promotion race to slime-ball Tobias Mehler. One night, a car thief sprays him with chemicals and he loses his sight. In steps Lurch-like Richard Stroh, who drives Furlong to a country Gothic mansion to meet his boss, Michael Madsen, leader of a satanic order. Madsen promises to restore Furlong's sight *if* he obeys their commands. Basically, he has to murder all those threatening to expose the sect, along with others who might impede his progress to the top. The common denominator among this group of madmen is ancient canes, each sporting a satyr's head that takes on a life of its own. Five hundred years ago, so legend tells it, a woodcarver was blinded in an accident. Evil woodland spirits impelled him to carve canes from forest trees. The man was eventually crucified for witchcraft and the canes, possessing devilish qualities, became lost in antiquity. Now Madsen and his brethren all own one of these ungodly canes. Several killings later, Furlong, dragged to the mansion, rebels at having to plunge his cane into West's heart. He has a fight to the death with Madsen and then wakes up blind, yet happy with his lot. Has he been dreaming these nightmarish experiences? Maybe not—the closing seconds

see rival Mehler, blinded himself, being offered the same deal by Madsen as was offered to Furlong at the very beginning. Although the film is a Canadian supernatural thriller that strays into *Devil's Advocate* domain, Bafaro competently directs. However, the movie contains a number of glaring faults. Madsen, blind in the opening sequence, regains his sight in a castle populated by German soldiers circa WWII. The jump in time-span from that period to the present is never explained. Furlong and West make a completely mismatched couple. She towers over him, while he wears a suit two sizes too big. Would a smart-looking glamour puss like West honestly get hitched to an ill-looking dude such as Furlong? Notice that West drives at least three different makes of car throughout the film. And Madsen's fake moustache and beard have to be admired for sheer audacity. Putting these to one side, *The Covenant* has enough satanic incidents and plot diversions to appease fans who lap up this fare. There are a couple of creepy interludes (West in an antiques shop, chased by a goblin; a baroque mural behind Furlong coming to life with fearsome figures) and the music, thankfully, is low-key. The denouement is nicely handled. It's nowhere near as bad as some reviews have suggested, not by a long shot.

Creature from Black Lake
McCullough Productions/Howco Intl. 1976; 91 minutes; Director: Joy N. Houck Jr.; Rating: ☠☠☠

Two students from the University of Chicago travel to the Louisiana backwoods to determine the existence of Bigfoot, otherwise known as Sasquatch.

Having received the classic low-budget treatment in 1972's *The Legend of Boggy Creek*, this is an early indie movie with a similar topic. Grainy photography and a rough and ready directorial approach give this tale some credence as actors Dennis Fimple and John David Carson drive into the Louisiana swamps in search of the legendary biped that has been prowling the backwaters for years. The creature's disruptive antics are covered up by the local sheriff (Bill Thurman), who prefers to turn a blind eye to the fact that he has a savage quasi-human wandering all over his territory. Grizzled, wild-eyed Jack Elam believes in the creature, as it grabbed his fellow trapper out of a boat and repeatedly attacks his shack in the swamps. So does redneck Dub Taylor also believe—his son and daughter-in-law were killed in a car accident following an encounter with the beast. The monster is really only seen in shadowy darkness, and in foreground shots, but this makes the picture all that more atmospheric and haunting, particularly when Fimple and Carson come under siege after pitching a tent by the Black Lake at night. The creature carries off Fimple, savaging him to the point that he has to be hospitalized (it doesn't stop him wanting to resume the hunt once he has recovered, though!). The townsfolk are probably played by a bunch of amateurs, judging by their forced performances, especially Catherine Hartt as a dizzy waitress. But this adds to the charm of an effective, if cheaply produced, excursion into the Bigfoot myth that is well worth catching.

Creature Unknown

Creative Light Entertainment 2004; 79 minutes; Director: Michael Burnett; Rating: ☠

A friends' weekend reunion in a wooded cabin turns to disaster as the three guys and two girls are threatened by a mysterious reptilian man-monster.

The creature turns out to be the twin brother of the one of the other guys who is dating his girl. Out of a fit of jealous rage, Chris Hoffman thought he bumped off (real-life) twin brother Matt Hoffman, but his body was dragged away and given an injection of reptilian DNA by a leather-clad female motorcyclist-cum-scientist working secretly in a hidden underground bunker in the woods. He recovered from his terrible injuries but, as a third-rate *Creature from the Black Lagoon* look-alike, he leaps around in the out-of-focus treetops, savagely attacking anyone foolish enough to wander into the woodlands. Two girls are torn apart in the opening few minutes, as eventually are most of the cast. If the plot sounds totally fatuous, so too is the acting, script, effects, music and direction in this lame-duck of a sci-fi thriller that wouldn't even have passed muster in front of a '50s audience. The bunker is blown to bits in the risible climax after a life or death struggle with the green, scaly terror in the laboratory, taking the creature with it, although Miss Motorcyclist has survived the explosion by giving herself a jab of her own monster-making formula. Some scenes of bloody gore sporadically perk matters up; otherwise, routine is too kind a word to use when describing this distinctly low-grade monster movie.

Crimson Force

UFO 2005; 92 minutes; Director: David Flores; Rating: ☠

An expedition sent to the Red Planet to tap a vast interior energy source gets caught up in a Martian civil war.

Crimson Force is without doubt a lamentable excuse for a sci-fi motion picture, starting off with some promise before going completely off the rails once the astronauts enter a colossal pyramid and encounter a bald-headed race with white contact lenses and black face paint. Everyone on Mars is at odds with one another regarding a massive ball of blue energy. Should they share it with the Earthlings or keep it for themselves? Hidden somewhere among all the triteness, pontificating, laughable costumes (the ridiculous wardrobe comes direct from either *The Mole People*, *Stargate* or both) and corny acting is the old chestnut about the Martians colonizing Earth when man was nothing more than a Pliocene ape. Hence we are all descended from this group of paranoid, Aztec-looking morons. The plot disappears in a sea of gobbledygook 30 minutes into the picture, and by the time David Chokachi and Teresa Livingstone make it back to Earth orbit for a bit of nooky, having placated the Martians, we are past caring whether or not they have had permission to use this energy source for Earth's benefit, whatever it may be. A poker-faced C. Thomas Howell, the argumentative ship's captain, has been left behind, but why is never made clear. Probably he wanted to consummate his relationship with a female Martian who has spent all of her screen time fluttering her eyelashes at him. *Crimson Force* is almost a textbook bad movie and can't even be classified as decent schlock—it's hard to fathom out why it was ever made in the first place. Perhaps it modeled itself on *Mission to Mars* (2000), another movie just as dreary. This kind of mawkish fare may have been par for the course in 1955, but certainly not in 2005. See this leaden-paced disaster at your peril!

Croc
RHI Entertainment/Thai Occidental 2007; 93 minutes; Director: Stewart Raffill; Rating: 🐊🐊🐊🐊

Ruthless property developers are using underhand methods to steamroll a young American's croc farm/zoo, leading to a spate of gruesome deaths by rampant crocodiles.

Yes, millions were spent on bringing *Lake Placid* to the big screen but, surprise, surprise, *Croc* wins hands down, proving without doubt that once in a while cheaper can be better. There are enough vomit-inducing dismemberments on display here to satisfy even the most gore-hardened freak, the Thai locations are splendid, the color photography vivid and the script fairly literate. On top of all that there are plenty of incidents to hold the attention. Gravel-voiced Michael Madsen turns up as "Croc" Hawkins, a grizzled hunter determined to kill the 20-foot saurian that has claimed the lives of dozens of people up and down the coast. Peter Tuinstra runs a local croc farm with his nephew and sister and is up to his eyes in debt. The local baddies want him out of the way, needing the land for development, and tax inspectors are on his back. Two of the bad guys turn loose three of Tuinstra's crocodiles one night and the zoo owner is then blamed when a couple go missing, the girl's leg washed up on the beach.

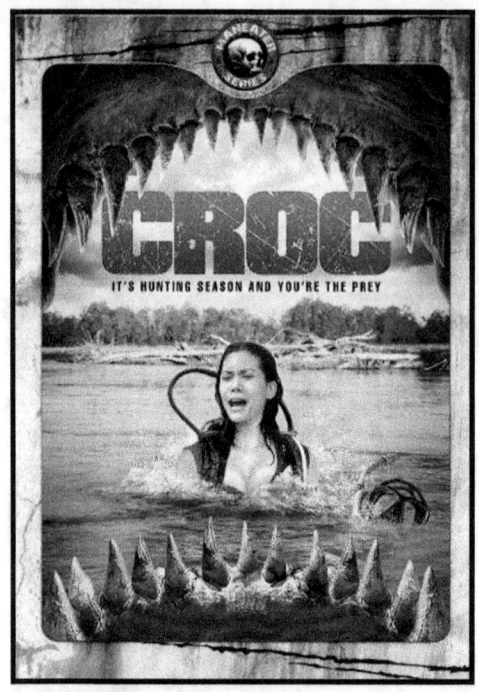

And a croc carries away a small boy. But the culprit doesn't belong to the zoo—it's the big male croc that Madsen has been hunting for years, and when a $50,000 reward is offered for its head, Madsen, Tuinstra, his family and Sherry Phungprasert, formerly from the Department of Animal Welfare, set off in a launch to hunt it down. The finale sees the group cornering the huge reptile in a vast cave, Tuinstra's leg clamped between its teeth. An explosive shell is fired into its mouth; the crocodile, fatally wounded, expires, releasing Tuinstra's leg and enabling the zoo owner to stagger free. The "jump-out-of-your-seats" opening sequence sets the pace as two fishermen dynamite a lagoon for their catch, the boat erupts and a pair of enormous jaws grabs them. Another excellent prolonged sequence shows the crooked developer meeting his hideous end when he dives into his pool, only to be chomped into little pieces; it is a gloriously over-the-top set-piece, compounded by his brother turning up to find not a blue swimming pool but one the color of ketchup, complete with body parts floating on the surface. *He* then suffers the same fate as *his* brother, the police discovering his chewed-off arm beside the lake of blood, still clutching a cell phone. Hokey in parts, like a throwback to a 1950s B movie, but unpretentious and fantastically true to its horror roots, *Croc* delivers—in spades!

Crocodile

Nu Image 2001; 93 minutes; Director: Tobe Hooper; Rating: ☠☠

Enraged at having its eggs shattered and stolen, a 20-foot Nile crocodile that has inhabited the Sobek Lake region for 96 years embarks on a rampage.

"I've survived 19 years in New York City. Murderers, rapists, muggers, you name it. And now I'm going to be eaten by a f—g monster?" So says Julie Mintz midway into Tobe Hooper's uninventive "giant crocodile" flick. What a great shame that old "Flat Dog," the name given the big reptile by the local rednecks, didn't finish off the entire cast by reel one. Pounding rock music over the opening credits introduces eight teens (five guys, three bimbos) intent on partying and getting it on celebrating college spring break. Yes, if anyone is aged 20 and over, they might just want to call a halt and proceed no further.

Following in the footsteps (should that read claw prints?) of *Lake Placid* and *Alligator*, Hooper's first direct-to-DVD feature offers nothing new in shocks, horror or gore. The eleven main cast members are whittled down to just three by the end (plus Princess the pooch), the remainder having been gobbled whole or chomped into bloody hunks of meat by the Croc who hasn't taken kindly to its eggs being taken away. The Croc homes in on the terrified, panicking, wailing teens because Caitlin Martin runs around oblivious to the fact that one egg on the verge of hatching nestles inside her backpack, placed there by moronic dude Greg Wayne. While the creature terrorizes the teens, who stumble through the dark lakeside undergrowth after their boat has been

rammed and demolished, Sheriff Harrison Young and the grizzled proprietors of a gator farm cruise the lake. One of them (T. Evans) is bent on revenge, as the beast killed his daddy and granddaddy. The director, bearing in mind his pretty impressive track record, does manage to pull off a few dramatic sequences to make audiences sit up with a jolt. Massive jaws rising up over Wayne, slamming down, taking him and half the jetty away; the monster smashing through the side of a general store; cutie Sommer Knight wriggling bloodily between huge teeth; and Rhett Jordan bitten in half are but a few examples. But leading characters Mark McLaughlin and Chris Solen (both vying for Martin's winsome favors) are so intolerably stupid that we certainly won't be rooting for them or anyone else for that matter. Old "Flat Dog," by the way, retrieves its newly hatched infant (handed over by a trembling Martin) and waddles back into the lake. Rated "18" in the United Kingdom, there's a lot less savagery on display here than in Thai Occidental's *Croc* (reviewed above) which, out of the two, is by far the better movie. This one comes recommended for booze and babe-loving 18-year-olds only!

Crocodile 2: Death Roll
aka: **Crocodile 2: Death Swamp**
Nu Image 2002; 89 minutes; Director: Gary Jones; Rating: 🐊🐊🐊

Following a bank robbery, four criminals board a flight to Acapulco, forcing the plane to crash-land in Mexico's Devil Swamp region during a storm. While attempting to reach a famed Mexican tourist spot, the criminals and the surviv-

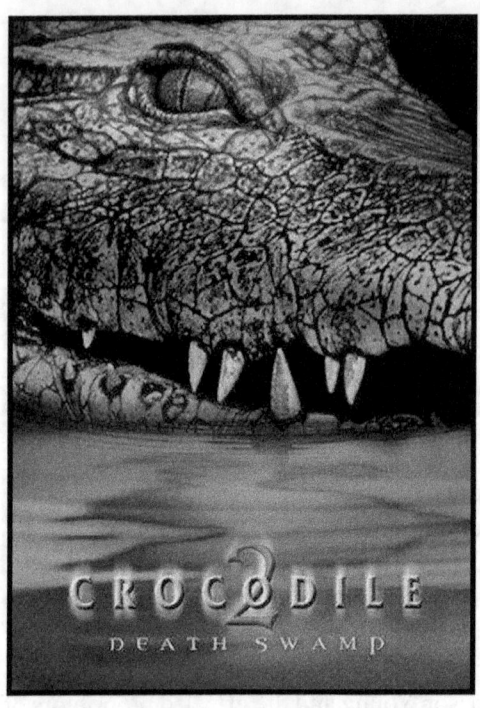

ing passengers are hunted down for lunch by an enormous crocodile.

It's all too easy to sit back and dissect a movie like *Crocodile 2*, picking on the bad points and ignoring the good, but director Gary Jones, the man responsible for the brilliant *Spiders*, has done a fair-enough job here, directing with pace and a keen eye on giant croc thrills. It's streets ahead of Tobe Hooper's *Crocodile* for starters and just as good as the hyped-up *Lake Placid*. First the minus points. There's far too much swearing—how many times can you shout "Motherf—r" before the word becomes meaningless? The opening bank raid is extremely violent. The underlying (and disturbing) verbal and physical brutalization of women present in the picture leaves an unpleasant taste in the mouth. Putting those aside, what we are left with is a meaty helping of humans vs. man-eating mother crocodile. Robber Darryl Theirse and his three utterly repellent sidekicks haul their loot (hidden in musical instrument cases) on board an airliner, force the plane to land in swamps during an electrical storm (the staging of the crash is frighteningly realistic when you take into account the budget), kill a smallish crocodile that strikes down one of their number, and wade off (with three surviving passengers plus stewardess Heidi Noelle Lenhart) in the direction of Acapulco, unaware that the dead infant's 25-foot mother is hot on their heels. Also roped into the action is Lenhart's boyfriend, Chuck Walczak, who offers boozy tracker Martin Kove $3,000 to fly out in his helicopter to the location where the plane came down in the hope of finding his girl and anyone else alive. Once Kove lands at San Christo and motors out into the swamps in a dinghy, meeting up with the stragglers, it's a case of who will survive and who won't as the colossal monster picks them off one by one. This leads to a prolonged confrontation in a ramshackle swamp dwelling that piles on the excitement, but unfortunately, includes an unpleasant assault on Lenhart by the truly repulsive, dead-behind-the-eyes John Sklaroff. After nearly everyone has disappeared down the creature's throat in grisly fashion and Kove (unwisely trying to outwit Theirse) has himself and his 'copter dragged into the waters by the mammoth reptile, Lenhart tosses a lighter into the methane gas-filled marshes and incinerates the beast, leaving her and Walczak to cozy-up in Acapulco. For lovers of the crocodile/shark genre of horror flicks, Jones includes an abundance of chomp-'em-up scenes to satisfy the blood-lust including Lenhart's co-stewardess swallowed whole, her chewed-up trunk washed up in a reed bed; one of the crime team ripped in half; another caught between fanged jaws, his almost-severed right arm dangling uselessly. The cast's not too bad either. Kove hones his grizzled Harrison Ford cigar-chewing character to perfection, Theirse is evil personified and gamine Lenhart looks gorgeous in a bikini. There are far more substandard indie efforts out there than this horror/actioner that, on the whole, gives audiences the required buzz, *and* we get to see a lot of the monster croc as well. Now that's got to be a bonus!

The Crows
Stream Films/SevenOne International 2006; 94 minutes; Director: Edzard Onneken; Rating; ☠☠☠

Crows that have become super-intelligent through an experimental research project at a hidden laboratory terrorize the inhabitants of Berlin.

It's hard not to compare *The Crows* with Hitchcock's *The Birds*, but whereas the latter movie had one of cinema's legendary directors at the helm, this German effort doesn't. Moreover, the dreadful dubbing (acceptable in 1966 but *not* 2006!) renders it comical at times, lessening the impact. Forty crows are treated with a serum injected directly into the brain to alter their metabolism, rendering them smarter than your average bird. They escape from a container truck and recruit thousands of others, all hell-bent on attacking consumers, picnickers and barbecuers, flocking over Berlin like a black cloud. Blonde Susanna Simon spends much of the film chasing around the countryside and the city, trying to warn people of the danger posed by the crows, even though she's six months pregnant. Dozy lawyer husband Stefan Jurgens doesn't believe anything that she's saying, scoffing at her silly speculations. In the meantime, the authorities are dumping meat laced with poison all over the city in an effort to kill the flying menaces. It really does sound too preposterous for words, but *The Crows* actually contains moments of undiluted suspense and terror. Effective sequences include the first attack at a children's party, the birds settling on telegraph wires in ones and twos while dozens more swoop over the roof of the house; the creatures swarming onto people enjoying the sun in Berlin's main park, clawing at their heads; a huge crow perched on a baby's pram, beadily eyeing the infant; and the crows in the hundreds, nesting in a derelict barn, just waiting. The final scenes show Simon and Jurgens driving a truck through thousands of the black monsters to coax, by means of a flashed signal, the original 40 crows back into the truck, to be re-programmed, so that they can instruct their winged brethren to behave themselves. The final shot of a large crow on its nest in the old barn speaks for itself—this is one problem that hasn't gone away! Moodily shot in somber colors, *The Crows* is at least offbeat in approach. After all, just how many horror films feature our feathered friends? The film's worth tracking down, even if it falls far short of the standards set by Hitchcock's 1963 masterpiece.

Cruel World
Primetime Pictures/Echo Bridge Ent. 2005; 88 minutes; Director: Kelsey T. Howard; Rating: ☠☠

Rejected by his hoped-for bride-to-be in front of an audience of millions, a deranged youth stages his own reality TV show in which nine contestants, after undertaking a series of punishing challenges, are brutally killed one at a time.

The teen horror bandwagon rolls remorselessly onwards, *Cruel World* swelling the burgeoning ranks, offering little in the way of freshness to this overdone genre. The film features loony killer (Edward Furlong), an even loonier brother (Daniel Franzese), nine shrieking teens and moments of gore. The opening sequence sets the rather nasty tone, as floppy-haired Furlong cuts the throat of the woman who spurned him (babelicious Jamie Pressly) and drowns her husband in a swimming pool. Then nine teens turn up at the house in a stretch limo, thinking they're taking part in a *Big Brother*-type reality show, the winner earning a cool $1 million. But Furlong has his own perverse agenda. Those rejected by their pals after a particular challenge are murdered by the lumbering, infantile Franzese, and those who dare to complain meet the same fate—stabbed, drowned, decapitated and buried alive. Challenges include being locked in coffins full of bugs crawling in green slime, eating raw meat, being tossed into the pool wearing a ball and chain, and fighting to the death with swords. It's one of those movies where we can tell what's going to happen before it does, with blonde Laura Ramsey the only survivor. Although Furlong's face appears on Laura Ramsey's mobile at the same instant a hand touches her shoulder at the very end. Is the madman still out there? Furlong's slobbish, chain-smoking, smirking creep performance spoils the picture. He acts the part well, but this is the kind of oddball most other men would love to kick hard

in the backside. After 10 minutes he's simply wearing on the nerves, and he's not menacing enough. A loud rock music soundtrack, teen-speak dialogue and typical teenage "Oh my God" performances all go to making this suitable for under-20s only.

The Cry
aka: **Cries of Death**
Fidelity Films/Santo Prods. 2007; 83 minutes; Director: Bernadine Santistevan; Rating: ☠☠☠

An ancient Mexican spirit, La Llorona, terrorizes the Spanish quarter of New York, possessing young mothers and forcing them to drown their children so that the spirit can once more experience the cry of pain and death.

Based on a Mexican urban legend, *The Cry* is stylishly directed by Santistevan utilizing vivid cinematography; artful flashbacks; a menacing, droning soundtrack; and a few scenes of genuine alarm. However, as flashy as it is, the movie emerges as a rather messy supernatural outing, hampered by a pitifully wooden central performance from Christian Camargo. He's a police officer desperately trying to solve the mystery behind 10 children that have gone missing in his neighborhood. He questions a young mother who has drowned her infant daughter in a bath, and after taking her to the station for interrogation, the woman's eyes scarily bleed as she complains of an insistent, throbbing voice in her head. Repetitive zooming-in on Central Park's murky lake, loud sobbing and whisperings in the air ("Cry with me." "Mine, mine, mine.") and several distorted monochrome shots of "something" homing in on mothers will have the audience thinking, "What's happening here?" All is more or less explained when Camargo and brash partner Carlos Leon visit an old Mexican witch (Miriam Colon). The crone relates the tale of La Llorona. Centuries ago La Llorona finds herself jilted by her lover and her son drowned in a river. Periodically her avenging spirit, drawing on water for her power, returns. The spirit compels mothers to kill their offspring in order that both she and they experience the cries and death struggles of the children. This particular storyline has all the necessary ingredients in place for a great modern-day horror film. Hammer Films, for example, would have had a ball working with this scenario in the 1960s. Unfortunately, *The Cry* goes all out for a fraught climax in which Camargo saves the one child that the demon is after. Is the boy a reincarnation of her long-dead son? All this occurs at the expense of the mother (Adriana Dominguez) having both eyes torn from their sockets and buddy Leon slain, his throat ripped apart. It also transpires (in flashback) that Camargo's deranged wife murdered their young son, but this seems to be a blind alley only included to tie in with the main plot. The movie features an interesting, original urban legend-type scenario, but it's not quite given the cinematic consideration it deserves. Many will hate *The Cry*, but audiences will have to admit that it's different from the normal run of shockers.

Danika
Blue Omega Ent./Roberts-David Films 2006; 79 minutes; Director: Ariel Vromen; Rating: ☠☠☠☠

A neurotic, emotional woman suffers from repeated hallucinations, premonitions and flashbacks that are somehow connected to her three young children and two-timing husband.

As contemporary psychological thrillers go, *Danika* scores highly, a powerful foray into one person's schizophrenic psyche. Marisa Tomei turns in a virtuoso performance in the title role of a housewife whose overprotective, almost smothering, nature toward her brood borders on the clinically obsessive. *Danika* requires two viewings at least to fully grasp the stream of pointers presented to the viewer, expertly blended by the director who has produced a gripping, haunting picture with real depth. And there are plenty of disquieting scenes to get our teeth into and get the brain working. Tomei is subjected to the sight of disastrous events before they happen—a violent bank robbery, a school bus exploded by a bomber, a small girl abducted and murdered. Who is the mysterious down-and-out she spots in a park (and who we see occasionally in the background)? What is the significance of her brother's death by automobile accident when she was six years old? Why are the rooms in her house sometimes empty, with no children around? Repeated shots of Tomei in her car with the children aged a few years younger appear, a rosary dangling from the windshield. Tomei's psychiatrist (Regina Hall) *could* also be the children's nanny. Her elder son's Spanish girlfriend has contracted AIDS. Her daughter is reading a schoolbook containing explicit adult material, the decapitated head of the girl's schoolteacher topples out of a shopping basket and a teddy bear seeps blood. "I'll always protect you"; "In this world, bad things happen"; and "I wish you could stop time at those moments when everything was happy and perfect" intones Tomei in voice-over narration, the intermingling pieces of the (obviously) irrational woman's existence slowly coming together as she frets over everybody and every single situation in her life. The conclusion, for once, pulls out all the stops and makes an indelible impact that lingers long in the memory. Tomei's husband (Craig Bierko) had been having an affair with her psychiatrist. Tracking the pair down to a motel, she stabbed him to death, drove off with her three children (when they were younger) and, distracted, jumped a red light, a bus ploughing into her vehicle, killing all three kids. However, Tomei, as penance for her actions, survived, now a shuffling, unglamorous bag-lady roaming the sidewalks in rags, her worldly possessions stuffed into a supermarket trolley, inhabiting a warped fantasy world, imagining what life *could* have been. A guilt trip of titanic proportions, maybe, but Tomei, Bierko and the three kids as they *would* have turned out (Ridge Canipe, Nicki Prian and Kyle Gallner) are totally believable, while Vromen's assured hand directs with verve and lashings of modern-day style, in glossy color with minimal use of music, seamlessly knitting together the mind-bending strands of the plot. No doubt about it, *Danika* is a 79-minute marvel of its type, ably demonstrating just what can be achieved on a low budget with talent at hand.

The Dark

Constantin 2005; 93 minutes; Director: John Fawcett; Rating: ☠☠

To cement their fragile relationship, a couple take a vacation in Wales, staying at an old shepherd's house. They face tragedy when their daughter goes missing.

The brooding talents of Sean Bean are utterly wasted in this incoherent supernatural drama that is all about the retribution faced if one's behavior

has caused undue suffering to a child. Therefore, the challenge is if audiences can interpret the convoluted plot and deduce the outcome by the end credits. Eighty-odd minutes of *The Dark* is a con-trick that leads us up the garden path as the wife (Maria Bello) has been dead all along, drowning to save the life of the daughter (Sophie Stuckey) she abused to a point where the girl took a drug overdose. Tied in with this family crisis is a 60-year-old tale related to Bean and Bello by bumpkin Maurice Roeves concerning a collection of religious fanatics leaping to their deaths from the nearby cliffs. These fanatics acted on instructions from an overzealous priest whose daughter drowned, her tormented spirit requiring a sacrifice in appeasement that now haunts the house. Umpteen shots of Bello stumbling up a rickety staircase in the dark to see what's going on in that creepy room outstay their welcome. The story is full of loose ends (are Bean and Bello separated, divorced? What exactly is their problem?), the interior photography is murky, and the normally reliable Bean looks ill at ease in the part. The splendidly rugged Welsh coastline, admittedly, is a definite plus. Like many modern-day horror/spooky kids films, the revelatory climax showing Bello's spirit trapped in the house with that of the shepherd's daughter is nicely handled and slightly goose-pimply, but regrettably it doesn't compensate for the preceding, sloppily edited 90 minutes, making the picture seem like a wasted opportunity for all involved.

Dark Breed

PM Entertainment 1996; 104 minutes; Director: Richard Pepin; Rating: ☠☠

A space rocket, Aquarius 7, crashes to Earth, the five male astronauts infected with a hostile alien parasite they have encountered in space. The sole woman on board is also infected, but by a peaceful alien who intends to destroy the others, called "The Dark Breed," before they can take over the world.

Not released until 2003, *Dark Breed* is a badly acted ragbag of a sci-fi movie using as its source material two classics—*Alien* and *The Quatermass Xperiment*. Unfortunately, it is light years behind both these movies in every department. When the Aquarius 7 puts down in a harbor, Jack Scalia, commander of Aquarius 2, is quickly on the scene and soon up to his neck in a lengthy car chase involving the five alien astronauts (all wearing yellow contact lenses) and the police. The sixth astronaut (Donna W. Scott) happens to be Scalia's ex-wife. She surfaces and begins her own hunt for her none-too-friendly male colleagues. The picture only picks up in the final 20 minutes after another protracted car chase and umpteen gun battles between the cops and the astronauts in a featureless warehouse district. A batch of alien eggs is located in a canister, and Scalia has visions of his own clash with an alien on *his* space mission four years back. It is revealed that the devious boss of Omega wanted the creatures brought to Earth anyway, to be used as killing machines. An alien looking very much like H.R. Giger's creation, but with a flattened head, crawls out of a corpse's ribcage and goes on a rampage before Scalia finishes it off with a bazooka. A greenish being emerges from Scott's body, kills Scalia's loathsome superior, then disappears, leaving husband and ex back in each other's arms again. Some arresting effects showing the parasites altering the astronauts' body shapes and a not-too-bad alien at the climax (even though it is a blatant copy) don't really make up for the desperate middle section, which fails to hold our attention and features awful performances from the entire cast. No wonder it took seven years for *Dark Breed* to get a release date!

Dark Wolf
DarkWolf Picture Company 2003; 94 minutes; Director: Richard Friedman; Rating: ☠☠

A detective, with the help of his girlfriend afflicted by lycanthropy, hunts down a ferocious werewolf that causes carnage on the streets.

Halfway into this picture, there is an explicit, full-frontal nude lesbian dance. This may be the one and only reason to catch this badly photographed werewolf outing, although it's unusual to see Hitchcock's one-time leading lady Tippi Hedren starring as an old tramp with clairvoyant powers who gets

slain in an alleyway. In fact, most of the film takes place in various dark alleyways (the whole of the action occurs during the night) as Ryan Alosio and cute-but-dumb female werewolf Samaire Armstrong comb the streets, searching for the wolf man when the moon is full. Various people are torn to ribbons (including Alosio's female partner) before the creature, after wiping out an entire police station, is shot in one glowing red eye and killed. Armstrong's one and only full transformation scene, although well-executed, unfortunately makes her look like an extra from *Planet of the Apes* with fangs. Alosio is as wooden as a board as the cop who, for a change, *does* believe in the werewolf legend. Surprisingly for a higher-budgeted horror thriller, this is distinctly second-feature fare and something of a letdown, even if the slayings are suitably grisly and the direction well paced.

Darkness Falls
Revolution Studios/Distant Corners Ent. 2003; 86 minutes; Director: Jonathan Liebesman; Rating: ☠

In the town of Darkness Falls, 1853, a kindly woman who gave children a coin when they lost their milk/baby teeth was horribly scarred by burning and hung as a witch. 150 years later, she returns to wreak vengeance on the town's inhabitants after a youth dares to look at her porcelain-masked face.

And to think that most people are under the impression that the Tooth Fairy is a benign fantasy figure, part and parcel of all children's formative years. Not according to this overwrought exercise. From a promising eerie first 10 minutes, in which, against local legend warnings, the youngster peeks at the wraith's mask when she glides into his bedroom to retrieve the last of his baby teeth, this hysterical offering very swiftly sinks into idiocy. Twelve years on, pill-popping depressive Chaney Kley still suffers from his harrowing encounter with the vengeful spirit and is called upon for help by childhood sweetheart Emma Caulfield. Her young brother (Lee Cormie) is in the hospital, unable to sleep because *he's* being tormented by the Tooth Fairy. He suffers from the "night terrors." Can Kley help the kid confront his demons? When the wailing banshee arrives in the hospital, fluttering around in tattered rags, all cinematic sensibilities are dumped and we are in for a rollercoaster ride of the overbearingly ludicrous kind. As police blaze away augmented by the sound of a hammering rock soundtrack, they're all, except one, wiped out. Kley, Caulfield, Cormie, doctor Grant Piro and one cop head for a lighthouse where they hope to drive the thing back to its netherworld using blinding light. "Go, go, go," yells Kley non-stop, followed by, "Let's go, let's go" as the creature's ruined features are at last revealed. Piro is whisked away to oblivion, and the far-from-friendly fairy is set on fire, vaporizing in the lighthouse's dazzling reflected beam. Even at a short 86 minutes, the movie seems twice the length and audiences could quite easily lose the will to live watching it. *Darkness Falls* was issued straight to DVD in Britain, and it's not too hard to comprehend why.

Dead Fire

North American Pictures 1997; 101 minutes; Director: Robert Lee; Rating: ☠☠

In 2062 Earth has been laid waste by decades of warfare, the atmosphere aflame with poisonous gases. Space station USS Legacy has the task of diverting a solar flare, dispersing the hostile ionosphere, thus enabling the planet to be repopulated.

The only snag is, criminal mastermind Max Frewer, in collusion with wicked colonel Rachel Hayward, takes over the running of the giant vessel so that he himself can wield undisputed power over the newborn Earth. However, the megalomaniac has a thorn in *his* side—Bruce Willis-type action-man Colin Cunningham. Cunningham climbs lift shafts; he guns down and roughs up the enemy before finally making it back to Earth in a shuttle with honeyed babe Monika Schnarre. This is after scientist C. Thomas Howell, sporting a blonde rinse, is brought out of frozen stasis and

changes the course of the solar flare so that it strikes the USS Legacy, blowing Frewer and his plans for world domination sky-high. One year later, Cunningham, Schnarre and their baby, cavorting in a green meadow, await the arrival of Howell as he lands in the cryo-bay cruiser. Lloyd A. Simandl, the brains behind the wonderfully bizarre *Ariana's Quest* (2002), produced this bog-standard sci-fi outing that has one or two imaginative moments conjured up by director Lee. These are squeezed between the dullish action sequences (Earth depicted as a ball of raging fire; the intricate design work of USS Legacy). Frewer is the only person around to elicit an animated performance (so does Howell, but *his* performance is so horribly hammy that audiences might want to avert their gaze). *Dead Fire* is a rarely seen Czech/Canadian collaboration that hardly merits a second viewing, if you can manage to track it down, that is.

Deadly Water
aka: **Kraken: Tentacles of the Deep**
Nu Image 2006; 88 minutes; Director: Tibor Takacs; Rating: ☠☠☠

Two groups of treasure hunters seek out fabled artifacts, including a priceless blue opal that lies in a wreck at the bottom of a Canadian lake, guarded by a gigantic squid.

Beginning with the horrendous demise of Charlie O'Connell's parents, both dragged beneath the murky waters of Desolation Passage by a monster squid, O'Connell, now an adult hunk, turns up years later to assist Victoria Pratt, Kristi Angus and Corey Monteith in retrieving a pile of Trojan treasure from a ship sunk in 1902. Limping baddie Jack Scalia and his motley crew are also interested, especially in a large blue opal that is worth a fortune. This is 1977's *The Deep* revisited, but this time with a decent monster and a brief running time. The villains wear black, O'Connell falls for Pratt (who spends most of the time flaunting her assets in a skimpy bikini top) and most of the cast are pulled into the lake by a mass of writhing CGI tentacles. We know that by the final reel, Scalia will be sucked under by those spiky tentacles (he is), that both male and female leads will end up in each other's arms kissing (they do), that the squid will be defeated (it is, entangled in a boat's cable drum and machine-gunned), that one valuable item will be retained by the hero/heroine (a Trojan mask), and that the opal will be returned to its rightful resting place

on the lake bed (it is, presided over by an army of baby squid). A leg ripped off here and a head there are included to appease any gore freak that fancies a creature-feature for a change. The underwater photography is passable if not luminous and, as giant squids go, this particular model isn't all that bad, featuring in a fair amount of the movie's running time (more so than in Paquin/Peach Arch's similar *Eye of the Beast*). Attractive Canadian location work combined with acceptable creature effects make this a monster movie that is easy on the eyes and not taxing on the brain.

Death Tunnel
Plus Entertainment/Dax Productions 2005; 97 minutes; Director: Philip Adrian Booth; Rating: ☠☠☠

Five sorority girls are blindfolded and locked up in cells inside an abandoned, reputedly haunted, asylum, as an initiation stunt. They face madness and death—"Five Floors, Five Girls, Five Hours, Five Ghosts."

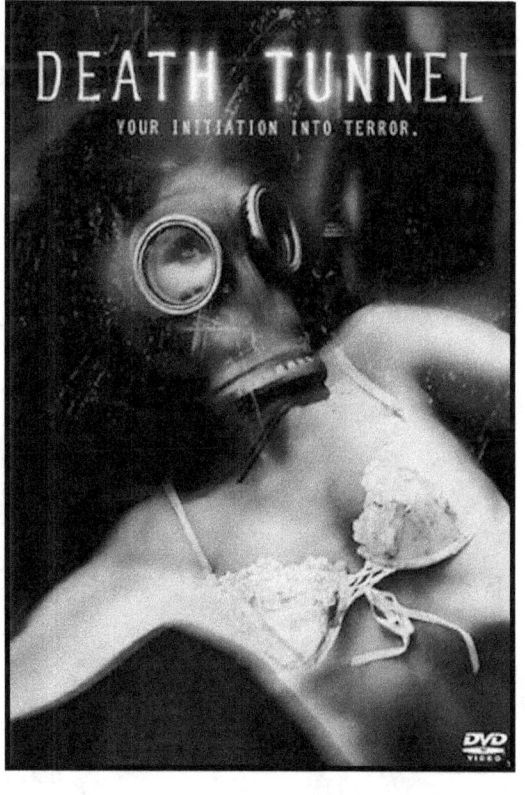

Filmed on location at the Waverley Hills sanatorium in Louisville, Kentucky, the massive, spooky building—its grim operating theaters cluttered with dusty, blood-smeared surgical/torture instruments, water dripping from scabrous walls—is an integral part of the production, much like the institution featured so skillfully in *Session 9*. But the relentless savage (and surreal) imagery, lightning-speed editing and intense color photography helps create a totally confusing narrative where audiences are left wondering just what the hell is going on. Such a pity! The storyline, although not exactly fresh, augurs well. In 1928, asylum-housed inmates suffer from the highly infectious White Death, 63,000 patients dying from the epidemic. To hide the horrendous death toll, the head doctor (Brian Dyer) deposits many of the bodies in a 500-foot dark, dank tunnel beneath the edifice, experimenting on and murdering those barely alive. The doctor lies to the authorities that his patients had in fact recovered and been released. Thus, the conniving medic benefits from further research funds that finance his lavish lifestyle. Therefore, are the five scantily clad bimbos menaced (Melanie Lewis, Yolanda Pecoraro, Kristin Novak, Annie Burgstede, Steffany Huckaby) the former inmates themselves, reliving past tragedies? Jason Lasater, the coordinator of this "truth or scare" shindig, is the grandson of the original doctor. Is he as mad as his grandfather? Why did Novak's grandmother wear a pendant with "RJV" inscribed on it, the initials of the hospital? Was she infected by the plague? Who is monitoring the girls' unrelieved terror on CCTV screens—Lasater and his buddy, or someone else? Is the malevolent asylum trying to claim the girls' souls? As the teens perish in the grisly manner of their original "selves" (pierced by a glass shard through the neck; jumping from the parapet; butchered by a figure in an anti-contamination suit wearing breathing apparatus; snapping a spine via hanging); the movie blitzes the viewer with a montage of alarming snapshots. These include grainy newsreel footage and yellowing newspaper articles (backed by thundering, heavy metal music) that show the sanatorium's chronically ill patients at the time it was in operation; extreme bloodletting (including a distasteful self-abortion scene); faded photographs of females resembling the five girls; and the apparition of the evil doctor himself putting in an appearance. The open-ended coda (all die—the asylum reclaimed them?) could well be classed as a cop-out. Even so, this hardcore teen horror picture shot in the frenetic style of *Hostel*, *Saw* and the remake of *House on Haunted Hill* will whet the appetites of those possessed of a more bloodthirsty nature, who savor their fare unsubtle and overstated, regardless of plot issues.

Deep Core
UFO 2000; 80 minutes; Director: Rodney McDonald ☠☠☠

Following a series of worldwide natural catastrophes caused by earthquakes, a giant boring vehicle burrows into the Earth's crust to plant four nuclear devices which, when detonated, will seal off the fissures that are leaking magma.

Was *The Core* based on this sci-fi actioner, coming as it did three years later? Was *Deep Core* modeled on Paramount's 1965 *Crack in the World*? Is McDonald's movie better than the other two? Well, as regards the disasters, all we get is a tidal wave, an erupting volcano, a collapsing building and a landslip over a freeway. The acting—Craig Sheffer (the machine's creator), Allison Saunders (the dolly-bird female lead), Harry Van Gorkum (the baddie) and Bruce McGill (the roughneck with a heart of gold)—is pretty poor. The script is okay after an initial 30 minutes of gibberish, and the effects, once the Series 2 vehicle is on its chosen task with Sheffer's team of oil-drilling buddies on board, are average. But unlike *The Core*, the pace moves along quickly enough; the rock-burrowing machine rumbling through tunnels on caterpillar tracks with its blue laser beam blasting the way ahead, is credible. Surely John Amiel's expensive 2003 version *must* have nicked that scene whereby the crew find themselves in a vast diamond-encrusted cavern over 100 miles underground. Mixed in with the "save the world from ruination" theme is a muddled sub-plot involving the Chinese and Sheffer's crooked boss (James Russo) that is superfluous (the Chinese want the machine for use as a weapon). It goes without saying that the nukes *are* detonated in synchronization, saboteur Van Gorkum sacrificing his life to save the planet. Resembling a typical '60s production in design and feel, *Deep Core* may be rough around the edges but it entertains for its 80 minutes. The one big bonus is that, unlike its million-dollar cousin, it *doesn't* feature a computer nerd to put a spanner in the works.

Deep Freeze
aka: **Ice Crawlers**
ACH/Regent 2003; 80 minutes; Director: John Carl Buechler; Rating: ☠☠

A company drilling for oil in the Antarctic disturbs creatures that have remained dormant in their icy lairs for eons.

Very much a routine monster-on-the-loose outing, the usual pack of misfits—research scientists (male and female), oil-drillers and the requisite computer geek—run around in confined passages as what appears to be a giant black rubber trilobite with a taste for human flesh devours them one by one. The company, Geotech, drilling for

oil on the ice shelf, has set off a series of tremors, awakening ancient monsters from a prehistoric age. Flown out to the base on behalf of the U.N. is a motley team of students, under orders to ascertain whether or not the company's operations pose an environmental threat. The first clue of danger occurs when people swim in the moon pool deep underground; one of the workers falls in and doesn't come out. A pre-Cambrian carnivorous arthropod worms its way into the base and goes on a rampage. It's actually an extraordinary but strangely endearing puppet that scuttles along corridors, as if worked by a clockwork motor. It is eventually shot to pieces after finishing off most of the cast in pretty gory fashion. For example a couple are in bed, and a man turns a woman over, only to see the thing clinging to her chest, eating greedily, then it's *his* turn! A much bigger version of the beastie turns up at the end but is blown to bits by Goetz Otto, along with the entire complex, leaving Allen Lee Haff and Karen Nieci the only remaining survivors. Give the director his due, the "female screaming" quota is cut down, a couple of the characters (team leader David Millbern and pill-popping Otto) have depth and some suspense is generated. Okay, the monsters are deliciously stupid, but *Deep Freeze* is entertaining although silly, the most stomach-churning scene in the entire production being when Norman Cole is seen in the shower, his torso (front and back) matted in thick body hair, almost like a werewolf. Is this real, or was it an effect, and if so, why?

Descent
Cinetel Films/Reel One Entertainment 2005; 90 minutes; Director: Terry Cunningham; Rating: ☠☠

A company specializing in deep drilling to tap the Earth's energy sources breaks into vast pockets of gas, causing the planet's tectonic plates to shift, creating a so-called "Ring of Fire" that results in worldwide destruction.

Readers may as well catch 2003's *The Core* (or better still, UFO's *Deep Core*) if you're a fan of sci-fi disaster movies, because *Descent* is a very uninteresting carbon-copy of both—same plot, different cast. Luke Perry plays the discredited scientist; Rick Roberts plays another scientist; Brandi Ward is the tomboy; Michael Dorn stars as a power-hungry general; and Mimi Kuzyk is the general's assistant. Two junk food-loving computer geeks help out, and there's a giant drilling machine called The Mole. The scene setting (mostly presented as TV newsreel footage) during the first quarter hour is fairly tolerable—fire erupting from a farmer's well, skyscrapers collapsing, a river of molten magma, sidewalks cracking and a bridge toppling. Then we are on familiar (and uninspiring) territory as our crew head off in the burrowing machine to plant a couple of 4,000 megaton nuclear devices 20 miles underground that, hopefully, will put a stop to the seismic disturbances. After a series of dull adventures (two colossal caverns are encountered), survivors Perry and ex-partner Ward float to the surface of the ocean in a capsule after The Mole becomes stuck on the seabed, both bombs successfully detonated and Earth saved from extinction. Quite obviously, Cinetel Films haven't learned from their past mistakes—*Descent* is a virtual rerun of *Scorcher* (2003), made by the same outfit, which itself was a mundane rip-off of the films mentioned above. *Descent* is moderately well produced and decently acted, but it's simply one "let's burrow into the Earth's crust and save the world" flick too many.

Devil on the Mountain
aka: **Sasquatch Mountain**
Grizzly Peak Films/Curb Ent. 2006; 90 minutes; Director: Steven R. Monroe; Rating: 💀💀

Following a bank robbery, a team of low-life thieves heads to the wooded hills with a female hostage, pursued by three cops, a tracker, a breakdown mechanic—and Bigfoot.

Shaky on-the-spot camerawork (to achieve a documentary effect), bleached-out colors, camcorder footage, time-lapse photography, a mentioning of aliens—director Munroe tries very hard to bring something new to the Sasquatch legend by dressing things up, but he only partly succeeds. After a group of villains disguised in monkey masks robs a bank, they crash their vehicle and grab buxom Cerina Vincent from the wreck of her car, taking off toward the woods. Sheriff Rance Howard, two deputies and grizzled tracker Tim Thomerson are quickly on their trail, unaware that a large hairy man-beast is shadowing their every move. Also in on the hunt is chain-smoking Lance Henriksen. In an *X-Files*-type pre-credits sequence he is repairing his wife's car at night when a vehicle collision occurs. His wife dies and a mysterious creature is captured on film, spotted in the background. Who out of this disparate bunch will avoid being mangled to death by the ferocious monster? The first hour of this lively but oddly filmed variation on the Bigfoot theme is moderately entertaining creature-fodder. But once the survivors seek refuge in a lodge, everything—inspiration, ideas, what to do next—grinds to a halt, the action bogged down in turgid, dialogue-driven scenes. Karen Kim and leader Craig Wasson eventually pump bullets into the creature and it later coughs up blood, expiring in a heap on the ground, crying for its companions. True to form, another creature is seen in the woods at the end. Attempts at injecting some social drama into the scenario (Henriksen is guilty over his wife's death and finds solace with his daughter) only serve as padding. Surely, Bigfoot (if he actually exists) is supposedly of a kindly, elusive disposition, not the raging flesh-eater depicted here. Not one of the best Sasquatch pictures ever made, *Devil on the Mountain* ultimately is a bit of a dog's dinner in all departments.

The Devil's Mercy
Red Duck Pictures/Peace Arch 2008; 90 minutes; Director: Melanie Orr; Rating: ☠☠

A couple and their 10-year-old son move into a rented apartment in a rambling house where the owner and his young niece are hiding a devilish secret.

A carefully paced occult thriller that limits the histrionics and gore, *The Devil's Mercy* tries its best to work up a mood of impending doom, but it's ultimately let down by the anti-climatic finale. Michael Cram, Deborah Valente and son Dylan Everett take up residence in a spacious apartment, the house owned by semi-retired Stephen Rea and his niece Hannah Lochner. The couple assumes that all is okey-dokey and that their new landlord is a swell guy, but the audience, from the start, knows differently. Rea is up to no good, entering into a pact with someone (the Devil?) that involves his niece and Everett. He religiously marks the days off a calendar, lights black candles, puts a hex on the couple to ensure they fall out with one another and keeps referring to an ancient

book listing people's names as far back as 1692. Obtaining a blood sample from Valente when she cuts her hand, overjoyed by the fact that Everett hasn't been baptized, pleased to note that Cram is floored by a bug confining him to bed and muttering to Lochner, "It will all be worth it," Rea skulks through the shadows like a man on a mission. And audiences will twig without too much bother that a sacrifice of some sort is being prepared, but for what purpose? Delving into the house's recorded history via the Salem Memorial Hospital, Valente turns up documents and photographs that throw light on the creepy Rea. The man (originally accused of witchcraft) is centuries old, as is his daughter (*not* niece), servants recruiting souls for their master in exchange for longevity. In that deflating climax, babysitter Siobhan Murphy is stabbed to death and Rea, after killing his daughter (at her request, to release her soul), promises to Everett (imprisoned within a pentagram) that he will save Everett's parents from dying if he gives his soul to "Him." The youngster agrees and Rea cuts his own throat, thus transferring his spirit into Everett. The evil lives on, as Valente discovers to her horror when she enters the darkened room and her son turns and faces her with malevolent eyes. Fair enough, *The Devil's Mercy* is not that dynamic compared with other devil-worshipping movies but, in its own quiet way, it is fairly involving. The ending, though, goes out with a whimper, not the expected bang.

Disturbance
aka: Choker
Artist View Entertainment
2005; 93 minutes; Director: Nick Vallelonga; Rating: ☠

As part of a pact with an alien race, a serial killer, condemned to die, houses one of their kind. But then he has to hunt down three others who plan on taking over the Earth.

We have yet another slant on *Invasion of the Body Snatchers,* and a mighty confusing one at that. When their human hosts become too uncomfortable, these particularly nebulous aliens drink copious amounts of water and "body-jump" by attacking another human and spewing forth green slime into the new host's body, leaving a string of bloodless corpses covered in odd blisters. Such activity has the police stumped. Paul Sloan is the strangler out to stop the possible invasion (he dribbles blue slime), but he cannot control his old urges and ends up murdering his assistant, Colleen Porch. *Disturbance* is heavy going for most of its running time, with the film's portly director Vallelonga starring as the government agent who knows all about the aliens, even though the police disbelieve him. After umpteen body-jumps involving that green goo, Sloan (released from police custody) and the alien leader have a multi-colored fight to the death in Vallelonga's swimming pool, where they both expire. But their race continues to survive—in the final shot, the agent's wife has golden goo seeping out of *her* mouth. As horror movies go, this one has all the trademark features found in a David Cronenberg 1970s flick. If only Cronenberg had directed, the results would have turned out a lot better than this garishly photographed mix of sci-fi and a murderer-at-large. This thriller resolutely refuses to grab the interest and ends up being both dull and unimaginative.

Dorian: Pact with the Devil
Cinema 4 Films 2001; 91 minutes; Director: Allan A. Goldstein; Rating: ☠☠

A decadent manager in the fashion world manipulates a young, attractive man into a life of hedonism. The young man becomes a famous celebrity while his portrait deteriorates, reflecting his sins and debauchery.

A flashy, trashy updating of Oscar Wilde's classic novel, fare for the MTV generation and virtually going straight to DVD, but any film featuring the mighty Malcolm McDowell (playing the Devil) has to be worth a look, surely. Ethan Erickson (wooden in his role) is the preening pretty-boy Louis, renamed Dorian by McDowell, suitably narcissistic in nature and taken under McDowell's wing on a promise of eternal youth, if he allows McDowell to claim his soul as his own. Each frame is filled with the beautiful wealthy set and their parties, highlighted by a semi-pop soundtrack. McDowell reinvents his *Clockwork Orange* persona with undisguised glee, and the women are gorgeous. Dorian rises to the top of the model world, all the while behaving like a spoiled brat, his portrait resembling something off the front cover of *Famous Monsters of Filmland*. Yes, it's a million miles away from Wilde's book and purists will balk at this particular rendition of his work, but it's reasonably entertaining for 90-odd minutes and McDowell makes it worth a look anyway.

dot the i
Summit/Arcane 2003; 92 minutes; Director: Matthew Parkhill; Rating: ☠☠☠

A feisty Spanish woman living with her love-struck, clinging fiancé starts a torrid affair with a young man she meets in a nightclub, but all is not as it seems.

Set in France and shot straight to digital, Parkhill's low-budget psychological flick intrigues and ultimately delivers a wallop in its revelatory climax. Natalia Verbeke, on a bet, kisses Gael Garcia Bernal at her hen party and then, totally smitten, embarks on a clandestine affair with him, even though it appears that someone is following them with a video camera, recording every incident. Lanky James D'Arcy, the girl's drippy fiancé, is unceremoniously dumped after Verbeke agrees to marry him, but once wed, she rushes back to Bernal. At the end of his tether and consumed with jealousy, D'Arcy films himself blowing his brains out. The sting here is that the whole charade is a set-up—the woman has been duped by both men all along, unwittingly starring in a film about a relationship on the rocks, to be screened at the Indie-Vision Film Festival. To make matters worse, Verbeke has fallen for Bernal big-time and is seething with indignity. Verbeke plots her revenge. D'Arcy is gunned down at the festival and Bernal's two dim-witted camcorder pals take the rap, Verbeke having planted a gun on one of them. This kind of suspense thriller with a twist in its tail reminds us of the films that William Castle churned out in the 1950s and 1960s. *dot the i* grabs from start to finish, with the director making full use of his limited finances to produce a little gem of a picture.

Dracula 3000
ApolloProMedia/Fiction Film 2004; 86 minutes; Director: Darrell James Roodt; Rating: ☠

In the year 3000, the crew of deep space salvage vessel Mother 3 boards the derelict hulk Demeter, adrift for 50 years in the Carpathian Galaxy, only

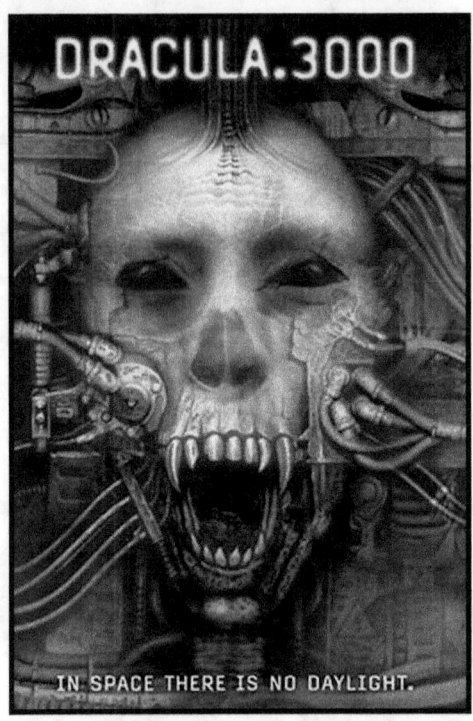

to encounter none other than Count Dracula.

The spirit of Bram Stoker most definitely *doesn't* live on in this insufferable "vampires in space" effort that would surely have the author spinning in his grave. We have bearded Casper Van Dien, as wooden as ever, joining the ranks of such luminaries as Edward Van Sloan and Peter Cushing, taking on the role of Abraham Van Helsing. Alexandra Kamp-Groeneveld plays a PVC-clad Mina and Grant Swanby hams it up as a whining, wheelchair-bound Arthur. Blonde Erika Eleniak turns out to be (a big bow to *Alien*) an android, sent to spy on the mission, while black dudes Coolio and Tiny Lister wisecrack their way through an execrable script. Langley Kirkwood plays Dracula (or Orlock), the chubbiest vampire since Lon Chaney donned a cape in *Son of Dracula*, and Udo Kier is the Demeter's captain, seen in intermittent video transmissions, acting as though he's having difficulty reading off the autocue. The plot? Apparently, 50 years previously, Kier made the mistake of stopping off at dying Planet Transylvania for a shipment of coffins, all filled with native sand. Dracula, it transpires, wanted to lie in infinite darkness after feeding off the blood of the Demeter's crew. Now Van Dien and company are up against the undead infection as the Count is revived and Coolio turns into the most ridiculous (and intensely irritating) bloodsucker the screen has ever seen. Eventually, Kamp-Groeneveld, Van Dien and Swanby are vampirized, all dispatched (along with Coolio) with a pool cue through the heart, and the sudden ending (hinting at a drying-up of production funds) sees Eleniak and Lister sloping off for some sexual shenanigans as the ship explodes on reaching the twin suns of Halbron. This eliminates the vampire leader, whose left arm has been severed after it was caught in a hatch door. With Swanby forever moaning, "We're all going to die" and Lister saying to Kamp-Groeneveld, "You're gonna vampire my black ass," it's no wonder many a purist will shrink at catching a single minute of this fiasco, which can't even be viewed as "tongue-in-cheek" horror fodder. At one point, Kamp-Groeneveld shouts, "This is so wrong." That statement just about sums up *Dracula 3000* to perfection; it will make audiences shudder with horror, but not that kind of shudder, and not that kind of horror!

Dracula's Curse

Asylum 2006; 107 minutes; Director: Leigh Scott; Rating: ☠☠

A group of vampire hunters known as "The Nine" forms an uneasy peace treaty with the undead clans that, after a period of five years, is broken by the evil Countess Bathorly.

Is Asylum's amateurish vampire tale a spoof that went badly wrong, even with Leigh Scott at the helm? Or is it simply a *vampire* movie that went badly wrong? Either way, in a nutshell, *Dracula's Curse* is so bad it's laughable in all the wrong places. Team leader Thomas Downey and his gun-toting posse of attractive (but dumb) female vampire exterminators, all resembling ex-porn starlets, call a truce in the war between the human race and the bloodsuckers. Five years on, the pact is violated when the wicked Countess (Christina Rosenberg) decides that she's had enough of being on friendly terms with non-vampires and wants to rule the roost. Rosenberg's acolytes abduct the girlfriend of one of the group and vampirize her. With a descendant of Van Helsing in tow (Rhett Giles), Downey sets off to defeat the Countess after she has done away with leading members of the vampire council. In the ensuing struggle between good and evil, it transpires that Downey is in fact Dracula. Fearsomely transforming into a *Jeepers Creepers*-type monster, Dracula kills the Countess and, inadvertently, his girlfriend (Eliza Swenson), who stares menacingly at the camera in human form as the end credits roll. Granted, *Dracula's Curse* is redeemed somewhat by Downey's startling change into "The Old One," a suitably freaky, cloven-hoofed, six-foot gray goblin with batwings (therefore elevating the film to two-star status!). And the second half of the picture is thoughtfully divided into book-like chapters. But the

acting is dire, the sound poor, Scott's direction disappointingly unsophisticated (and we all thought Ed Wood and Jerry Warren were the bottom of the barrel), the makeup on the level of a series of Halloween masks (with the obligatory *Nosferatu* clone) and the color washed-out. This clumsy effort is best viewed after a few drinks. Stone cold sober, audiences may want to pass it by.

Dragon

Asylum 2003; 90 minutes; Director: Leigh Scott; Rating: ☠☠☠

In olden times, a kingdom wages war with the Dark Elves and an evil sorceress who controls a fire-breathing dragon.

Princess Amelia Jackson-Gray, two escorting knights (Matthew Wolf and Jon-Paul Gates) and forest dwellers Jeff Denton, Jason DeParis and blonde Rachel Haines trek through gloomy woodlands to enlist the help of Lord Blackthorn in defeating both the elves and the dragon. En route, they encounter witch Eliza Swenson and her aide (Jessica Bork), argue among themselves, indulge in a great deal of gibberish relating to spells and riddles and ward off marauding elves, eventually, with the assistance of Swenson. They even slay the dragon with a magic scepter after everyone except Jackson-Gray, Wolf and Denton have perished. The curse is then lifted, and the elves bow in acquiescence to their new princess. Yes, *Dragon* is typical of the sort of "U" certificate second-feature we would find showing in any British cinema during the 1960s. This is the type of movie where audiences of the day were quite happy to ignore Swenson's quite obviously fake white contact lenses, were not too bothered by the sight of a sub-Harryhausen monster, lapped up the numerous talkative interludes delivered by a labored cast and were entertained by the black-faced, pointy-eared protagonists. Listen, why spend millions on fairy tale efforts such as *Legend*, *The Princess Bride* and *Dragonslayer* when independents can produce fare like *Dragon* for peanuts? Really, there's not that much to choose between the big budget and the low budget. Any 21st-century computer wizard with the right hardware could drum up a dragon similar to the model on display in this picture, and the creature is engaging enough to amuse the youngsters. However, Swenson's necromancer won't scare anybody over the age of eight. In addition, this has got to be the most gore-free picture the company has ever produced. So there you have it—swords and sorcery for the under-12's by courtesy of Asylum's stock ensemble of writers/actors/producers and directors (many of whom have cameo roles in these movies), incorporating a number of incidents that older buffs may find to their liking. In its own economical way, this is a charming little fantasy number best viewed in the company of popcorn-loving, cola-swigging kiddies.

Dungeons & Dragons 2: The Elemental Might
aka: Dungeons & Dragons: Wrath of the Dragon God
Skyline Films/Studio Hamburg 2005; 105 minutes; Director: Gerry Lively; Rating: ☠☠☠

A former soldier and four heroes journey to a distant land to steal a black orb in the hands of a wicked sorcerer. The sorcerer wishes to awaken a mighty dragon, commanding the monster to lay waste to the kingdom of Ishmir.

A direct-to-video sequel to 2000's *Dungeons & Dragons*, undoubtedly made to delight all devotees of the sword and sorcery game. But what about those who don't care about the game? The profusion of fanciful place-names littering the dialogue won't signify a thing, and neither will the characters and their machinations. No matter, the simplified "good versus evil" plot means that we can sit back and enjoy this colorful fantasy on a *Lord of the Rings* level, but *not* on a *Harry Potter* level. Thankfully, on this occasion, there are no kids in the way to spoil the action. Bruce Payne (reprising his role from the first movie) plays the sorcerer, determined to remove Ishmir from the map by rising from its mountain lair a colossal dragon. Mark Dymond, Ellie Chidzy, Tim Stern, Steven Elder and Lucy Gaskell are the five sent by Lord Roy Marsden to retrieve the orb before Ishmir is destroyed. Dymond's wife (Clemency Burton-Hill) uses spells to guide them into one of the undead, where the warriors battle winged monsters and assorted CGI beasties before the disturbed dragon attacks Ishmir. But the dragon is quashed by the orb's mystical power and Payne, one arm sliced off, kicks his heels in a dungeon. The movie dazzles with a cornucopia of skullduggery involving Payne's ghoul-faced

ally; magic tomes prophesying ancient legends; weird and wonderful creatures; a cave emitting green, poisonous gas; and spooky dungeons deep beneath a statue's base. Unfortunately, the script contains incomprehensible (to non-aficionados) jargon and even teleportation. It's all a bit hard-to-swallow, like a convoluted picture book coming to life on the big screen. In its favor, *Dungeons & Dragons 2* contains picturesque, striking photography, decent effects and a fantastic dragon. Against it, Dymond and Payne make a pretty limp-wristed hero and villain. At least the film adopts a more serious tone than similar fodder, and adults should therefore appreciate the picture as much as the younger generation.

The Entrance
Jove Pictures 2006; 81 minutes; Director: Damon Vignale; Rating: ☠☠☠

A 17th-century sorceress, originally a possessed nun in 1612, demands continual sacrifices over the centuries to appease her wrath at being exorcized by a learned monk.

Shot digitally, this Canadian psychological-cum-supernatural thriller is high on atmosphere, low on cohesiveness. A distraught stranger, ex-drug dealer Michael Eklund, visits policewoman Sarah-Jane Redmond. According to his far-fetched yarn, he and three other men, all sporting dubious pasts, have been kept prisoner in a basement under a multi-storey parking lot, playing a series of games in which the losers die. Those that perish are shown scenes of their crimes via a movie projector (people overdosing on drugs; a young boy raped by a child pervert) before they vanish into a supernatural black hole. Eklund has been allowed to escape creepy janitor Ron Sauvé on condition that he returns with a new sacrifice. A debt to be paid, but to whom? Abducting the disbelieving Redmond, the druggie takes her to the parking lot and drives off, leaving her alone to battle sinister influences perpetuated by the witch and her demon acolyte. *The Entrance* is one of those convoluted exercises in haunting terror that audiences will never fathom unless they give it their absolute undivided attention. Some notable sequences include black and white shots of a monk scribbling texts and exorcizing a woman roped to a bed; the witch seen in flashes, showing off her staring eyes and fanged teeth; a circular symbol known as Baal-berith tattooed on the back of Sauvé's hand; and Redmond compelled to experience her own rape, meeting her attacker face-to-face. This is all very puzzling. Redmond's father is another victim of the mad sorceress (projected grainy images of the man gunning down a colleague), and in the last moments, Redmond goes to shoot Eklund, realizing too late that the sins of those slain have been passed to her. "You pay for your past misdemeanors," seems to be the film's message in a cheaply produced offering containing a sparse, dreamy score that exposes the stark surroundings. The film features a good performance from Redmond as the cop, but she *doesn't* meet with a happy ending. At least watching her up against the forces of evil, one can easily forgive some of the gaping holes in the plot.

Epoch: Evolution
UFO 2003; 94 minutes; Director: Ian Watson; Rating: ☠☠☠☠

Ten years after an alien monolith, the Torus, appears on Earth, two more emerge from deep underground, in France and Russia, coinciding with an outbreak of hostilities between the United States, Russia and China. Is it the intention of these structures to destroy the planet or prevent a catastrophic war?

The Torus resembles a 400-foot high black jagged spinning top standing on a narrow base—expanding burn rings radiate out from these alien artifacts, and when they meet, Earth will be annihilated and terra-formed into a world suitable for another species. Doctor David Keith's son was conceived in the original Torus and now possesses otherworldly powers. A group of religious fanatics employ an assassin to kill him and Keith, seeing them as a threat to civilized society and their own ambitions, while the Chinese also view the alien monoliths as a threat to *their* ambitions. Tied in with this is a crystal containing strange markings, discovered near a Greek monastery in the 13th century, that turns out to be a key that enables Keith and dishy anthropologist Angel Boris Reed to open a portal situated at the top of the Russian Torus to unravel its secrets. *Epoch: Evolution* has a rushed feel to it, the general tenor of the narrative not made clear until 40-odd minutes have passed. The action jumps all over the place from one country to the next, as weather patterns develop into chaos due to the effect of the rings, but at least the movie moves quickly and features excellent CGI effects—a "Space Defense System" space station taken out by a Chinese missile; the interior of the Torus (a series of garishly lit passages, home to a jellyfish-type being); the monolithic forms rising majestically out of the ground; and, of course, the by-now obligatory opening shots of our solar system, a hallmark of this brand of sci-fi. The space hardware looks like the real McCoy as well. Keith's son saves the day, standing before the Torus in Russia. Aware of the boy's alien conception, that he is "The One from Within," the monolith disintegrates, exposing a gleaming spaceship that leaves Earth with its French counterpart in search of another planet to lay waste and re-populate. World War III is canceled as a consequence. Cramming in religious themes (the French look upon the monolith as a holy relic; ancient Greek scrolls foretell of the coming of the Torus) and world politics (the world's peace is in jeopardy due to the big nations' refusal to converse with one another), Watson's energetic movie rises above the rest of the pack (almost epic in scope for an indie production). It is more involved than most and, although leaving a lot of loose ends dangling, makes for thoughtful science fiction entertainment.

Evilenko
Pacific Pictures/MiBAC 2004; 111 minutes; Director: David Grieco; Rating: ☠☠☠☠☠

Dismissed from his teaching post for making sexual advances on a 12-year-old female pupil, a rabid communist-cum-pedophile becomes one of Russia's most notorious serial killers.

Move over Hannibal Lecter, Malcolm McDowell is on the prowl! The British actor radiates pure depravity like no other, playing Andrej Romanovic Evilenko, who between 1984 and 1992 raped and murdered 55 girls, boys and women by strangulation and the blade, eating parts of their bodies for good measure. Although based on fact, the movie is presented as horror fiction, McDowell first seen in Kiev, 1984, sporting a pudding-basin haircut, his magnified eyes staring unblinkingly from behind large spectacles, virtually hypnotizing his intended victims before pouncing. An uncharacteristically dowdy Frances Barber is McDowell's unsuspecting wife, while Ronald Pickup is a homosexual psychoanalyst (and political activist) who thinks he *may* know who the merciless killer is (he guesses correctly, catching the monster in the act of abusing a young girl; he's then slaughtered with a cutthroat razor). Laconic magistrate Martin Csokas is on the sadist's trail, completely befuddled as the mutilated corpses turn up on a regular basis. Naturally, the content is discomforting, the killings not overly graphic, although one scene is not suitable fare for those easily upset—McDowell uses his wiles and "kindly old uncle" routine to lure a schoolboy into a toilet on a train, butchering him. It's the *thought* of

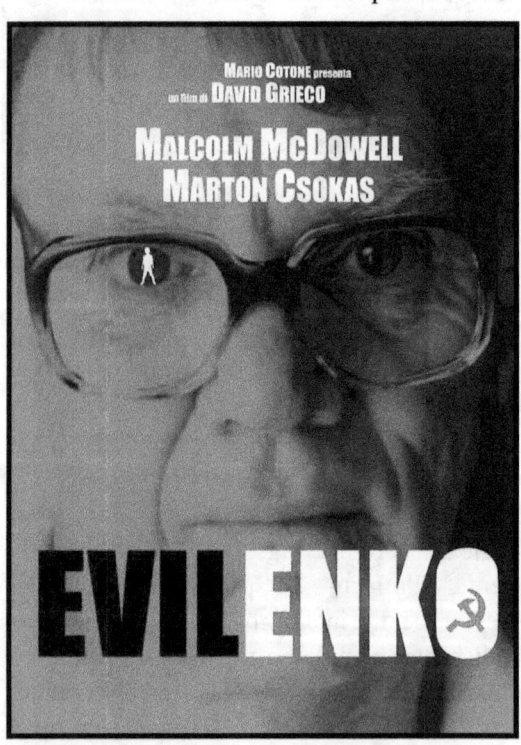

what the man does to his victims that unsettles the nerves, especially the one time that a police officer describes to Csokas the state of a girl's body and how it has been violated. Eventually caught in 1992 after committing a murder on the grounds of an army barracks and being spotted by a soldier, McDowell is interrogated in true *Silence of the Lambs* fashion, chillingly reeling off with cocky ease details of every single crime committed: names, dates and locations. Blessed with a haunting, low-key soundtrack and bathed in somber colors to match the dour, bleak mood and wintry streets, *Evilenko* is nothing short of a minor masterpiece of horror *film noir*. McDowell, who has made a specialty out of portraying the kind of people you wouldn't want to meet, is absolutely mesmerizing as the cannibalistic madman—baleful eyes on the lookout for prey, a disconcerting habit of sucking in his lower lip. Perhaps this is what Alex from *A Clockwork Orange* would have turned out to be like 30 years on!

Fall Down Dead
New Films Intl. 2007; 93 minutes; Director: Jon Keeyes; Rating: ☠☠☠

A psychopath known as The Picasso Killer has been at large in a city for nine months, carving up his female victims into grotesque poses in imitation of some form of perverted art.

Rheumy-eyed Udo Kier has cornered the market for continental nutcases, playing them for decades. So no surprise then that he turns up in this low-budget serial killer flick, portraying a murderer who slashes women to death with a cut-throat razor and keeps various body parts in his apartment (check out that chess board with fingers replacing the traditional chess pieces!). Kier hacks his way through 93 minutes of standard killer-on-the-loose action without a single drop of blood staining his expensive coat. He is homing in on waitress Dominique Swain who, after witnessing a particularly gruesome slaying in an alley, finds herself holed up in an office block with cowardly security guard David Carradine, two cops (R. Keith Harris and Mehmet Gunsur) and three other people. And a city on/off blackout isn't helping matters! Will they escape from the madman's indestructible clutches or won't they? After several graphic and extremely bloody set pieces (including a man whose face has been skinned, and Monica Dean's head cleaved in half), Swain and Gunsur, who have formed a close bond (she fancies him, he fancies her), live to tell the tale, even though the trick climax has Kier (surviving a roof fall) sneaking into Swain's flat and snipping off a locket of her daughter's hair, to be used in his latest artwork. How many of these types of movies can you make while keeping everything fresh? Keeyes' flashy direction and artful lighting effects stick to the rules and generally come up trumps, making audiences forget (apart from Kier) the mediocre acting (Carradine appears to have had one drink too many, stumbling around and slurring his lines). And the Master of Suspense would be less than pleased to discover that the block that serves as the main setting is called "The Hitchcock." An ear-splitting soundtrack jars on the senses, Swain's spunky heroine isn't *that* convincing, and too many similar shots showing the beleaguered cast wandering through one empty corridor after another occur. Notwithstanding these faults, *Fall Down Dead* is marginally better than the usual run of slasher fare. Kier's chilling delivery of lines such as, "You will be my masterpiece, my Mona Lisa" evokes memories of those continental horror masterpieces of the 1960s, of which at times this picture oddly resembles.

Falling Fire

Producers Network/TMN 1997; 93 minutes; Director: David D'or; Rating: 🙎🙎🙎

Due to Earth's failing resources, astronauts maneuver giant asteroids into the planet's orbit in order to exploit their mineral wealth.

A sci-fi conspiracy thriller, *Falling Fire* attempts to throw into the pot environmental and religious issues and comes up with a talkative mix of varying ideas that it tackles in a somewhat heavy-handed manner at times. Attempting to guide an asteroid Earthward by controlled atomic detonations on its surface, members of a space station carry out the tricky task. The erratic supervision of highly strung Captain Mackenzie Gray hampers the mission, which is also under threat from a saboteur (Zehra Leverman), the daughter of religious fanatic Christian Vidosa, who wants the colossal rock to collide with

Earth, seeing it as God's retribution for mankind's sins. The rich, meanwhile, are leaving instructions for their bodies to be placed in a state of cryogenic suspension (at a price), their revival to take place following the ensuing cataclysm. After the ship has survived a reactor overload and several crew members are done away with by Leverman's devious machinations, the saboteur is exposed as the spy and jettisoned into space, the religious fanatic shot and the asteroid safely blasted into Earth's orbit. The acting flight commander (Michael Paré) escapes in a shuttle as the space station ploughs into the colossal ball of rock, the resulting explosion guiding the asteroid on its chosen trajectory above the planet. Some impressive shots of the asteroid and the space station, including a couple of effective space walks, compensate for the draggy, preachy interludes that bog the movie down. But on the whole, *Falling Fire* is an intelligent addition to the "Earth is in danger from a meteorite/asteroid" genre.

Fear Itself: Dark Memories
aka: **Ring Around the Rosie**
Poligon Films/Run Ent. 2006; 87 minutes; Director: Rubi Zack; Rating: 💀💀

Following the death of her grandmother, a publicist and her boyfriend drive out to the country to put the family house in order, but the woman soon becomes entangled in a harrowing series of events linked to a past tragedy involving her long-dead sister.

Not even the burly presence of Tom Sizemore (playing a hick psycho) can raise this supernatural "things that go bump in the night" potboiler above the level of average, as we once again are treated to the much-favored "woman in peril" setting that regurgitates all the old tricks in the book to scare an audience. Such as Gina Philips' sister (Jenny Mollen) appearing at the house, then sometimes disappearing. Then we are barraged with all the usual suspects—the spirits of two young girls (the sisters when they were younger?); a corpse-like face in the bathroom mirror; windows clattering during the night; an ancient wooden door leading to who-knows-where; flickering lights; clumping footsteps; and handyman Sizemore forever muttering something about, "I won't let you fall." What the significance is of the decomposed corpse of a deer shown at the beginning

I've no idea. It's placed there for shock value, probably, as is the scene when the actress screams "Rats!" at deafening volume when a dozen of the much-maligned rodents spill out of a cupboard. It's very easily a third of the way in before we can deduce the storyline, the movie practically giving the game away early on. Philips is caught up in a terrifying paranormal past/present situation. Sizemore murdered her 11-year-old sister 17 years previously, and Philips is enacting the circumstances leading up to her sister's death at the hands of the sick, sex-obsessed loner (she plunges backwards from a window). Boyfriend Jeff Batinkoff turns up at the end to take Philips away from the accursed place, the sister's spirit now at peace as it vanishes into the woods with the girls' treasured doll, Sizemore's nearby shack long-abandoned and empty. For a pleasant change, the film is embellished with a decent score, although a little too loud and over-elaborate at times. But this alone doesn't make amends for dismal performances all round (apart from Sizemore) and an over-familiar plot that, to be truthful, has been done to death and in much better productions than this one.

Fear of the Dark
Constellation/Faulkner 2003; 86 minutes; Director: K.C. Bascombe; Rating: ☠☠☠

When his parents go out for the evening, a 12-year-old boy diagnosed as having a morbid fear of the dark is terrorized by "the night things" when a storm causes a power failure.

With this cheap and cheerful "creepy house" thriller, director Bascombe ingeniously plays on most youngsters' nocturnal fears of what is in the closet, what lies under the bed and what is that shadowy form in the corner of the room when the lights go out. So in one way or another, we can sympathize with Jesse James as he notices strange shapes on the walls, is afraid to descend the cellar steps, has odd scratches on his back and suffers recurring nightmares relating to an incident when he was a toddler (of being dragged across the cellar floor by an unseen boogeyman). His babysitting brother (Kevin Zegers) scoffs at what he regards as silly childish notions, but he soon has a reality check when he himself is subjected to the same kind of spooky occurrences that have scared his baby brother witless. The director throws everything into the pot as the tension escalates—flickering on/off lights, weird marks, writhing outlines on the walls, thunder and lightning, furniture moved out of position, distorted shots of the landing and hallway, doors banging, the TV channel switching from a cartoon to a horror movie and zombie-like figures appearing at will. All this culminates in Zegers' girlfriend (Rachel Skarsten) entering the scene and all three being attacked by rabid dogs, hordes of cockroaches and living corpses. Young James, in the nick of time, reconnects the lights and these hostile phantoms vanish into the ether. We don't receive an explanation for the cause of all this paranormal activity, simply that the older brother, in the final frame, is now being tormented by these "night things" in the darkness of *his* bedroom, forced into believing James' stories. A tinkling *Halloween*-style piano track heightens the suspense in some scenes, and the two screen brothers actually mouth lines of an articulate nature. Considering the low-budget feel, this is quite acceptable horror fare if one can get past that ghastly opening yodeling title music.

Fido

Anagram Pictures 2006; 93 minutes; Director: Andrew Currie; Rating: ☠☠☠☠

In the suburbs of Willard, families employ zombie helpers to carry out the household chores, their flesh-eating tendencies kept in check by electronic collars.

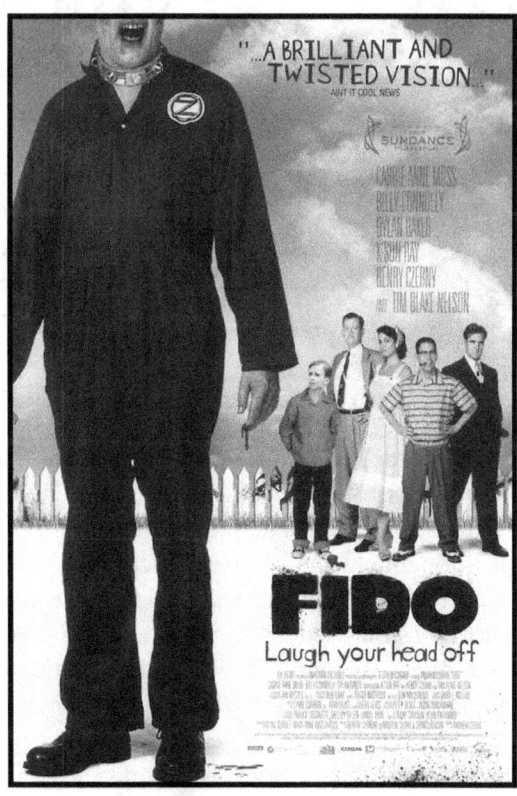

If the term "cute" can be applied to any horror-comedy, than *Fido* fully deserves that accolade, a pastiche of 1950s suburbia photographed in rich colors that kicks off in spoofing 1950s newsreel black and white fashion. A viral space dust has settled over America, reanimating the dead who have to be cordoned off from towns in the aptly named Zombie Lands. If fitted with an electronic collar, however, some gray-faced specimens can be controlled via remote control handsets and serve a useful purpose in society, such as delivering papers and milk, and mowing lawns. Young Dylan Baker christens his personal zombie (Billy

Connolly) Fido. When troublesome brothers Aaron Brown and Brandon Olds tamper with Connolly's collar, he reverts to type, ripping the arm off an old woman who then becomes a zombie herself. To protect his new (and unusual) friend, Baker decapitates the lady and disposes of her body, and the remainder of the picture is taken up with Zomcon's head honcho (Henry Czemy) and the police trying to locate the killer while the zombies are in revolt. After Baker's Dad dies, his mother (Carrie-Anne Moss) gets a little *too* close to Connolly, emotional-wise (anything else would be unthinkable!). When odious Czemy is zombified, his daughter (Alexia Fast) leads him around like an obedient dog. And the end shot sees Connolly stroking Moss' new baby, the zombie having truly taken the role of her dead husband. *Fido* is a lovingly crafted parody of

'50s life, smoothly combining humor, romance and horror, and although some might think it plain daft, it's a daftness that pokes gentle fun at the zombie genre which, let's face it, is no bad thing.

First Born

Blueprint/Virtual Studios 2007; 95 minutes; Director: Isaac Webb; Rating: ☠☠☠

A New York ballet dancer becomes pregnant and takes up residence, in a large house, miles away from the city. Following the difficult birth of her daughter, she starts to imagine that malign forces are contributing to her fragile state of mind.

Is *First Born* merely a study of post-natal depression, a supernatural thriller, a psychological drama with hints of devilry, or something else? All these elements are included in the convoluted plot that has Elisabeth Shue ensconced in her vast, very cold (in atmosphere) house. Businessman husband Steven Mackintosh works late into the night and sinister Kathleen Chalfant, employed as a home-help and babysitter, acts as though she practices the black arts in her spare time. Feeling increasingly isolated and prone to sweaty nightmares, Shue's perfectly structured world seems to be disintegrating around her. Director Webb's well-directed movie throws in plenty of tidbits to keep us guessing as to what's going on here. Why are white mice (a witch's familiar in olden times) scuttling around? Why does a raggedy baby doll keep appearing and where did it originate before Shue picked it up from a subway carriage? Who is the mysterious

"Jenny," a teenager who used to live in the house but now no longer exists? Is she the girl Shue spotted on the subway train, holding the doll (or baby), then vanishing into thin air? Why did Chalfant place infant's hair and a dummy in a bag under the baby's crib? When Shue attends a business party, how come all the rooms are suddenly devoid of guests except for one? Was Chalfant telling the truth when she claimed to police that a carving knife was found in the crib? A plethora of questions leads to no real satisfying answer, even though the director goes in for the compulsory shock ending. Shue is seen burying the omnipresent staring-eyed doll under the lawn, and Mackintosh arrives home to find the doll in the crib. Has Shue finally flipped and buried her baby alive? The actress (a little bit on the well-built side to play a ballet dancer) turns in a fine performance as the mother under enormous stress from Lord-knows-what, and Chalfant is appropriately creepy as the wizened housekeeper who *could* be nursing a dark secret. It's a real shame the viewer isn't let in on the secret, if in fact there ever was one. It's that kind of a picture—teasing, tantalizing but ultimately a tad disappointing.

Five Across the Eyes
Trauma One Ent. 2006; 94 minutes; Directors: Greg Swinson and Ryan Thiessen; Rating: ☠☠

Five girls driving back from a football game become lost in the dark. They desperately try to shake off their tail, a female homicidal killer who, for reasons of her own, is hell-bent on capturing and torturing them.

It's a well-worn cliché that many products churned out by independent film producers appear as though, all told, the amount expended only came to a measly $100, even if a larger sum of cash was actually spent. Well, this one *does* look like a $100 movie and it surely can't have cost a lot more. Shot in grainy *Blair Witch* mode, 95% of Swinson and Thiessen's hysterical horror show takes place within the confines of Sandra Paduch's car, the remaining 5% outside of it. No plot as such, and no characterization either—Paduch,

Danielle Lilley, Mia Yi, Angela Brunda and Jennifer Barnett drive endlessly down badly lit country roads, chased by psycho Veronica Garcia with a rifle, she nursing a severe attitude problem. When their vehicle breaks down, runs out of fuel, gets a puncture or is forced off the road by Garcia's car, the girls are subjected to prolonged bouts of torture from the mad harridan. She shoots to wound and helps herself to a toolbox, carrying out some pretty basic dental surgery on one of the petrified girls. Discovering three corpses in the trunk of Garcia's vehicle, the teenagers try one more time to flee but are caught yet again by the killer. Finally, they manage to turn the tables on their dogged pursuer who is rendered unconscious by a hammer-blow to the head. Each of the five, hyped-up for revenge, stabs her repeatedly with a screwdriver, setting fire to the mutilated body after it has ceased twitching. *Five Across the Eyes* doesn't offer any kind of a motive for Garcia's abhorrent penchant for lustful infliction of pain on others. The movie's simply an excuse (and seems to be the target) for a certain section of movie-going clientele to revel in firsthand. We are given five young women in extreme tremors, fearing death at any moment—vomiting, urinating, spitting out loose teeth, blood oozing from cuts, constant screaming, bickering, sobbing and near-nakedness (as when Garcia orders them to strip at gunpoint). Quite a list for any sadist to get his (or her) teeth into! There's no escaping the fact that it's a nasty little number, albeit a tolerably constructed exercise in camcorder frenzied savagery, and it won't appeal to everyone's tastes. "I'm having a nervous breakdown," shouts Lilley at one point. Audiences could easily experience one too, sitting through this picture.

For Sale By Owner
aka: **13teen**
Chheda Films 2005; 90 minutes; Director: Pritesh N. Chheda; Rating: ☠☠☠☠

In the town of Emeryville, a serial killer is at large, carving the number 13 on the victims' chests.

A main cast of three, minimal music, a terse script and a surprise coda all go toward making *For Sale By Owner* a brilliant, low-budget horror suspenser that lovers of the rare and unusual should seek out forthwith. The events in this artful little shocker unfold over one rainy day and night. Alone in a house (is it hers?), child social worker Amanda Brown has an unwanted visitor in the form of bulky real estate contract specialist John Lansch. He's there, so he asserts, to close a deal on the sale of the property. She denies all knowledge of any sale. As the rain continues to pour down, he asks to stay inside until his ride appears, and after a few reservations, Brown nervously agrees. But is there more to this pair than meets the eye? Chheda calculatingly shoots in close-up and odd camera angles to get right inside the heads of the menacingly quiet Lansch and sassy, on-edge Brown. She also suffers from disturbing black and white flashbacks to when she was a young girl, visions of abused, sobbing children tantalizingly thrown in for good measure. And just who is "Angela," the friend she keeps phoning? Is Lansch (in the middle of a custody battle over his daughter) the killer that has been terrorizing the town? The arrival of morose Marc Hustvedt, sent to repair a faulty security chip, throws an almighty spanner in the works. Is he the murderer? Tension and mind-games between all three build to a crescendo, when the director opens up a Pandora's box of revelations. "Angela," the supposed person Brown has been talking to all along, is her old rag doll; Lansch is informed by his boss by mobile that the owner of the house left on vacation some time ago; a bloodstained knife is discovered in Lansch's case; and Brown, in those troubling flash-

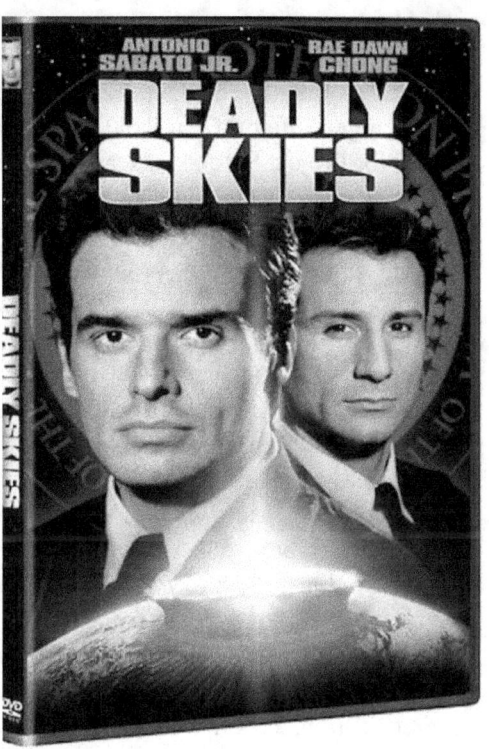

backs, was apparently raped 13 times as a youngster by her guardian priest. Brown, it turns out, is the serial killer. The woman's tortured past unhinged her to the point of schizophrenia, and she stabs Lansch to death. She in turn has a road sign plunged into her chest by the limping, battered Hustvedt (the result of a baseball bat attack), revealing the number 13 tattooed on her skin as she lays dying in a pool of blood. A marvelous exercise in how to produce a classy thriller on shoestring finances, Chheda's psycho picture, it must be said, puts a lot of those highly expensive serial killer movies made over the past few years firmly in the shade.

Force of Impact
aka: **Deadly Skies**
Black Lagoon Pictures/Insight Film Studios 2007; 89 minutes; Director: Sam Irvin; Rating ☠

An asteroid the size of Texas, dragged out of orbit, heads toward Earth, bringing with it death and destruction.

There are a great many science fiction disaster movies relating to the Earth under threat from approaching meteors/asteroids/planetoids stretching back several decades, but none worse than this turgid effort. Viewing *Force of Impact* is roughly the equivalent of wading through treacle. And don't be fooled by the initial four minutes showing lumps of burning rock raining from the skies, because nothing of any consequence follows; the action grinds to a halt after 30 minutes. Hidden behind a colossal meteorite is a rogue asteroid that endangers life on Earth, and only inventor Antonio Sabato, Jr., who used to work for Project Safe Skies, can save the day with his super-duper laser gun. Trouble is, smarmy General Michael Moriarty has his eyes on said laser for use in warfare as a weapon of mass destruction, so Sabato sabotaged the project on ethical grounds. Enter astro-scientist Rae Dawn Chong who, unable to convince the authorities that the world is doomed in 20 hours, breaks into the Air Force Base housing the laser with colleague Dominic Zamprogna, Sabato and Michael Boisvert pursued concurrently by Moriarty and a gang of militia. It's not giving too much away by revealing that Chong and Sabato save the day, aiming the laser beam at the asteroid on orders from the U.S. president, blowing it into a million little chunks of harmless debris. Apart from the sluggish pacing, the acting is pretty dreadful throughout. A tired-looking Moriarty slurs his lines, Sabato's pretty-boy looks belie his lifeless performance, and Chong (previously spotted in 1985's *Commando*) should, in all honesty, be held to account for crimes committed in the name of bad acting. Shrieking her clichés ("It's a matter of life and death!"), constantly repeating what someone else has just said (Sabato: "We did it." Chong: "Wow! We did it!") and screeching excitedly "C'mon, c'mon, c'mon, c'mon" and "Please, please, please, please" when the going gets tough, all spoken with a deadpan expression. She even coos, "That is *so* nice" when Sabato invites her into his pad at the end for some post-asteroid lip action. This is one actress who should return to drama school forthwith and immediately brush up on her dubious technique. *Force of Impact* is the dullest of the dull. Any film that makes *Savage Planet* seem mildly diverting by comparison can't have a lot going for it, and this picture doesn't.

Frankenfish
Bayou Films/Silver Nitrate 2004; 84 minutes; Director: Mark Dippe; Rating: ☠☠☠

Genetically mutated giant fish that have the ability to breathe underwater and on land cause terror among the inhabitants of an isolated Bayou community.

It's all the fault of big game hunter Tomas Arana and his Chinese mobster pals. To liven up his appetite for sport, Arana unleashes the fish (scientifically bred with a species of killer snake) into the swamps without realizing how large and voracious they would become. Following the discovery of the chewed-up corpse of a local fisherman, detective Tory Kittles and biologist China Chow from the Department of Fisheries take a small launch up river to investigate. In no time at all they find themselves battling for their lives against the 12-foot-long predators. Arana's original research boat is also discovered, the bilge area full of rotting corpses. Most of the action in *Frankenfish* takes place at night as, one by one, every member of the cast except for Kittles and besotted chick K.D. Aubert is finished off by the over-large fish in a grisly manner—a hippy decapitated, the headless trunk spurting jets of blood; a woman ripped apart; a man swallowed whole; and others dragged to their deaths by the ravenous creatures. Even the delectable (but lesbian, judging by her chat-up conversation with Aubert) Chow has half her head blown away when a shotgun goes off by accident.

"Oh man, we are f—g fish bait," cries the wimpy lawyer as boats are smashed, one houseboat set ablaze and another pulverized to the point of submersion beneath the swamp waters. Hammy villain Arana and his mob arrive on the scene near the end, only to be gobbled up by a 25-foot monster specimen that meets its blood-spattered demise when it hurls itself into the rotor blades of Kittles' boat. This leaves time for the cop to engage in a bit of lip action with sexy bedraggled Aubert. The final shot is of the lawyer stuck on a muddy bank, the victim of a pack of baby flesh-eaters that swarm over his body. *Frankenfish* is well acted and scripted but permeates an air of "It's all been done before." More should have been made of the mutant fish themselves. They look great *when* we are allowed to see them, which isn't often. So the movie drags in places. The one big plus is Kittles. It's nice to have a black main character carrying a film for a change, the actor shining in his role as the detective-cum-medical examiner, slightly Vin Diesel in approach and none the worse for it.

Frankenstein
Flame TV/L.I.F.T. Productions 2004; 88 minutes; Director: Marcus Nispel; Rating: 🩻

In New Orleans, a serial killer is extracting various organs from his slaughtered victims. Unbeknown to the police, the murderer is 200 years old, one of a number of super-beings created by a Dr. Victor Helios, alias Frankenstein.

A *Frankenstein* flick in name only, adapted from a Dean Koontz novel, with none other than Martin Scorsese as executive producer. Yet despite these illustrious personages, director Nispel's addition to the longest-running saga in horror film history is an utter shambles, for many reasons. Koontz apparently disassociated himself from what was to be a two-parter, hence the yawning, open-ended and abrupt ending that comes as a complete cop-out. A police partnership comprising Adam Goldberg and Parker Posey are on the trail of a killer whose recent victim has had his heart torn from his body. Another cop (burly Michael Madsen) tries his hardest to interfere in their investigations. Things take an ominous turn when a morgue assistant claims that the victim possessed two hearts, an unusual number of teeth and had a high bone density, giving him abnormal strength. Meanwhile, incarcerated in his splendid Gothic mansion, a sinister 200-year-old surgeon (Thomas Kretschmann) has not only created his own beautiful wife, but the results of his handiwork (also two centuries old) are roaming the city, hunted by none other than Madsen, who stores their livers, hearts and other body parts in his decrepit apartment. He also has the power to reproduce, something sinister writhing inside his abdomen. On the side of good is Kretschmann's original creation, Vincent Perez (cloaked and scarred), who finally defeats Madsen in an old warehouse, pushing him from a gantry to his death. As the killer lies dead, a gaping hole in his stomach (what was it that crawled out?), the film suddenly (and annoyingly) closes with a discussion on how to defeat the evil doctor before he populates the world with his "children." Photographed along the lines of *Se7en* in grungy, dirty color, with New Orleans' baroque architecture standing in for the Universal and Hammer villages of yore, this *Frankenstein* suffers from disjointed scenes (many simply fading into black), a predominance of close-ups (to get that all-important *film noir* effect, no doubt) and, even at a short 88 minutes, an unbelievable amount of superfluous padding. Why have a sub-plot involving Posey's autistic brother when it isn't followed through? Why that drawn-out funeral parlor interlude? Why the arty opening shot of kids playing under a hose? Why the endless discussions about whether Goldberg should "get it on" with Posey? Unwanted scenes never hampered the old *Frankenstein* flicks. They simply got on with it. What's more, this misguided picture isn't remotely enjoyable as a piece of horror cinema. It's bleak, dull and uninteresting. It *is* possible to produce a modern-day variant on the old legend and come up with a winner (see the review below). But this version fails on all counts; dig out those Universal and Hammer classics, and you'll see what I mean.

Frankenstein Reborn
Asylum 2005; 84 minutes; Director: Leigh Scott; Rating: ☠☠☠☠☠

Incarcerated in an asylum for the criminally insane and accused of a wave of brutal slayings, Dr. Victor Frank (Rhett Giles) relates to a psychiatrist the chain of events that led to the creation of a crazed monster following a series of medical experiments to restore paralyzed limbs. At the same time Frank tries to convince the authorities that this supposed creature is out to get him in revenge.

Frankenstein meets the slasher/splatter exploitation movie genre in this phenomenally violent, twisted and gruesome updating of the old Mary Shelley story, a no-holds-barred effort from Asylum filmed in just two weeks with great panache. Giles is attempting to cure spinal injuries (and ultimately to reanimate the dead) by perfecting "biological nanotechnology" on a paraplegic (Joel Hebner), rejuvenating the man's dead cells, but his experiment has disastrous side-effects. The doctor's evil and deep-rooted homicidal (and sexual) fantasies are transferred via computer into Hebner's system, causing the man to have nightmares and become disoriented, now desiring the experiments to end. Giles refuses and shoots him dead. Hebner's body, with the aid of brain surgeon Jeff Denton, is then resurrected as a deformed monster that acts out Giles' murderous visions by first killing Denton, followed by slaughtering both his detested associates and various women. All this mayhem helps the doctor rebuild his dead girlfriend (Eliza Swenson), using female body parts. A little girl eventually befriends the monster after her babysitter becomes a victim, the child assisting the police in establishing Giles' lurid tale as fact, not the ravings of a madman. Told in a series of confusing flashbacks after a nauseating opening few minutes of butchery, the movie suffers terribly from a muffled audio track in places, which detracts (but not that much) from oodles of bloodletting—limbs torn from bodies; bloody autopsy-type dissections; a decapitation; brains blown out; female nudity; drug usage; and kinky sexual activity. From the energetic direction and acting, though, audiences get the impression that everyone had a ball making the flick. Livelier than the likes of Kenneth Branagh's intense but boring *Mary Shelley's Frankenstein*, this film comes closer in feel to Richard Cunha's memorable schlock feature *Frankenstein's Daughter* or, dare we say, *I Was a Teenage Frankenstein*. This could be, low-budget enterprise or not, one of the most inventive *Frankenstein* movies ever produced, since it is so wildly over-the-top in all departments. The monster itself is suitably grotesque, a ragged, skull-faced version of Christopher Lee in Hammer's 1957 classic *Curse of Frankenstein*. *Frankenstein Reborn* is sick—but slick!

Frayed

Lock It In Ent. 2007; 111 minutes; Directors: Norbert Caoili and Rob Portmann; Rating: ☠☠☠☠

In 1994, a mentally disturbed eight-year-old boy suffering from a severe personality disorder bludgeons his mother to death with a baseball bat. Eleven years later, the youth escapes from a mental institution in Washington and embarks on a killing spree.

First things first, *Frayed* opens with one of the most shockingly brutal murder scenes depicted in a modern-day horror film, all the more nauseating *because* of its singular matter-of-factness. Get past this without closing your eyes and you may think you're in for a standard "psycho-on-the-prowl" feature that nods its head firmly in the direction of *Halloween*. But *Frayed* is much more than that and needs at least two viewings to unravel its multitude of riddles, red herrings and twists, some of which can be recognized and some that can't. Tony Doupe plays a police officer who has remarried following the violent, unsolved death of his wife. At the same time the daughter Alena Dashiell is out with her girlfriend and two guys cuddling-up in tents, Aaron Blakeley, her schizophrenic brother (who hasn't spoken a word for the length of his duration), is being transferred to a maximum security hospital. He kills his two guards and breaks out. He dons a raggedly stitched sackcloth hood painted like a clown's face and runs riot with a screwdriver, remorselessly stabbing to death (in another scene guaranteed to bring on revulsion) a driver, a gas station owner, Dashiell's girlfriend and the two boyfriends, a few law officers, and his father's second wife (Kellee Bradley) before cornering his sister in the house. She calms her demented sibling down and plays him his favorite tune from a music box, only for him to stab himself before being shot by his father. The surprise ending is then revealed. Doupe in fact slaughtered his wife who caught him in the act of abusing their son, the little boy locked away for a crime he didn't commit. In the final frame, audiences are left in no doubt that the pedophile, like a leopard, hasn't changed his spots, sneaking into his other son's bedroom. However, scattered throughout *Frayed*'s running time are clues (presented mainly in flashback or flashes) that hint that not all is as seems in this movie. Are Blakeley and the hooded maniac one and the same person? Bearing in mind that he's a schizo, the killer may be one of his many personalities, a figment of his warped imagination. Did Doupe shoot his son on a lonely stretch of roadside and *then* assume the role of the masked lunatic? Has the whole thing been dreamed by Dashiell as a guilt trip over her brother's imprisonment and her father's perversions? Did *any* of the murders take place at all, with the possibility that Dashiell conceived them in her mind? What is the significance of the Memorial Day Softball Tournament photograph dated 1974 shown time and time again, other than the fact that every person in it (they're all connected in one way or another with the storyline) except Dashiell is dead? A conundrum indeed! For devotees of films, horror or otherwise, that make you think, then this well-executed, darkly shot chiller offers the necessary stimulation. If not, audiences might find it all a bit too much to take in.

Gargoyle
aka: **Gargoyle's Revenge**
Avrio Filmworks/Cinetel Films 2004; 87 minutes; Director: Jim Wynorski; Rating: ☠☠

CIA agents converge on Bucharest to deal with the high-profile kidnapping of an ambassador's son. They find themselves involved in a centuries old religious drama concerning a fearsome creature resurrected by a Satan-worshipping priest that, with its offspring, will conquer the world.

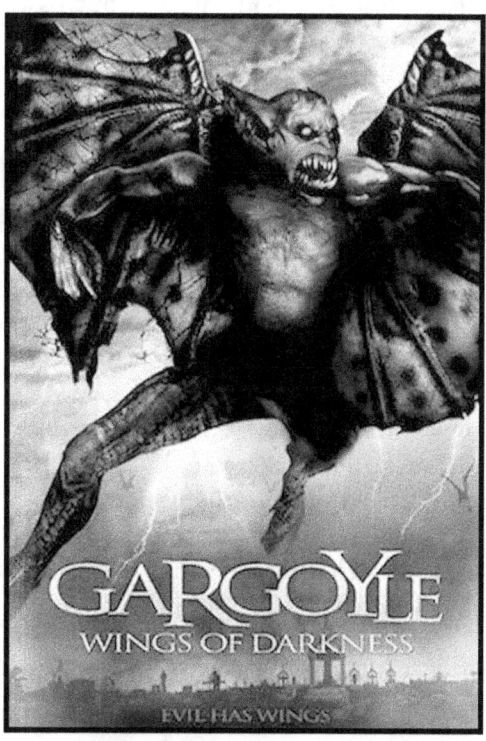

It is very tempting to dismiss *Gargoyle* as a crashing disappointment. But let's delve deeper into *why* it's such a crashing disappointment. Peel away the glossy location photography (shot in Romania) and an inventive winged monster (looking as if it's just flown in from a Ray Harryhausen '70s *Sinbad* outing). What we are left with is an uncoordinated mix-up featuring so many half-baked ideas filched from all manner of genre flicks that everything ends up a complete disaster. Never was the phrase "the total doesn't add up to the sum of its parts" truer than in this case. This movie urgently needed a binding agent! The imaginative *Van Helsing* styled pre-credits sequence shows a Gypsy girl in Romania, 1532, fleeing down a track in a wagon, a winged demon hovering in the night sky. Nearing a church, the creature is dispatched by a priest firing an arrow from a large crossbow. With a signpost marked Carpatia and Vasaria added to a mob of torch-bearing villagers, it's a simple matter of deduction to put a finger on the film's source references, but after this splendid opening few minutes, everything takes on an air of desperation as we flash forward four centuries. Michael Paré and Sandra Hess are two CIA agents who uncover a plot cooked up by priest Fintan McKeown to unleash thousands of gargoyles onto the population. But *Gargoyle* tries much too hard to be all things to all people, unsuccessfully blending gung-ho CIA action, gunfights between rival drug gangs, religious mumbo-jumbo, embarrassing romantic flirtations, car chases and creature-feature mayhem. Terrible acting (Paré goes through the motions like a walking plank) and the pulverizing background choral cacophony make *Gargoyle* such a bane to sit through. It's all here in one form or another—Castle Orlock, the Dracula society, shades of *The Omen*, mutterings about the blood of Christ and an egg-hatching scene set in a Gothic chamber copied direct from *Alien* that verges on the criminal. Vacant-looking Kate Orsini, a church restoration specialist, rushes around with a giant crossbow, its arrows dipped in the blood of Jesus, the only projectiles that can kill the big mother gargoyle (CIA machine-guns finish off the hatchlings). Paré, face as immobile as one of the church's stone statues, intones, "Give me the god-dammed flamethrower" and "Wells, I've got blood" with all the conviction of a rank amateur. Of course, we have to be treated to the sight of a surviving flying gargoyle as the end credits run. Deeply buried in this unappetizing soup is the germ of a decent, straightforward monster picture. Unfortunately, as another old saying goes, "too many cooks spoil the broth." Substitute "cooks" with "ideas" and you'll see why *Gargoyle*, despite a higher-than-average budget, is unattractive, derivative hokum, poorly conceived by its makers.

The Gathering
Granada 2002; 92 minutes; Director: Brian Gilbert; Rating: ☠☠☠☠

Coinciding with the accidental discovery of the remains of an ancient church mysteriously buried below ground in England's West Country, a young American girl turns up in the village of Ashby Wake and triggers off a series of strange events.

Unaccountably shelved shortly after release and edited down to 86 minutes, this underrated supernatural drama delivers the goods in a subtle manner and is none the worse for this careful approach to its subject matter. Crumbling figures carved into the walls of the gloomy crypt and the people gazing at a statue of Christ on the cross bear an uncanny resemblance to shabby-looking strangers seen wandering around the village. Petite Christina Ricci, hit by a car but oddly surviving without serious damage, is taken in by the family responsible. Ricci begins having premonitions concerning the couple's asthmatic boy, that he is under threat from a lunatic in their midst. The film's premise is at least different—decaying bas-reliefs depict the people who watched Jesus die on the cross and thus they are condemned to wander forever like lost souls (attending scenes of mankind's suffering such as Kennedy's assassination, the atomic bomb tests, hangings by lynch mobs, etc.). Ricci is one of the "watchers," redeeming

her tortured spirit at the end by saving the disturbed loner from being murdered at the hands of a local man abused as a youngster by some of the village's leading figures. The lad guns them all down, the strangers watching from the sidelines, blank-eyed and emotionless. The semi-tragic ending, with Ricci free of her curse and leaving the family she has come to love, works like a treat. The young actress turns in a satisfying performance as a bewildered "lost soul," and the understated direction produces a satisfyingly modest but effective chiller that entertains and enthralls.

Ghost Lake
American World Pictures 2004; 107 minutes; Director: Jay Woelfel; Rating: ☠☠☠

In 1904, the town of East Rushford was buried under 40 feet of water following the construction of the Rushford Dam. Every 13 years the spirits of the long-drowned inhabitants rise from the waters to claim the souls of the living.

In many ways, *Ghost Lake* is your archetypal indie horror movie—clodhopping direction, bland color photography, a bit suspect technically, confusing plot, sufficient but not great acting, corny script and hoary-looking '80s-style ghouls. A longer-than-average running time, a respectable audio level *and* multi-image/split screen effects differentiate it from the normal run-of-the-mill

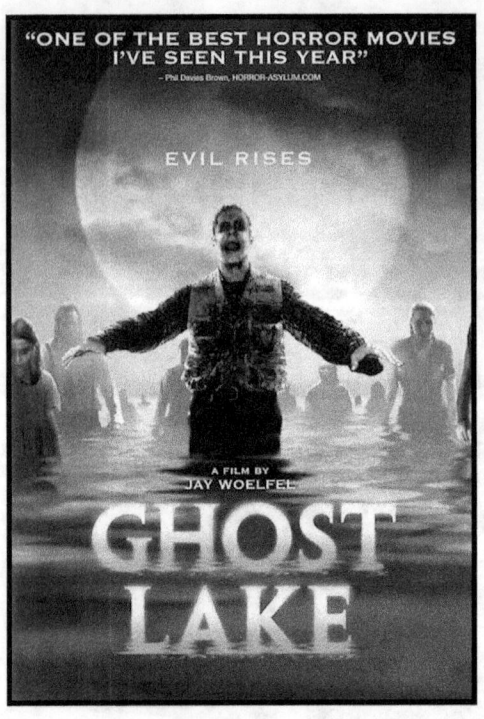

product. But that doesn't mean to say audiences can't be entertained by this variation on *The Fog* and others of its ilk, even though the storyline veers all over the place at times. Tatum Adair is a young woman (and a pretty promiscuous one judging by the opening "sex in a car" scene) who, full of guilt following the death of her parents by gas poisoning, decides to spend some time to reflect on the tragedy in the family's lakeside lodge. Picking up loner Timothy Prindle en route, Adair is then plagued with supernatural visions. Her dead parents appear, she dreams about a town submerged beneath flowing waters, a mysterious eight-year-old girl comes and goes, fishermen vanish into the lake and are rammed by a phantom boat, and zombie-like corpses roam the woods at night. Is Prindle (Adair has a raunchy sex frolic with him as well) "normal" or something more sinister? Is the little girl (Azure Sky Decker) a ghost? Does the grouchy deputy sheriff know more about the sinister events unfolding than he lets on? Why are rotting bodies now being washed ashore? The number 13 figures strongly as a plot motif—every 13 years 13 of the town's decaying members, led by a vengeful fisherman, emerge to claim another 13 victims on the 13th of the month. Adair is among the chosen 13, *if* we can make sense of all that is happening. Prindle and the sheriff both turn out to be members of the undead, while Decker is in fact a twin, her sister having drowned in the misty lake. After several confrontations with these lost souls, Adair, with the help of Decker, somehow breaks the 100-year-old cycle and returns to the family home, her parents' spirits absolving the girl of all guilt over their deaths. The jellified/liquefied ghouls are appropriately tacky, but no more so than in countless other zombie thrillers. Adair proves to have a fine figure and, believe it or not, there are one or two moments of bona-fide shock. Okay, *Ghost Lake* is cheap, but it seems to be aware of its limitations and ends up being rather enjoyable in a cheesy kind of way.

Ghosts of Goldfield
North American Pictures/Barnholtz Ent. 2007; 88 minutes; Director: Ed Winfield; Rating: ☠☠

Five teenagers decide to shoot a commercially backed video in a reputedly haunted hotel, only to find that the sole "occupant" is terrorizing them, the vindictive spirit of a woman murdered by the building's owner in the early 1900s.

There's actually one solitary ghost on offer here—it's Ashly Margaret Rae, a young woman who had an affair with the hotel's barman and bore his baby. When owner Chuck Zito found out (he was madly in love with the girl) after a maid snitched on the couple, he killed the newborn and threw the body down a mineshaft, then tortured and murdered Rae. In a fit of rage, the barman (Roddy Piper) placed a curse on the maid, who turns out to be none other than the grandmother of Marnette Patterson, the team's leader and the one person who is therefore connected to the hotel. A camcorder haunted house movie for the camcorder generation, Winfield's direction hardly differs from the video footage this gang is shooting. But if audiences can put up with the continual swearing, the witless dialogue ("This place is totally freaking me out.") and the annoying characters (bespectacled nerd Scott Whyte; flighty bimbo Mandy Amano; self-satisfied jock Richard Chance; wimpy cameraman Kellan Lutz), there *are* moments of promise. Patterson

has repeated visions of past events in the hotel, filmed in saturated sepia tones; room 109 must *never* be entered; the interior of the hotel is suitably eerie; Steven Yeaman's score is an effective low, menacing drone and Rae's gray, harpy-like wraith, wild, staring eyes, flowing hair and broken teeth isn't the kind of spook anyone would want to bump into during the night. If the movie had been made on a bigger budget, with better stars and a decent script, it might have been a winner. As it is, the very *cheapness* of the production works against it, and the verdict? Just one more "teens in peril" offering for a younger audience. It's not giving all that much away to reveal the conclusion. Despite Patterson attempting to appease the angry spirit by handing Rae a silver locket containing her grandmother's photograph, hell hath no fury as far as this particular ghost is concerned and the teenagers perish gruesomely, one by one, Patterson destined to haunt the hotel for all eternity. The end credits, also in sepia, relate the tragic history of the Goldfield Hotel, built in 1903 during the gold rush era in Nevada. Supposedly based on true events, *Ghosts of Goldfield* is light years away from classics like Robert Wise's *The Haunting* (as are most modern-day supernatural thrillers), but in the context of how it was made, it isn't too bad, providing one or two hair-raising sequences for buffs to get mildly excited about.

The Glow

Studio Products 2002; 89 minutes; Director: Craig R. Baxley; Rating: ☠

A couple (who never knew their parents) rent a swish apartment after the husband encounters a group of track-suited but inexplicably fit old folk while out jogging. The building's other residents are mainly a group of eternally youthful-looking oldies as well, exhibiting disconcerting behavior patterns.

After they move in, strange things happen. The genuinely younger tenants seem to vanish without trace; a creepy old janitor appears to be hiding some dark secret in a basement stuffed with black bin liners; and a surgically enhanced Dina Merrill is taking an unhealthy interest in Portia de Rossi's pregnancy. In the meantime, obsessive jogger hubby (Dean Cain) is becoming far too cozy with an attractive blonde jogger while his wife, after losing the baby, begins to be threatened by the sinister Merrill and her clan, all apparently over 100 years old but looking 30 years younger.

This clumsily handled fantasy/mild horror flick travels up one cul-de-sac too many. For instance, why does the female jogger suddenly disappear? Are Merrill and company extracting some kind of fluid from their tenants in order to maintain their youth, before dumping the desiccated corpses in the basement? Why was Merrill so upset over de Rossi's pregnancy? What *is* that pink concoction they continually swig back? Why is the fact that de Rossi and Cain never knew their parents relevant to the plot? Needless to say, the couple escapes the clutches of the oldies after they have been strapped to operating tables and had tubes inserted into their necks. Merrill and her gang are eventually herded away by the police. The final reel hints that there may be more of these track-suited centenarians running around the streets of New York. But by then the viewer would have probably given up on this incomprehensible cut-price take on *Rosemary's Baby*, the glamorous de Rossi about the only thing to hold the attention.

Grayson Arms
aka: **Lethal Eviction**
Sidekick Entertainment 2005; 97 minutes; Director: Michael Feifer; Rating: ☠☠☠

The Grayson Arms apartment building is sold to new owners who haven't ascertained why their tenants are dying off like flies in hideous circumstances.

Does a tortured spirit inhabit Grayson Arms? Audiences would think so from the pre-credits sequence showing a workman pushed to his death from a window ledge by a half-seen black figure. But no, it's not a ghost, just someone from among the bunch of loonies who rent rooms in the block—a lonely girl and her unstable sister (both played by Jennifer Carpenter); campy crossdresser Andy Martinez, Jr.; three beer-swilling dudes; elderly female resident Michael Learned; and doctor Judd Nelson, who is keeping tabs on Carpenter and her sister. Are new owners Stacey Dash and James Avery behind the demise of Learned (heart attack) and Adam Huss (a lethal injection), the disappearance of Carpenter's self-harming twin and the near-drowning of Nelson? After 30 minutes, the killer's identity is revealed (but we can easily guess who it is anyway). Carpenter has no twin sister. She's a schizo on the lam from an institution, tracked down by discredited psychiatrist Nelson who wants to root out the overwrought girl's deep-seated problems by further therapy. Anyone stupid enough to antagonize her is eliminated pronto. For those horror buffs that sat through innumerable psychodramas in the 1960s, *Grayson Arms'* final act strays into Hammer domain, containing echoes of *Fanatic* and *Hysteria*, not to mention William Castle's *Homicidal*. A basement climax (complete with burnt corpse) sees the certifiable Carpenter plunging a knife into Nelson before Avery guns her down. Not all is done and dusted though. At Carpenter's funeral, her bereaved boyfriend (Todd Babcock) sees another girl in black wander away from the graveside. Yes, it's the dead girl's *real* twin and she's schizophrenic as well, arguing with herself in two different voices as she leaves the graveyard. Feifer's direction, more or less, copies everything that has gone before; and the acting isn't much up to scratch. Nevertheless, *Grayson Arms* has a slightly kooky flavor to it and mostly succeeds in avoiding the usual clichés found in these psycho movies. It's strictly middle-of-the road stuff, not all that bad for its type.

Grindstone Road
Red Duck Pictures/Peace Arch 2008; 93 minutes; Director: Melanie Orr; Rating: ☠☠

Following a car accident in which a couple's 11-year-old son is coma induced, the pair moves into a dilapidated house. Scarcely five minutes later the spirit of a young boy who went missing years ago torments the woman.

The opening scene of the car crash down a misty, isolated road will have audiences thinking that perhaps this is a portent of good things to come.

Wrong. As soon as Fairuza Balk and Greg Bryk take up residence in their new, tumbledown home, *Grindstone Road* heads down all too recognizable "spooky house" territory. It's a case of, yes, we *have* seen this all before, so just how well put together is yet one more revamp on a well-known plot? We encounter dripping water, the dark cellar, the spectral face in the mirror, the nightmare visions, the bathroom sequence (Where would these movies be without a bathroom sequence?), the spectral figure (filmed in ghastly Day-Glo colors) present during happenings connected to past happenings and the elderly neighbors (Walter Learning and Joan Gregson) who, despite outward appearances, are not quite as wholesome as fresh apple pie. The much-trusted, indispensable creepy events are strung together unevenly. The story goes that a boy (Dylan Authors) disappeared years back and a local teacher (Zachary Bennet) hung himself because of his alleged abuse toward the kid. But how come this missing boy has the same name as Balk and Bryk's son and was the same age? If audiences manage to stay with it, they'll probably deduce that the gray-haired folks next door were the boy's parents, abusing, torturing and finally killing him. They bumped off the teacher as well to make it look like suicide, therefore using him as a cover-up for the crime. The murdered boy returns from the grave reminding Balk that she used to play with him when she was a child, and his parents are the real monsters here. The hyperactive finale has the repugnant oldsters, their foul deeds discovered, attempting to silence Balk and Bryk, but instead winding up dead. The lad's spirit is then freed from its curse (along with Bennet's) and the couple's son wakes from his coma. Direction-wise, the movie is adequately presented. But acting-wise, Balk as the pill-popping, angst-ridden mother is a disaster. In one key sequence, she is on the bed with her husband trying to relate, between sobs, her feelings over her son's accident. You cannot understand a single word the actress says. This kind of mumbling, hard-to-hear delivery is a scourge of modern-day cinema and can wreck what might have been a pleasant enough 90 minutes of supernatural hokum. But wreck is exactly what it does in this case.

Guardians

Lightning Rod Studios/Shoreline Ent. 2009; 92 minutes; Director: Drew Maxwell; Rating: ☠☠

An elite team formed to combat supernatural forces that threaten the world enters the township of Twilight Cove. There the inhabitants are under threat from scaly creatures that have been summoned from another dimension by an occultist.

Watching *Guardians* is akin to sitting through one of Ed Wood's or Jerry Warren's efforts from the 1950s—muffled, stilted dialogue, wooden acting, static direction, a blank look on the actors' faces and less-than-sparkling cinematography. What saves the day are the flamboyant CGI-animated monsters—man-sized, tailed, scaly gremlins armed with rows of ferocious teeth that leap around, causing havoc with their deadly claws. A certain Dr. Strand (Bryce Lord) has used the text of an ancient book to lure these things from another dimension, no doubt in order to conquer the world. Action hero Shannon Watson and his team, which includes a weird, psychic kid (Nick Driessen) who has the ability to foresee trouble, drive into the body-strewn town in a large truck. Their mission is to rescue the townsfolk holed up in a school, slay the beasties and gain control of the magical tome from Lord. Victims who have survived but have been injured by these creatures turn into rabid zombies as their blood has become contaminated, and the numerous monster-perspective shots are deftly (and cheaply) handled. Simply smear red paint over Plexiglas and hold it steadily (or as steady as you can) in front of the camera lens! After a great many deaths, Watson eventually discovers that by pouring a mixture of contaminated blood and a green liquid brewed from the book's instructions onto bullets and weapons, he can vaporize the monsters, the zombie humans and, finally, the demonic Lord. The pre-opening sequence showing Watson and company in an abandoned church putting paid to a vampiress in her coffin is well managed for a cheapie. The trick ending (the book coming to life in Watson's hands, his boss stating, "The psychics are after it") hints at a sequel that will probably never see the light of day. Low-budget daft sci-fi maybe, but the pace doesn't drag and those eye-catching monsters lift the movie out of a rut to the level of average entertainment for the bad flicks buff.

Hangman's Curse
aka: **The Veritas Project: Hangman's Curse**
Namesake Entertainment 2003; 106 minutes; Director: Rafal Zielinski; Rating: ☠☠

A nerdy student, bullied at college, capitalizes on the suicide-by-hanging of his uncle 10 years earlier by creating a legend whose sole purpose is to put terror into all those who cross his path.

With a title that could so easily have featured in a 1950s horror movie and a promising opening scene showing a youth hanging himself from a gloomy upstairs room, audiences may think that this is one teenage horror outing that tones down on the bozos, the bimbos and the gross behavior of all concerned, delivering something worthwhile for a change. Unfortunately, it doesn't. A family team—Mom (Mel Harris), Pop (David Keith), son (Douglas Smith) and daughter (Leighton Meester)—form "The Veritas Project," experts at sniffing out the paranormal and seeking the truth behind strange happenings. Rogers High School calls the bunch in, all incognito, to find out why the high school jocks are succumbing to hallucinations, rendering them unfit to play. Does the legend of Abel Fry, the guy who hanged himself, have anything to do with it? Who is marking the insides of lockers with a drawing of the hangman, said owner falling ill soon afterwards? Are those two far-out Goths behind it all? What are those odd noises emanating from the "forbidden wing" and grates in the walls? To the accompaniment of blaring heavy metal music, Smith and Meester rummage around in places where they're not supposed to be, while Keith's nutty professor friend (Frank Peretti) irritatingly spouts streams of scientific jargon ("It's pheromone that's causing it," he shrieks frantically) relating to a mysterious powdery substance located in the victims' lockers. The pentagram crops up somewhere, as does a play entitled *The Curse of the Hangman,* before any supernatural leanings the film may have harbored are tossed out the window in favor of—spiders! Yes, the college geek, Daniel Farber, as revenge for his uncle's death and being bullied, has hatched a plan to exploit the "dead uncle's spirit" angle and infest the wall cavities with thousands of arachnids that contain, in their venom, a hallucinogen. Once the chosen victim was bitten, he (or she) experiences violent hallucinations (corpse-faced ghouls) and goes into a coma. After being caught, Farber decides to do the decent thing by pressing a large wolf spider to his chest, thus expiring in the "Witching Chamber." Meester, covered in bites, is rescued and survives, as do the two Goths. *Hangman's Curse* is lukewarm teen horror fare being far too long, lacking in spooky thrills, suspense and even gory moments. Okay, it might have something of importance to offer about the effects of bullying, but the finished article seems unable to handle the message persuasively by intertwining this central idea within a twin ghost/deadly spiders framework. The picture simply doesn't cut it as horror entertainment, but one thing *is* in its favor—the college kids are far less obnoxious than usual!

Haunted Boat

Hannibal Pictures 2005; 91 minutes; Director: Olga Levens; Rating: ☠☠

Six teenagers board a small motor launch and head off for Catalina Island. But on the voyage, strange happenings occur that have no rational explanation.

The Blair Witch Project meets *Ghost Ship.* Cheaply made (and boy, does it look it), this supernatural sea-going outing has three guys and three girls cruising out to sea to the usual sounds of thumping rock music. However, this is a boat with a difference. The uncle of one of the guys is found dead on the vessel, his decomposed corpse lying undiscovered for weeks, and the cabins, reeking of decay, are strewn with garbage. Adrift on the ocean after the engine packs up, a series of odd events take place. A ghostly face appears at the windows; one of the lads dives overboard and never returns; the group tells ghost stories; the other two males go off in a small rowing boat to look for help and *they* don't come back; a thick mist encloses the boat; one of the girls has a seizure follow-

ing an epileptic fit; a creepy stranger looking like an extra from Wes Craven's *The Hills Have Eyes* turns up, administers some aid to the sick girl, gets back in his boat and fades into the gloom; a dead bird is found on deck; a black cat appears out of the blue; and another of the girls electrocutes herself. The remaining 30 minutes leave audiences wondering whether the survivor, dark-haired Courtney Scheverman (a dead ringer for Demi Moore), is suffering from multiple hallucinations as reality merges with fantasy (the two missing males come back, then vanish, then reappear). The denouement, that she was the only one allowed to survive a series of unnatural (and unexplainable) trials and tribulations, and that her friends all died on the trip, comes as no real surprise. The final seconds see her diving into the harbor to rejoin her phantom pals on the ghost ship that sails out to sea and gradually disappears. Obviously produced on a minuscule budget, *Haunted Boat* does have its moments of interest and is moderately entertaining in a cheapo kind of way, even though the camcorder style of filming grates after a while, as does the muffled soundtrack and grainy imagery.

Haunted Forest
Fotocomics Productions/Mainline 2007; 81 minutes; Director: Mauro Borrelli; Rating: ☠☠☠

In remote mountain woodlands, a living tree demands blood sacrifices as revenge for the murder of a young Indian girl's lover in 1887, the girl's spirit protecting both the tree and the forest from interlopers.

Living tree movies are hard to come by. The classic is, as all '50s buffs know, Allied Artists' *From Hell It Came*, released in 1957. But that was a walking tree monster. This incarnation is merely a gnarled face and two arms dangling from a trunk. Although *Haunted Forest* once again explores the overused "lost-in-the-creepy-woods" scenario so loved by cheapo film directors, it's surprisingly fresh and intricately plotted. Half Cherokee Sevy Di Cione is determined to discover the whereabouts of a burial chamber underneath the roots of a mystical tree, having his grandfather's journal as proof of its existence. Trouble is, he's roped in two of his empty-headed pals (Adam Green and Edoardo Beghi) to help him (more like hinder him) in the search. Also in on the hunt is mad tracker Mark Hengst, and two girl nature lovers crop up to add some female spice to the group. Legend has it that if a person finds a splinter embedded in their flesh in these woods, they fall sick and are earmarked as a sacrifice, doomed to be dragged into the ground by gray limbs and there to be planted like human saplings. There's a lot going on over the 81 minutes. A ghostly girl is spotted, eyes look out from the undergrowth, maggots crawl among the carpet of dead leaves, the sinister tree is located, Di Cione has a tussle with the reanimated corpse of the long-dead Indian girl, and several bodies lie entombed beneath the ground, twigs growing out of their flesh. Botanist Jennifer Luree is the only one to make it out alive, all the others sacrificed to the tree, with Di Cione plunging a stake into the trunk, which spouts blood. As he foolishly crawls inside a hollow opening to investigate, he becomes entwined in a web of finger-like branches and then swiftly cocooned, becoming part of the tree that lives on. Borrelli's camerawork wobbles all over the place at times and the frenetic climax has an almost hallucinogenic feel to it, but taking everything into account, *Haunted Forest*, conceived along the lines of an adults-only Grimms' fairy tale, is quirkily different enough to intrigue and excite the horror taste buds.

Hellhounds
Muse Entertainment Enterprises 2009; 92 minutes; Director: Ricky Shroder; Rating: ☠☠☠

A Greek warrior has to enter the labyrinth of Tartarus in order to regain the soul of his murdered virgin princess bride, a soul that has been claimed by Hades.

"You know Kleitos, none of this would have happened if you'd bedded me when I gave you the chance." A priceless line, perhaps unfitting for a slice of Greek mythological hokum such as *Hellhounds*, but within the context of this

movie, it works beautifully. This lively fantasy adventure is *Jason and the Argonauts* minus Ray Harryhausen's monsters, Bernard Herrmann's music and an all-star cast (although any genre fan tuning in would acknowledge that Todd Armstrong's stiff performance in *Jason* is the equal to anything on offer here). On his wedding day, jealous suitor James A. Woods poisons Scot Elrod's lovely bride (Amanda Brooks). A seer who lives in the woods (Indra Ové, sporting black contact lenses) tells Elrod that he has to travel to Tartarus, the Prison of the Souls, where Hades intends to claim Brooks' virgin spirit, which hasn't, in this instance, entered the Elysian Fields. The only way the Greek can bring his bride back from the dead is to drink a protective magic elixir, take her body to the labyrinth's gateway inside a volcano, make off with her soul and return it to her body, where the two will merge and she will be as before. Elrod's subsequent adventures include crossing a gloomy River Styx, getting lost in the maze, fighting two huge loping hounds with glowing eyes, warding off mutants inside a skull-shaped mountain and dealing with traitor Woods. Restored more or less to normal life, her blue spirit hovering uncertainly between good and evil, Brooks and Elrod emerge from barren Tartarus. Demonically possessed Woods, ordered on the threat of eternal damnation by the ghoulish Hades (Oltin Hurezeanu) to fetch Brooks back to him pronto, pursues the lovers with three of the bloodthirsty hounds. But he is defeated when Elrod slices Woods' enchanted staff in two and the villain is savaged to mincemeat by a surviving hound. The creature's blood is then fed to the princess and she is finally herself again. Ben Cross appears briefly as Brooks' father, the king, his role in the Oscar-winning *Chariots of Fire* a dim and distant memory. The stilted dialogue matches the wooden acting to a tee and the whole shebang (filmed in Romania at a cost of $2 million) has the look and feel of a continental 1960s co-feature. What a shame Charles H. Schneer wasn't around as producer! Nevertheless, *Hellhounds* entertains and, apart from one scene of yucky gore (which might put you off spaghetti), is okay fare for the juveniles. Even grown-ups might get some pleasure out of watching it.

Hellraiser: Hellworld

Dimension/Castel Film Romania 2005; 91 minutes; Director: Rick Bota; Rating: ☠

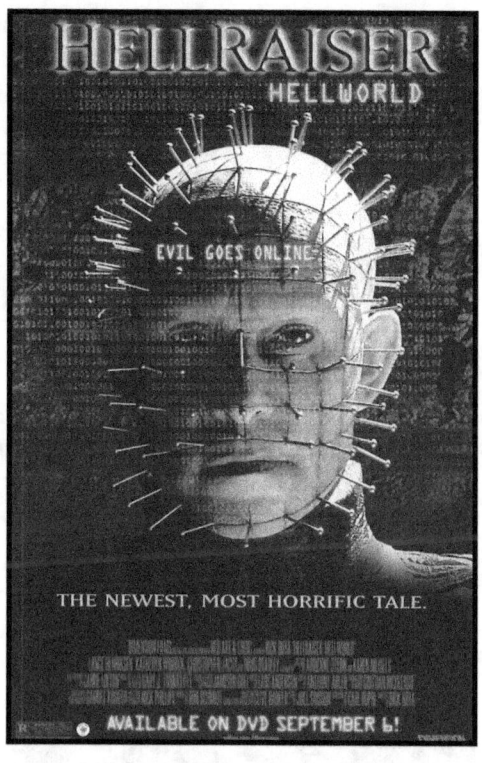

Following the mysterious death of a teenager, five of his friends attend a Hellworld convention, held in a rambling house. There they find themselves trapped in a version of hell presided over by the dead teen's insane father.

Hellraiser, when first released in 1987, was an inventive shocker of its day, featuring a gallery of grotesque mutants (the Cenobites) released from the underworld by Sean Chapman and his infernal puzzle-box. Several straight-to-DVD follow-ups have been produced over the interim period. Rick Bota's trashy entrant reducing Clive Barker's original concept to the level of a teenage slasher flick, and a poor one at that. If you enjoy partying-on, boozing youngsters and earth-shattering rock music, interspersed with a few moments of bloodshed, overloaded with dopey teen-speak and old hat situations, you might gain a shred of merriment from watching defenseless teens Kathryn Winnick (the blonde piece of totty), boyfriend Henry Cavill (the self-obsessed jerk), Anna Tolputt (the punkette), her boyfriend Khary Payton (the black dude) and angst-ridden Christopher Jacot up against the party's host, a wooden Lance Henriksen. The man is seeking redress after his son paid with his life by summoning Pinhead and his pals via the puzzle-box, a device that has the ability to open a gateway to hell. The five get ensnared in a series of traps laid by glum-looking Henriksen—Tolputt is manacled to a chair, the blood drained from her body by twin rotating saws; Payton is decapitated; Cavill has the ever-present smirk wiped off his face when a meat-hook lodges in his back; and Winnick is almost buried alive. All the while, Pinhead and two Cenobites watch ominously from the sidelines. However, what the kids have actually been put through has been a continuing nightmare. The teenagers, drugged by Henriksen, were buried alive at the beginning in coffins, each containing a ventilation pipe and cellphone, the ghastly deaths an illusion produced by their own agitated imaginations. Only Winnick and Jacot make it unscathed, freed by the cops and cruising off together as Henriksen, on the run from the police and holed up in a seedy motel, is sliced into segments by a Cenobite. Visually and orally, *Hellraiser: Hellworld* is an unqualified pain to sit through, badly acted, clumsily directed, unnecessarily noisy, the shock sequences offering nothing we haven't seen a thousand and one times before. Even horror-mad teens may wish to avoid this hodgepodge of a carve-'em-up movie.

High Plains Invaders
Castel Film Romania 2009; 90 minutes; Director: Kristoffer Tabori (K.T. Donaldson); Rating: ☠☠☠

In 1892, the mining town of Avaranth, Colorado, finds itself overrun by alien invaders, who landed to feast on uranium ore.

The leaden skies of Eastern Europe (the movie was shot in Romania) stand in for the bright blue skies of Colorado, the Old West looking like a dank part of that particular area of the world. The townsfolk speak in hilarious forced American accents, especially rootin' tootin' Calamity Jane-clone bounty hunter Sanny Van Heteren. Sounds like a recipe for disaster? Not quite, because what saves *High Plains Invaders* from being an unpalatable mix between a Western actioner and *The War of the Worlds* are the aliens. CGI conceived, these huge biomechanical insectoid creatures scuttle around on four blade-like legs, a long, whiplash tail emerging from their oval bodies that can fire off projectiles, their front ends opening like a peeled orange to reveal rows of teeth and mandibles. Not only do they look great, we see an awful lot of them. No scrimping occurs on the visuals in this wacky sci-fi offering. It's standard sci-fi monster fodder but directed with pace and flare.

The aliens descend from a massive global ship just as train robber (and eventual hero) James Marsters is about to be strung up. One of the things crawls into town, kills a few locals and then proceeds to bury itself in a deep shaft, hunting for the precious uranium that will give it sustenance. A tremendous opening sequence for an independent production such as this could not be imagined. Marsters, ex-lover Cindy Sampson, Van Heteren and a few others hide in the jailhouse, and then it's simply a question of what can be done to halt the invasion in its tracks and who gets out alive in the process. A nice touch is the complete lack of understanding exhibited by Marsters and company as to the origin of these otherworldly raiders, scientist Sebastian Knapp having a stab at it, saying that they "come from the stars." Knapp is the sacrificial lamb in the end, luring the alien hordes into town with a cartload of uranium ore. As the ship hovers over him and hundreds of the invaders, he dynamites everything in sight (including himself and the spaceship) while Marsters and Sampson ride off into the sunset, or what passes for a sunset in the bleak wasteland of Romania. An aspect of the storyline not taken up is the fact that one of the victims has strange sores breaking out over her body. This is quickly mentioned but subsequently dropped. So forget the distinctly un-American depiction of the West, the European cast laughably acting as though they were *real* cowboys (and cowgirls) using those god-awful accents. It's the aliens that win the day and steal the show here, the remarkable effects emerging as the winner above everything else.

Hoboken Hollow
American World Pictures 2006; 98 minutes; Director: Glen Stephens; Rating: ☠☠☠

On a run-down ranch in the Texan backwaters, itinerant drifters seeking employment are tortured and butchered for kicks.

This slasher-fest, which makes *Hostel* look tame by comparison, should carry a Government Health Warning, as in: "Do not view this movie on a full stomach." Some of the disturbing sequences include people's body parts repeatedly inflicted with pain from a cattle-prod; a knife plunged into a foot; a worker hung, drawn and quartered, his flesh cooking in pots and left in strips to dry; another worker having a tooth yanked out with pliers; a dismembered foot in a bucket; a brutal rape involving that cattle-prod; blood dripping from spiked bodies into tins and jars; body parts fed to pigs; and a man's legs repeatedly stabbed. A high gore quotient to be sure, but can *Hoboken Hollow* really be classed as entertainment? Moreover, what are Dennis Hopper and Michael Madsen doing appearing in this horrible show of a picture? Having said that, in its own trashy, low-grade way, Glen Stephens' revamp of *The Texas Chain*

Saw Massacre and others of its ilk should appeal to those who find all this human blood and guts fare palatable. Hillbilly C. Thomas Howell (sporting *very* bad teeth), his pug-ugly wife, retard brother and another relatively normal couple take in homeless migrants to work on the ranch. If they step out of line or complain, they are literally dead meat (or catfish bait, as one of the drifters says). Ex-Iraqi war veteran Jason Connery, on the hoof himself, becomes an unwilling victim in this gruesome situation. A sub-plot involves Lin Shaye and her hulking, dim-witted son (Mark Holton) stalling on selling their property to a developer. After a series of stomach-churning sequences in which most of the workers are disposed of (bodies either carved up or dumped down a well), Connery succeeds in escaping and Howell is murdered by Holton for helping Connery get loose. It then transpires that Shaye and her son (who only *pretends* to be an imbecile) are in on this killing spree, as is the sheriff (Hopper). Based on supposed fact, none of this deranged bunch of ghouls was ever brought to trial. The final shot of a young female deputy lying in a pit full of half-dead humans for company hints that they were left to carry on with their ghastly deeds. Get the sick bucket out if you're going to put yourself through this "in-your-face" bloodbath. You'll need it!

The Hole
aka: **After the Hole**
Pathe/Canal 2001; 102 minutes; Director: Nick Hamm; Rating: ☠☠

A mentally disturbed schoolgirl lures three classmates into a disused underground bunker for a short break, the purpose being to make them suffer through her own jealousy of their love lives.

Efficiently put together as it may be, there is something not quite right about this psychological horror drama, despite an unsettling performance from young Thora Birch as the "ugly duckling" schoolgirl totally infatuated with the school's heartthrob, Desmond Harrington. After cajoling him, Keira Knightley and Laurence Fox into the bunker for a bit of excitement, three of them die horribly when they find the door to their prison locked. Maybe it's the incessant swearing or Knightley's constant mugging at the camera that is so off-putting, or the general loathsome air of most of the leading characters involved. Birch, though, is terrific, hoodwinking her psychiatrist (Embeth Davidtz) in the final reel over the real cause of the deaths of Harrington, Knightley and Fox. Birch is responsible, having possessed the key to the bunker's hatch all along, while Knightley expires in agony from poisoning, Harrington kills Fox in a rage and then dies by falling off a ladder. To cover up the truth of the matter, Birch even pushes her doting boyfriend/best friend/accomplice into a river to stop him from blabbing to the police. He was in on this little scheme himself, an experiment in human behavior under pressure. The final close-up of Birch's cherubic features as she talks to the police, a combination of innocence and knowing slyness, watched by her slowly comprehending psychiatrist, chills the spine. Otherwise, this is an uneasy mix of teen horror, rom-com and detective thriller that doesn't quite gel as it should.

The Hollow
Platform Ent./Speed Productions 2004; 83 minutes; Director: Kyle Newman; Rating: ☠☠

Halloween night. The great, great grandson of schoolteacher Ichabod Crane takes a party of youngsters out on a hayride to re-enact blood-curdling happenings in the town of Sleepy Hollow. He finds himself on the run from the legendary apparition known as the Headless Horseman, who carried off the original Crane to regions unknown in the 1700s.

Tim Burton's *Sleepy Hollow* (1999), although pictorially lavish, didn't count as one of the director's more memorable achievements, and Newman's cheapo follow-up doesn't really improve on the fanciful tale. In some ways this is a shame as the opening credits (shot in sepia tones) display a great deal of imaginative flair. The clichés are all here to appeal to the teens—rock music soundtrack, bonehead football jock Nick Carter, long-suffering girlfriend Kaley Cuoco, nice Kevin Zegers (the descendant of Crane) whom Cuoco fancies, Judge Reinhold, Zeger's abusive father, the unavoidable sex scene and unkempt groundskeeper Stacy Keach trying his best to warn the townsfolk of the dangers of the Headless Horseman

("He's after a head," snarls Keach to all and sundry). The bulk of the action takes place virtually over one night (Halloween) when the Horseman with the Jack-o'-Lantern features and glowing eyes appears out of nowhere and beheads various people who cross his path. The collected heads are fed to a magical vine growing on the phantom's grave. Unable to cross a bridge spanning the river because he will lose his powers, the Horseman meets his end when Zegers plunges an ancient sword (taken from Keach's ancestor's grave) into the wraith, throwing him onto the bridge where the thing immediately goes up in flames, a smoldering mess. Not much here to get excited about, probably due to the fact that the insubstantial storyline isn't the greatest piece of horror/fantasy fiction to hit the screen. Zegers and Carter argue incessantly over delectable but dizzy Cuoco, battered-looking Keach keeps cropping up as the harbinger of doom and even the gore quota is low on the scale, disappointing since the protagonist lops off heads for his own amusement. *The Hollow*, sadly lacking in genuine thrills, scares and suspense, just about manages to hang in there for its brief running time, that pumpkin/skull visage with the fanged jaws about the only point of interest for die-hard indie horror fans.

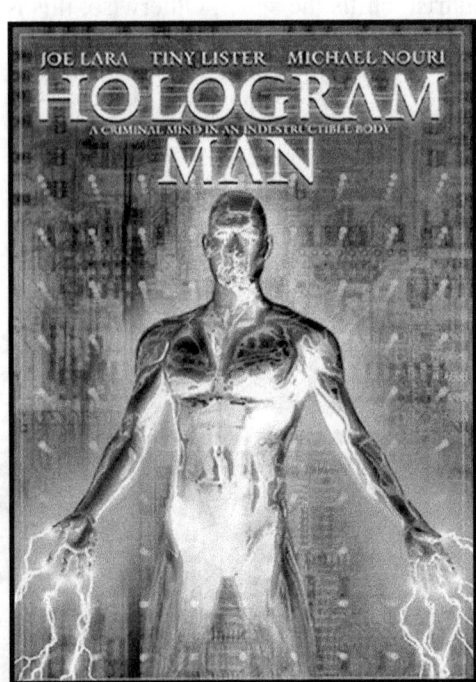

Hologram Man
PM Entertainment 1995; 101 minutes; Director: Richard Pepin; Rating: ☠

In futuristic Los Angeles, a violent gang boss is placed in a holographic state for five years as punishment. When his release is turned down, an accomplice sets him loose as the indestructible "Hologram Man," the criminal intent on taking control of the city.

I caught this movie as a late-night showing on the Arabian MBC2 channel. After an opening 15 minutes containing nothing but gun battles, explosions and vehicles crashing into one another (plus a *Speed*-type bus chase), my wife declared her non-interest in the subject and retired to bed. In hindsight, I wish I had followed her. The 1990s specialized in big, brash no-brainers such as *Demolition Man* and *Total Recall*, and independent PM Entertainment's addition to the mix is like all the rest. A total lack of wit, intelligence and humor is on display, with one explosive shoot-out following another in rapid succession, featuring characters audiences cannot possibly relate to, crummy special effects and dated sets. It's a joyless exercise all round. Beefy Evan Lurie plays badass Norman "Slash" Gallagher (don't ever call him Norman!) who is placed in holographic suspension as punishment for his crimes. When his sentence is completed, a panel of judges rejects his plea to be released, ordering him to be reprogrammed; however, a saboteur within the CALCORP organization decides to throw in his lot with Lurie's mob of misfits, transferring the criminal's holographic entity from the main computer to the gang's. Emerging into his headquarters surrounded by a blue glow, red electrical bolts crackling from his fingertips, Lurie is plastered in synthetic skin to contain his energy and enable him to manipulate physical objects. Quickly relieving a bank of $100 million, the maniac then kidnaps various city officials in order to control Los Angeles. Long-haired Joe Lara is the thorn in his side, a cop who is determined to bring Lurie to justice one way or another. When Lara is fatally wounded, his girlfriend (Arabella Holzbog) places *him* in the holographic machine, restoring his life force and therefore setting the scene for one hologram man vs. another. *Hologram Man* is comic book stuff verging on the moronic, a terrible (and very loud) score underlining the endless, repetitive gun battles. Michael Nouri, playing Lara's oily superior, is the only actor around to turn in a believable performance. Lurie just doesn't cut it as a villain, despite his pumped-up physique. He's too well spoken and his refined features aren't thuggish enough. In the dying seconds, after the crime lord has vanished in one almighty blast, the hazy form of Lara simply walks away, which any self-respecting sci-fi fan should do to avoid this twaddle. A tantalizing electrically charged sex scene between holographic Lara and his girl is the only piece of imagination on show here.

Homeworld

Rhinomotion 2008; 104 minutes; Director: Phillip Hudson; Rating: ☠☠

In the year 3037, a spaceship crash lands on a planet called New Eden, its crew sent there to destroy the Mendax, an alien race that is controlling Earth's inhabitants by mind manipulation.

Audiences will have to be fully alert and possess a considerable amount of patience to sit through

Hudson's slice of almost incomprehensible sci-fi baloney that tries hard to tease and intrigue, but the film falls flat. The opening sequence is admittedly a corker as Captain Vance Harvey's ship spirals out of control over the alien world, crashing into the rocky terrain. Moreover, there are one or two well-photographed scenic shots of the wooded, mountainous terrain and a weird-sounding soundtrack. But that's just about it in a tale that probably would have done *The Outer Limits* or *The Twilight Zone* some justice over the course of an hour, but not at 104 minutes on the big screen. For practically the entire length of the picture, Lt. Beau Ballinger, Corp. Bronston DeLone, Sgt. Larissa Kasian (the token chick) and doctor Kenneth Sears run around in the dense woods, seeking God-knows-what (The Mendax? Other humans? The Mendax city?). Sears, overacting to the point of pantomime, kills the injured Harvey with a rock and the team encounters two aliens dressed in Stone Age costumes, both wearing bug-masks to honor their dead—or are they human? And what about those green crystals sprouting from the ground that have the ability to protect people's minds from corruption? Inserted into the "action" are scenes of each crewmember transmitting bulletins on board ship and scenes of Ballinger in a room conversing with his image in a mirror—or is *that* an alien? Further complications arise when both of the captured Mendax turn out to be human, one of them the captain of a previous vessel that landed on the planet with an identical crew to the present one. Therefore, is the existing crew clones of the first team, and are the aliens up to their old tricks of mind games, using their influence to confuse the ultimate aim of the mission—the release of two canisters containing a virus that will annihilate the Mendax and save Earth. The deranged Sears turns out to be the only human among this disparate bunch, finally releasing the virus into the atmosphere, and the last few minutes has Ballinger talking with one of the aliens (who looks as though it has wandered in from the set of a *Dr. Who* production), the creature stating that Earth's inhabitants cannot be now controlled by them. There's nothing essentially wrong in coming up with a thought-provoking sci-fi concept once in a while to offset all the mindless pap, but *Homeworld* lacks the cohesive touch to tie up those loose plot threads and ends up a rather boring muddle. Once, in this instance, is definitely enough.

House of Blood
aka: **Chain Reaction**
Film J Productions 2006; 103 minutes; Director: Olaf Ittenbach; Rating: ☠☠☠☠☠

A prison van collides with a doctor's car on the highway, the doctor and the escaping inmates heading into the woods, making for the Canadian border. They stumble across a strange cabin housing even stranger occupants.

Director Ittenbach's rough-around-the-edges horror movie is definitely for buffs who like their fare dished up raw, bloody and undiluted. Those of a more delicate disposition should steer well clear. Four prisoners plus Dr. Christopher Kriesa chance upon the Olde Worlde building deep in the misty woods, the residents dressed in colonial attire, speaking in a medieval dialect ("Aye, understandeth I, but understandeth thee what happen could when thee here stayeth"). Chains are on the walls and restraining ropes adorn the beds. Profanity spouting, gun-happy Simon Newby (exhibiting a severe case of overacting) orders Kriesa to operate on his brother's badly shattered arm. The medic hacks it off using a mallet and a large knife, the graphic bloodletting acting as a catalyst for these weird folk to transform themselves into rabid vampire mutants who slaughter the prisoners. Kriesa escapes with the help of Martina Ittenbach, playing

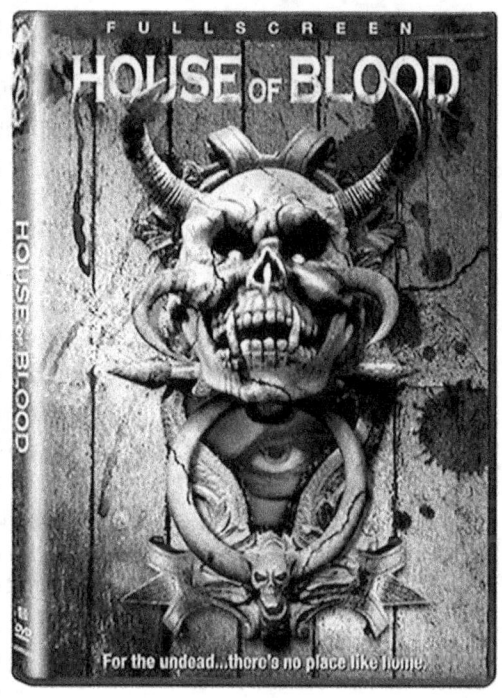

Alice, one of the people managing to control their innermost monstrous selves. Events then take a mysterious turn. A S.W.A.T. team arrives on the scene, arrests the doctor, fails to locate the house, and Kriesa, unable to convince the police on the feasibility of his story, is packed off to a prison in Seattle. But the incidents he has just been put through happen again. Another van/car crash occurs, the prisoners break free and Kriesa finds himself caught up in a nightmarish form of déjà vu as the cabin and its collection of scary inhabitants return to feast on a new batch of humans. Again, the doctor takes flight with the winsome Alice, and out on the highway the two observe a third collision involving a prison van. The very final scene is of Ittenbach finally unleashing the beast within her as a prisoner shoots her. Many unanswered questions exist in this movie. Why is Kriesa reliving these gruesome events, and what is the connection between him and Ittenbach in the sequences (shot in monochrome) showing the doctor, as a small boy, receiving a pendant in the form of an ornate cross from the girl? But put this aside and we have spades plunging into heads, a vampire sliced in two, a chainsaw carving up torsos, flesh hit by bullets in fountains of blood, heads ripped off, dismembered body parts being eaten, plus an unflinching operation on a scrotum. The acting is terrible but comes secondary to the gore-laden effects, filmed with a certain amount of over-the-top relish. Okay, there's nothing of a cerebral nature here, but in its own carnage-laden style, *House of Blood* entertains more so than a lot of other, higher-budgeted splatter-fests.

House of the Dead
Brightlight Pictures/Boll Kino KG 2003; 90 minutes; Director: Uwe Boll; Rating: ☠

Five teenagers charter a boat at great expense in order to attend a rave party on an island. When they arrive, they find that the partygoers, who reside in an ancient house, have all been turned into zombies.

Look, Uwe Boll can dress this zombie flick up however much he likes—*Matrix*-type shoot-outs in slow motion, constant insertion of clips from the video game (on which the movie is based), buckets of gore and a techno-beat soundtrack. It still doesn't disguise the fact that his effort is very much overworked fare that will have fans of the zombie genre muttering: "Just how many more times can you show countless scenes of teenagers being chased by zombies before it all becomes repetitive?" So on this particular island, Tyron Leitso, Will Sanderson, Ona Grauer, Enuka Okuma and Sonya Salomaa are the two guys and three dolly birds up against the zombie hordes presided over by shaven-headed lord and master David Palffy. He, with his skeletal crew, came to the island centuries ago and has to feed off the flesh of the living to prolong his existence, as do his minions. Sequences standing out include near-nude females attacked by the mummified dead; an old house containing decaying body parts; numerous (and very drawn-out) battles between zombies and humans; the boat's captain gunning down the creatures as they try to board his vessel; and interminable shots of survivors running through the dark woods, hounded by the lurching flesh-eaters. *House of the Dead* is tedious and yawn inducing, a bad, sad reflection on today's horror output and zombie actioners in particular. Viewers have to be real die-hard zombie fanatics to gain any enjoyment from this clichéd horror farrago.

The House of Usher
Abernathy Productions 2006; 81 minutes; Director: Hayley Cloake; Rating: ☠☠☠

A young woman attends the funeral of her best friend, who apparently expired under mysterious circumstances. The woman becomes embroiled in a continuing family curse.

Edgar Allan Poe's classic tale of madness is given a modern, indie treatment in what turns out to be a proficiently directed horror thriller containing a sparse, quirky score that complements the doom-laden plot. Izabella Miko travels out to the Usher mansion to be present at her friend's funeral, meeting up with the dead girl's brother, writer Austin Nichols (playing Roderick Usher), who used to be her boyfriend. But all is not well in the diminishing Usher household. Black-clad Beth Grant, resembling the evil Mrs. Danvers in Hitchcock's legendary *Rebecca*, hovers in the background, making it plainly clear that she resents Miko's presence in the house. Pallid Nichols, suffering from an incurable disease (or so he claims), receives regular injections to combat the effects of neurasthenia, aided by sporadic immersions in an isolation tank bathed in blue light. His illness, however, doesn't prevent the guy from making Miko pregnant. By then the poor woman has discovered the Usher's terrible, incestuous secret. Over the decades, each female family member has given birth to twins, who have themselves mated and had twins, and so on, and so forth. Miko's pal (Danielle McCarthy) *isn't* dead at all. She is carrying her brother's baby and, out of her mind, self-aborts with the aid of a coat hanger to try to end the curse. The loathsome Grant, angry at what the girl has done, leaps out of a window to her death; the insane McCarthy and her brother both drown in the isolation tank (which takes the place of a coffin). The final shot sees Miko in the hospital, the ultra-scan showing twins growing inside her—the curse lives on! Granted, there's no Vincent Price around to hold our attention, but nevertheless, this is an atmospheric, unorthodox re-visioning of the Poe story that works well within its budget limitations. Many other Poe filmic adaptations exist on the market that are much worse than this outing.

How to Make a Monster
Creature Features Productions 2001; 90 minutes; Director: George Huang; Rating: ☠☠

Three computer geeks concoct a violent video game that spirals out of control when the cyber-monster created by the game takes on a life of its own and goes on a rampage.

Executive producer Samuel Z. Arkoff updated his hokey old 1958 B thriller (which featured the Teenage Werewolf and Teenage Frankenstein) for the 21st-century computer generation. Software company Evilution employs

three techno-buffs (tough-guy Tyler Mane, black dude Karim Prince and nerdy Jason Marsden) to design a violent computer game for the kids. Once completed, a force from within the computer takes control of an interactive suit, slices up Mane and sticks Prince's head onto Mane's decapitated body. Result? A robotic killer at large in the complex, with Marsden, boss Steven Culp and assistant Clea DuVall fighting for their lives against the unstoppable foe. Stan Winston designed the heavily armored monster in this comic book twaddle. Huang directs with some flair, and the thumping title music by David Reynolds is a real bonus for lovers of blood-tingling soundtracks. But this will only appeal to addicts of 18-rated video games and a few hardcore horror fanatics.

The Hunt
American World Pictures 2006; 90 minutes; Director: Fritz Kiersch; Rating: ☠☠☠☠☠

Two men and an eight-year-old boy venture into an area of restricted woodlands known as Casper Lease to shoot a video on a deer hunt. They disappear, prompting a huge search by the police and the man who financed the video, hoping to capitalize on its commercial potential.

Based on a true series of events which took place in 1999, Kiersch's alien-conspiracy thriller, shot *Blair Witch*-style for maximum impact, may be an indie movie but it's one that pulls the viewer into its anxiety-ridden action, the final revelatory surprise coming like a bolt out of the blue. The movie flashes backwards and forwards between the search for the missing trio (taking place over several days, filmed as a pseudo-documentary TV news bulletin) and the reason for their disappearance, pieced together from video footage recovered from the sole survivor (young Mitchell Burns). We see Joe Michael Burke (the hunter), Robert Rusler (the cameraman) and Burns (Burke's stepson) heading off to the woods to produce a hunt video that they reckon will be a major seller. On entering the woodlands, things take a nightmarish turn for the worse—a truck is parked, the approaching hulking driver warning them to keep out; deer are spotted but remain tantalizingly elusive; they stumble across a strange circle of electronic gadgetry, with mounds of a queer powdery substance on the ground; the 15-foot-high fence partly enclosing the woods is designed to prevent anything inside escaping; their compass readings go haywire; a deer's body is found, one leg torn off, a wooden post plunged into its neck; odd scratch marks appear on trees; a pair of prison-issue shoes is found near an old shelter, together with a chopped-off finger; a pale figure is seen flitting around at dusk; and at night, men drive into the woods on buggies, followed by a helicopter, and then drive off. In the

meantime, to add to the mystery, the story rapidly jumps forward, concentrating on Cliff De Young's own futile investigations (he was the hunt's investor) in tracing the two missing men from the videotape found on Burns. The hillbilly café assistant uncomfortably denies seeing the threesome on their way to the woods, even though he is seen on the tape. De Young is informed that the owner of the pickup has died. The payoff comes as a complete bombshell. Casper Lease happens to be an area designated for the study of an extraterrestrial life form that inhabits the woodlands, the powers-that-be allowing the outer space visitors to feed off both the deer and prisoners who are brought there by the authorities; the driver they encountered is a trustee, guarding the creatures (which resemble hairless, three-fingered bony humanoids with fangs) against trespassers. The boy is spared after the men are slaughtered, and although De Young presents his findings to the National Security Agency: UFO Division (which includes a photograph of one of the alien beings), his notes are shredded, as this is one cover-up that must never be made public. De Young's character and his wife died in an accident in 2001, the police hurriedly pulling the plug on the case while the young boy and his mother live incognito at an unspecified address somewhere in America. A lot of bigger-budget efforts could learn much from this highly recommended "it really happened" sci-fi suspenser that engages the attention throughout, making audiences want to experience it all over again once that eye-opening ending has unveiled itself.

Hybrid

RHI Ent./Paquin/Peace Arch 2007; 90 minutes; Director: Yelena Lanskaya; Rating: ☠

At the Olaris Biomedical Center, the victim of a fire who has lost his sight is given the eyes of a wolf in an experimental transplant operation. When he recovers, the man inherits the attributes of the donor.

We won't see any werewolf in the anemic *Hybrid*, another straight-to-DVD disaster that bodes well for about 15 minutes before nose-diving rapidly into absurdity. Corey Monteith, the recipient of the eyes, possesses yellow orbs, eats raw steak, has enhanced color vision, can see in the dark and sleeps curled up on the floor. He also suffers from repeated newsreel footage (no, that should be visions!) of wolves attacking stampeding buffaloes. Befriended by an attractive Indian girl (Tinsel Korey was the one who ran over the wolf that became the donor for Monteith's new eyes), he escapes from the hospital ward, visits the local zoo, is recaptured, savages a doctor and escapes again, followed by the usual posse of weapon-flourishing, thick-brained cops. The final soul-destroying 10 minutes has Monteith running around in the woods, chased by the law. He massacres the lot of them and is last spotted loping over hearth land in the company of a pack of wild wolves, covered in blood, his admiring Indian girlfriend (who claims to enjoy an affinity with nature and animals, thus sympathizing with Monteith's plight) and an old Indian shaman looking on. If just once Monteith had transformed himself into something resembling a werewolf, this lethargic effort could have been saved. But he doesn't. In trying to be fresh, all we end up with is a low-budget variation on Asia's *The Eye*. The interesting "use of animal transplants on humans" angle is quickly dropped and female research scientist Justine Bateman is the only cast member to give any semblance of acting. Korey is attractive but inert and Monteith is as wooden as the trees he runs through. After the movie finishes, older (and wiser) horror buffs will no doubt groan in despair, casting their minds back to the glory days of Lon Chaney, Jr., Oliver Reed and even Michael Landon, when wolf men were *real* wolf men, not the feeble specimen on display here.

Hydrosphere
aka: **2103: The Deadly Wake**
Producers Network/Danforth Studios 1997; 100 minutes; Director: Philip Jackson; Rating: ☠

A captain, whose previous vessel sank under mysterious circumstances, is given the position of navigating a 100-year-old ship, the Lilith, to Nigeria. He's unaware that there is a death-dealing cargo on board that could spell catastrophe for the planet.

Not even the talents of Malcolm McDowell can save *Hydrosphere* from being perhaps the nadir of the actor's career, a total fiasco of bad performances, cardboard sets (bathed in an orange tint), cumbersome direction and dialogue containing pages of 22nd-century hogwash. Bearded McDowell is delivering a consignment of synthetic protein to war-torn Nigeria, oblivious to the fact that dozens of barrels in the hold contain something much more sinister—Clarion, a biological plague agent that can cause widespread death in 20 minutes and rapidly poison the world's oceans if submerged in seawater. Conniving boss Gwyneth Walsh and new president Sandy Kaizer plan to destroy the ship by planting two bombs on board and thus wipe out the planet. But stooge Michael Paré decides to switch sides, helping, with second mate Heidi von Palleske, to defeat Boudicca, an indestructible PVC-clad female cyborg that prances around like a demented dancer, launching mini-rockets and firing bullets. Meanwhile, the ship's crew, a group of criminals, is released, siding with the beleaguered captain, and a rat bites Ensign Hal Eisen. Oh yes, I nearly forgot the 86-year-old "Baby" in the bell jar, a "neural computer" communicating via the radio operator's lips. It all sounds completely absurd and it *is* completely absurd. None of the plot makes the slightest bit of sense (Are we in the middle of a global war? Who controls the planet? What has Nigeria got to do with this?). Paré acts as though he's in a trance and all we can really do is sit back, ignore the unfathomable storyline and admire Walsh's shapely legs, because there's nothing else to admire in the picture. Futuristic sci-fi actioners don't come any worse than this joint Canadian/British effort.

I Am Omega
Asylum 2007; 90 minutes; Director: Griff Furst; Rating: ☠☠☠

One of the few survivors from a plague that has turned the human race into flesh-eating mutations battles for survival on the outskirts of Los Angeles.

First, Vincent Price in *The Last Man on Earth* (1963); second, Charlton Heston in *The Omega Man* (1971); and last but not least, Will Smith in *I Am Legend* (2008). Now Mark Dacascos in *I Am Omega*. Mark who? Well, if imitation *is* the sincerest form of flattery, then anything American International and Warner Bros. can do, Asylum can do as well, if not better, in the most important department of all. The undead mutants featured are heaps better than those appearing in the previous, far more expensive, renditions of Richard Matheson's celebrated cult novel. Erupting from the earth, their blotchy skin, blood-drooling mouths, blank eyes and oddly serrated skin guaranteed to put the wind up any sane person, these creatures are the stuff of nightmares. Dacascos, living alone in his barricaded house, his only companion a life-sized dummy, surrounded by fencing, alarms and lights, is a pill-popping nervous wreck following the slaughter of his wife and child at the hands of the flesh-eaters. Entering the city through storm drains and planting bombs with timing devices near gas mains (his ultimate plan is to incinerate the mutants in one almighty inferno), his structured world is turned upside down when he receives a message from a distraught woman (Jennifer Lee Wiggins) on his laptop, pleading for him to take her to Antioch where, she says, thousands of other survivors are living in the mountains. She is immune from the disease. Two ex-soldiers next turn up and drag the protesting Dacascos off to L.A. to locate the girl who they want for sexual pleasure. The movie then runs its course in a series of confrontations with the undead, Dacascos ending up with Wiggins after the two maniacs have been killed and Los Angeles blown to smithereens. Photographed in muted color and ruined by one or two silly moments (how come Dacascos has the strength to jump-start a car after being shot in both legs by loony Geoff Meed?), this cheapo is, to be quite honest, far more entertaining in its sub-George A. Romero style than Price's and Heston's efforts, and the movie even gives Will Smith a run for his money (but that's not too hard a feat, is it?).

I Know Who Killed Me
360 Pictures 2007; 104 minutes; Director: Chris Sivertson; Rating: ☠☠

A young girl is abducted and tortured by a serial killer, but she is mysteriously released with her lower right arm and lower right leg amputated. On the road to recovery, she claims to be a different person altogether, much to the puzzlement of an FBI psychiatrist and her parents.

Blue, blue everywhere, but audiences can quite easily *get* the blues sitting through this overworked retread of countless psychological thrillers stretching back over decades of horror filmmaking. Throwing everything into the brew in the hope of tantalizing, intriguing and scaring an audience, director Sivertson's mess of a movie is a perfect showcase of how these modern-day psycho flicks simply end up becoming an incoherent, unfathomable jumble. Complex plot structures and symbolism are nothing new. Geniuses like Hitchcock and Bergman frequently dabbled in storylines that worked the mind but always made sense in the end (*Vertigo* and *The Seventh Seal* are two classic examples). Nowadays, *nothing* seems to make sense. Lindsay Lohan stars as a promising piano student who, much to the dismay of her teacher (Michael Adler), decides to quit her lessons to concentrate on writing. In the meantime, a serial killer is at large, one girl's mutilated body discovered with the fingers and toes missing. Then it's Lohan's turn to suffer a very nasty torture-porn sequence before being found barely alive in a ditch. Fitted with prosthetic limbs, she contends in the hospital that she is *not* the daughter (Aubrey) of Neil McDonough and Julia Ormond (she is now Dakota), doesn't recognize her boyfriend and starts having repeated visions of a girl resembling herself being victimized by the madman. Yes, the color blue predominates to the point when audiences feel like screaming. This, together with so many uncoordinated sequences and awkward flashbacks (is Lohan acting  out a part in one of her own stories?), makes for tiring viewing, especially approaching the inevitable showdown with the killer where Lohan mumbles her lines to a point where the dialogue is virtually unintelligible. Hidden among the tangle of pseudo-symbolic blue images, red herrings (a video clip on stigmatism) and grisly mutilations is a half-decent scenario of sorts. Lohan had a twin sister, Ormond's baby dying at birth. McDonough stole one of the twin baby girls from a druggie mother and paid the woman money. The music teacher is the psycho, murdering his protégées who don't match up to his expectations (he wears a blue ring, hence the omnipresent "blue" motif), and the twins each experience the other's pain. In time-honored fashion, Lohan (as Dakota) lops off her tormentor's right hand, stabs him to death, uncovers her sister's comatose body in a glass-lidded coffin and lays down with her—to die? The much-vilified Lohan, mostly famous for her offscreen antics rather than her onscreen contributions to celluloid, actually puts on a fairly respectable show, despite her less-than-flattering dark brown rinse. Maybe the film would have profited from a more proficient actress in the role, and certainly a more adroit director at the helm. Given hardly any screen time in British cinemas, *I Know Who Killed Me* is a bit of a disaster, saved from a one-star rating by some vibrant color cinematography and Lohan's edgy performance.

Ice Spiders

Sci Fi Pictures/ACH 2007; 88 minutes; Director: Tibor Takacs; Rating: ☠☠☠

Six different species of spider, genetically altered to be used by the military as both invincible fighting machines and bulletproof vests made from their skin, escape from a mountain laboratory and go on a rampage in the ski resort of Lost Mountain.

Eight Legged Freaks in the snow, *Ice Spiders* offers up the standard post-2000 theme of scientists tampering with DNA to produce animal warriors at the expense of innocent lives. In the Pine Mountain government laboratories, mad doctor David Millbern injects six spiders with DNA extracted from fossilized arachnids, accelerating their growth rate to a stage where the insatiable creatures burst out of the lab and, impervious to the cold conditions, begin to prey on skiers in the nearby Lost Mountain resort. Patrick Muldoon, the local ex-ski champion lumbered with the unenviable task of instructing a group of rowdy teenagers, fancies dishy doc Vanessa Williams (who was in on the spider experiments, but only up to a point). When cocooned corpses are found hanging in the trees and dismembered bodies of technicians lie in bloody heaps on the lab floor, Williams, Muldoon and company find themselves in retreat as the spiders attack both the resort and a stranded school bus full of those obnoxious teens. Okay, there aren't a vast number of spiders on display in this low-budget offering, but those that are

"*Eight Legged Freaks* meets *Hot Dog: The Movie*"

there scuttle around convincingly enough, gorging on ravaged flesh and entrails. The gore count is pretty high in this picture. Incredibly, *Ice Spider*'s soundtrack is curiously muted (even the heavy metal music near the end), a miracle in this age of the ear-busting audio track, and there are some novel perspective shots seen through the arachnids' eyes, appearing as distorted glass images. Granted, the dialogue is crass ("Awesome," repeated over and over; "This is totally not cool."), but we come to expect this in modern-day horror movies, unfortunately, and the acting is perfunctory to say the least. Nevertheless, Takacs, who directed the excellent *MosquitoMan*, handles the action with spirit. The snowy mountain scenery is beautiful and the finale (one surviving spider driven away in a steel container after Millbern met his nemesis) satisfactory, the army cover-up stating that everyone at the resort suffered from a mass hallucination, imagining the whole thing. *Ice Spiders* is a nifty little creature-feature that doesn't outstay its welcome.

Insanitarium
Stage 6 Films/Benderspink Prods. 2009; 89 minutes; Director: Jeff Buhler; Rating: ☠☠☠

A young man purposely carves himself up and acts like a madman in order to get institutionalized. His goal is to find out why his unbalanced sister has never been released from a mental hospital.

Samuel Fuller's 1963 classic *Shock Corridor* clashes with the zombie genre in a frenetically paced horror outing that has raving doctor Peter Stormare, assisted by equally raving nurse (Molly Bryant), injecting his patients with an experimental drug, stripping away the last vestiges of reason and turning them into flesh-devouring maniacs sporting white, staring eyes. Dark-haired Jesse Metcalfe plays the man infiltrating Stormare's establishment, teaming up with another investigator (Kevin Sussman), the two sneaking around the corridors at night, attempting to discover the secret behind the medic's unethical experiments and rescuing his sister (Kiele Sanchez) in the process. Once Metcalfe has revealed himself to be an impostor and the inmates break free, all semblance of plot and characterization is quickly dispensed with as Buhler creates one bloody scene after another. Patients are eaten alive, a nurse has her arm ripped off by a Hannibal Lecter clone housed in a cage, the walls are covered in crimson,

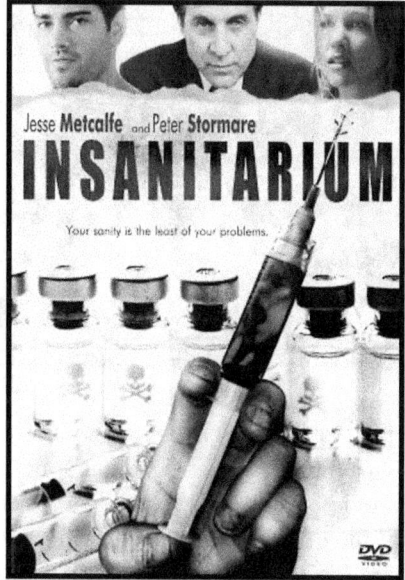

scalpels are wielded and, for cat lovers, there's one scene guaranteed to have audiences phoning to contact the nearest animal protection league. The open-ended finale features a score of blood-smeared lunatics, led by the mad-as-a-hatter Stormare, charging out of the institution and attacking the police as Metcalfe and Sanchez make their getaway. No finesse, no suspense, no drama—just a modern-day gore-fest for those who get their kicks out of fodder such as this. It's put together with ghoulish style, but the film lacks heart and depth. But then, are those qualities needed in movies like *Insanitarium*?

Intermedio
aka: **Dead and Dying**

Asylum 2006; 82 minutes; Director: Andy Lauer; Rating: ☠☠☠

Two guys and their girlfriends head off to a cave system on the Mexican border to buy drugs. They become prey to the tortured souls of the dead—the "In Betweens"—in the gloomy passages.

Yes, it's another "kids running for their lives in tunnels" horror movie, this one, coming from Asylum Productions, better than most, featuring a well-endowed foxy female (Cerina Vincent) and liberal doses of gore. Vincent, boyfriend Callard Harris, Edward Furlong (a childhood friend of Vincent) and Amber Benson descend into the complex of passageways via a trapdoor, exchange cash for dope with two dealers and are hunted by nebulous phantoms evoked by withered-looking Steve Railsback. The story goes that if anyone captures a dead person's blood before it hits the ground, the blood catcher is protected from evil while at the same time is able to control that person's spirit. Puritanical Railsback did just that to his own son, cutting his throat because of the boy "messing with sluts and druggies" and preserving his blood in a vial. Young Railsback now haunts the caves like so many other victims. In the pre-credits sequence, Vincent and Furlong's fathers met the same fate on a similar mission 18 years previously, one of the reasons why they want to investigate the place. Once one of the drug dealers dies horribly (a length of chain, swung by a skeleton, penetrating his left eye), the group charges willy-nilly through the galleries (Benson

hobbling madly on crutches) chased by the wraiths, separate, meet up, enter a heavily padlocked building from one opening, exit through another, re-enter the same rooms via a third trapdoor, exit by way of a crawl-space, shadowed by the ghostly son who, it turns out, only wants to help them escape from his father's clutches. Furlong and Vincent alone emerge bloodied, bruised but alive from the caves, the rest slaughtered by the ghouls; Railsback, his precious vial broken by his son, ripped apart by the demonic spirits. Those demonic spirits are really only shown as a quick blue skeletal blur, but never mind, this is a lively enough show, even though it's really hard to understand why top-heavy Vincent (after boyfriend Harris is killed) would want to fall into the arms of slobbish Furlong. No wonder Harris and Benson return from the grave, their ravaged countenances staring in disbelief through a window at the couple, in each other's arms, on a bed! If alert, keep a keen eye on a major blooper eight minutes in when the film's image is reversed for about 15 seconds. Vincent's T-shirt, stretched over her ample chest, is the giveaway!

Isolation

Filmfour 2005; 95 minutes; Director: Billy O'Brien; Rating: ☠☠

On an isolated Irish farm, a genetically modified cow, bred to supposedly increase fertility, gives birth to a calf that contains six parasitic fetuses.

Alien transposed to a rural farm setting, as farmer John Lynch discovers that a newly born calf contains six mutated infants—five are dead, but a sixth slithers away, forming the basis for what happens. Lynch, vet Essie Davis and doctor Marcel Lures, who were experimenting on the cows to increase the livestock by scientific means, are at the mercy of the creature, as are squatters Sean Harris and girlfriend Ruth Negga. Shot in grainy, murky color to mirror the dull gray skies of Ireland, there is gore aplenty as the little slimy monster swims around in the slurry, chomping and burrowing into humans and cattle, leaving only Negga (who has been bitten but survived, but *may* be infected) the sole survivor. Four months later, she's in the hospital having a pregnancy scan and told that her baby is normal—but is it? *Isolation* does its best to pile on the shocks and suspense, but the movie's biggest handicap is the creature itself. In its tiny state, it resembles an oozing, bloody bone with

spindly legs, but at the climax, where it's man-sized, the monster looks like a tangle of spare ribs with one bovine eye staring balefully from the center. Forcefully directed by O'Brien, *Isolation* (not given a wide release in Britain) would have been a minor, classy shocker if only the protagonist were a humdinger. Unfortunately, it isn't, and that's where the film falls down, through its own lack of imagination or resources.

Jolly Roger: Massacre at Cutter's Cove

Asylum 2005; 80 minutes; Director: Gary Jones; Rating: ☠☠☠☠

Two teenagers unearth a pirate's chest half-buried in the sand. On opening the lid, they unwittingly unleash the ghoulish spirit of Roger Laforge, Jolly Roger, a legendary pirate who was murdered by his ship's crew and is now thirsting for revenge.

"You took my treasure, matey, but not again." "They say some guy dressed as a pirate did this." "Ho ho ho." "Mmm. Is that a musket in your pocket or are you just happy to see me?" Yes, we're not talking *Treasure Island*, Robert

Newton and Long John Silver here. Asylum's campy, trashy horror parody (surely it has to be!) reaches new heights in decapitations (16 and counting) as the festering buccaneer (a heavily disguised and costumed Rhett Giles) slashes his way through the town of Cutter's Cove, slaughtering the descendants of those who took his looted gold all those centuries ago and used it for their own selfish means. Asylum movies equate to buckets of gore and naked breasts—audiences get more than their fair share in these fun-packed 80 minutes. Heads are lopped off at the rate of one every few minutes, an arm is yanked out of its socket and faces and torsos are carved into ribbons. A near-the-knuckle sex romp appears at the start and the extended, near-pornographic lap-dancing sequence midway in is guaranteed to have most male viewers in urgent need of an ice-cold shower (Bernadette Perez—phew!). Tom Nagel and Kristina Korn play a couple of teens on the run, Thomas Downey is the bemused sheriff, Pamela Munro the obstructive mayor and Kim Little appears as Downey's assistant. A little conviction to these outlandish goings-on comes from the usual bunch of company regulars. The pirate (quite an endearing character, it has to be said) is defeated at the end when Nagel cuts his head off, only for the monster to return to claim *his* final heads—Downey's and Korn's. The yellow light Giles installs in his victims' eyes contrasts with his single glowing red eye. The actor probably had a ball in the role, as did the props department whose job it was to manufacture all those severed heads that are heaped grotesquely in the pirate's chest. This is one of Asylum's zanier efforts, its tongue set firmly in its cheek; peppered with lines like those quoted above, how could it possibly be otherwise? And that opening/closing pulsating rock track will delight all metal freaks.

Journey to the Center of the Earth
RHI Entertainment/Reunion Pictures 2008; 90 minutes; Director: T.J. Scott; Rating: ☠☠☠

An heiress enlists the aid of a professor and his nephew to trace the whereabouts of her explorer husband, who disappeared into the bowels of the Earth four years previously.

Over a dozen film adaptations of Jules Verne's novel have been made, stretching right back to 1909 (*Voyage au Center de la Terre*), but none are quite so topsy-turvy as this made-for-TV offering. The standard-bearer still remains, 50 years on, Fox's lavish, carefully paced fantasy—James Mason is commanding (and underrated), Pat Boone delivers his best-ever performance, eye-catching subterranean set designs inspire and Bernard Herrmann's evocative score remains one of his best. Here, Iceland is substituted for Alaska, waspish Professor Lidenbrock becomes bullish Professor Brock (Rick Shroder), Axl changes to Abel (Steven Grayhm) and, from the Fox movie, female lead Arlene Dahl transforms into Martha, the heiress (Victoria Pratt). And Verne would surely have turned up his scholarly eyebrows at the thought of his tetchy professor being cast as a pugilist! All said and done, this version retains the Victorian setting as the trio plus Russian guide Mike Dopud trek into the Alaskan wilderness to locate a mine entrance only visible one day of the year. Once inside, the foursome descend into the Earth's depths via galleries and vast caverns, emerging

at an underground lake bathed in electrical light. Menaced by winged dinosaurs (Archaeopteryx?) and a Mosasaurus (*not*, as stated, a Plesiosaur), the picture then takes a downturn when Pratt's husband (Peter Fonda) is introduced into the story, a self-appointed figurehead lording over a lost tribe of Indians. Following a tussle with the surly natives, the explorers, together with the tribes' unofficial chief, make good their escape. However, Fonda, dynamiting the entrance to a hidden exit passageway to keep the Indians at bay, is inadvertently left behind as the four head down the tunnel flooded by the explosion. They are expelled by a vortex up into the lake at the surface, and Pratt, rid of her megalomaniac husband, decides to hitch up with Shroder on his next journey to the East Indies. Nicely photographed, scenes imbued in sepia/pastel colors to complement the period feel, Scott's effort is ruined in the first 25 minutes by some bouncy, distinctly un-Herrmann-like music, unable to sustain that all-important air of fantasy and awe after Fonda and his Indians are found. Taking untold artistic liberties with such a legendary piece of work will dismay many traditionalists, but if audiences can put Fox's classic aside for a moment, they might well enjoy this 90-minute juvenile adventure that is imaginative in parts, uninspiring in others.

Kaw
S.V. Scary Films/Reel One Ent. 2007; 92 minutes; Director: Sheldon Lewis; Rating: ☠☠☠☠

Flocks of ravens, infected by mad cow disease, turn on the population of a small American town.

It evokes Hitchcock's *The Birds* 50 years on, a gritty horror movie (filmed in Scotland) that includes one-time Hitchcock stalwart Rod Taylor playing the town doctor, complete with pork-pie hat. Now if that isn't an homage to a vintage classic, what is! As was the case with the master's own ornithological horror masterpiece, a steady build-up of suspense and terror occurs. Sheriff Sean Patrick Flanery investigates the mysterious death of a local farmer while noticing an ever-increasing number of ravens appearing on trees, buildings and in the sky. Grizzled bus driver Stephen McHattie is the first to escape the pecking terrors. Midway into the action, Flanery's wife Kristin Booth discovers that these birds are infected from diseased cattle. Two Amish farmers (John Ralston and Vladmir Bondarenko) are also aware, but being religious zealots, they think the whole thing is an act of God, punishment for man's misdeeds and loose morals. Lewis makes excellent use of Scotland's bleak, wintry landscapes and shoots the ravens in full-frame to present them as a truly terrifying predator, not simply a winged menace. The scenes of hundreds of the creatures emerging like a plague of black bats from misty woodland and the night sky are the stuff of nightmares. Although the gore quota isn't excessive, what exists will upset some viewers. Other nods in the direction of *The Birds* are an explosive gas station climax outside a diner, a school bus under attack from hundreds of stone-carrying birds and a complete lack of any explanation regarding the ravens suddenly dying in the thousands. Finally the icing on the cake occurs when Flanery and Booth return home, walk slowly upstairs and open a door. Audiences can guess what happens next! A wink reminding audiences of the horrors that Hitchcock subjected Tippi Hedren to in his picture is revisited. Try to ignore Ralston's hysterically false Amish whiskers (the glue is actually visible if you look hard enough) and enjoy this downbeat horror yarn that packs quite a punch. It's a real treat for older buffs to see veteran Taylor back on the big screen after a hiatus of many years. The maestro himself would have been proud of this one.

Killer Bees
Regent Entertainment 2002; 95 minutes; Director: Penelope Buitenhuis; Rating: ☠☠

On Honey Festival Day, the town of Sumas is under siege from a deadly swarm of African killer bees brought over illegally from South America by truck.

When will filmmakers ever learn that bees do not make good movie monsters. Think back to *The Deadly Bees* (1966), *The Savage Bees* (1977) and *The Swarm* (1978)—duds, each and every one of them. *Killer Bees* is not any different from the rest: average plot, adequately acted and with mediocre effects. It's the old, old tale of the pompous town mayor ignoring the advice of the sheriff (in this case, C. Thomas Howell) to take necessary precautions against an attack of killer bees, putting public relations before public safety. Only when several farmers, an elderly woman and the local high-school jerk have been stung to death, and a black cloud of the insects descends on the town during the festival, does the hairpiece-wearing official realize that something is seriously wrong. Naturally, he meets his end, covered in bees, as he tries to drive off. The main swarm is incinerated inside a hall after Howell and bee expert Fiona Loewi (who has a crush on the soon-to-be-divorced law officer) set fire to the building. There's nothing new here, the thrills are few and far between and the photography colorless. Yes, it's one more "bee" movie to join all those other worthy contenders for the title of the most uninteresting insects-against-man feature ever produced.

King Cobra
Trimark Pictures 1999; 93 minutes; Directors: David and Scott Hillenbrand; Rating: ☠☠☠

Cross-bred from an African King cobra and a Diamondback rattlesnake, a 30-foot reptile escapes from a laboratory and causes terror in the small rural town of Fillmore.

No wonder this particular snake is so dangerous. Apart from its size, Dr. Joseph Ruskin has pumped the reptile with increasing doses of "aggressive serum" and vast quantities of testosterone, as well as tampering with its brain chemistry and neural transmitters, although why is never explained. Two years on from the lab explosion that frees the monster, we are in the town of Fillmore preparing to celebrate Brewfest, and straight away we can see where this restyled copy of a '50s B movie is coming from. Yes, despite local doctor Scott Brandon, cop girlfriend Casey Fallo, Japanese snake expert Pat Morita and Ruskin (wearing an eye patch) all warning the mayor of the gigantic reptilian menace slithering around in the surrounding woods, the man in charge loftily declares that the show *must* go on, regardless. Profit-before-lives becomes a much-favored plotline following in the shadow of *Jaws*. Not even the discovery of two huge snake skins, a larger-than-normal fang and a couple of gruesome deaths (Brandon's father is swallowed whole by the beast) convinces the overweight head of the community that the festival must not take place. But it proceeds, come what may. It contains dialogue of the caliber of, "We're gonna kick some ass!" as the townsfolk, rifles ready, comb the woodlands. When one of them stumbles across a colossal skin and declares, "We're gonna need bigger guns" (*Jaws* again!), audiences might be lulled into thinking that this is yet another of those no-brainer clunkers. But no, the mighty hissing cobra, when fully on display in the film's final third act, is effectively realized, towering over its victims, fangs dripping venom. Some genuine tension arises in the build-up to the snake's multiple attacks, backed by (you've guessed it!) a *Jaws*-type soundtrack. Morita, Brandon and Ruskin eventually trap the monster in a tube where it is gassed but not necessarily killed (they never are in these modern-day horror flicks!). And check out Brandon's flying dropkick on the cobra's head as it wrestles with Morita, a gem of a scene. More carefully paced than most other giant creature vs. man efforts, efficiently acted and boasting an eye-catching monster, *King Cobra* will not disappoint fans of this type of fare or anyone else wishing for 90 minutes of monster-snake thrills.

King of the Ants
Asylum 2003; 102 minutes; Director: Stuart Gordon; Rating: 🌟🌟🌟🌟

A mild-mannered painter and decorator is turned into a psychotic killer when he is double-crossed and tortured on instructions from a ruthless property developer.

Anyone of a nervous disposition, allergic to scenes of graphic violence in the tradition of *Saw* and its sequels, should stay well away from *King of the Ants*. A chilling journey into how a series of escalating events can forever change one man's life, this psycho-drama with horror overtones is briskly directed by Gordon, with a sparse but effective soundtrack and riveting performances to match. Chris McKenna plays a decorator, innocently going about his business, when he has the misfortune to cross paths with hulking sadist George Wendt. The mountainous thug has a proposition for him to spice up his mundane existence—spy on his boss' accountant, a man who is investigating Wendt for corruption. But following a meeting with Wendt's chief, the equally odious Daniel Baldwin, McKenna, on promise of a payout of $13,000, murders the accountant. To his alarm, Baldwin doesn't cough up the money, so McKenna attempts to blackmail him by threatening to expose his crooked dealings using evidence contained in an incriminating file. What follows is a descent into hell. Held prisoner in an isolated desert house, the decorator-turned-murderer is savagely and repeatedly beaten around the head with a golf club to render him into the state of a vegetable but, totally deranged (he has visions of mutants baying for his flesh), his swollen, bloody, drooling features a mass of ugly lumps, he rips Wendt's throat out with his teeth, escapes, roams the streets looking like the victim of some heinous act, recovers in the arms of the accountant's widow and exacts a terrible revenge on those who, through their own violent actions, have caused his rebirth into an inhuman killer. The final 15 minutes forcibly emphasize the film's inhumanity. Wendt's frozen corpse (kept in a freezer) is decapitated and the head thrown on a fire. Baldwin's two henchmen are bludgeoned with a mallet, paralyzed and locked in the house, which is then set ablaze. Baldwin is doused in fuel and set on fire, McKenna tossing a lighted match. The movie successfully dwells on the darker side of human nature (McKenna's all-too-realistic murder of the accountant fills him with both revulsion and euphoria at the same time) without compromising its moral stance on such appalling deeds. For a low-budget nihilistic shocker of this type, it packs one hell of a punch but is certainly not suitable for those prone to a weak stomach. The movie doesn't make for comfortable viewing.

King of the Lost World
Asylum 2005; 90 minutes; Director: Leigh Scott; Rating: ☠☠☠

A passenger airliner crashes into an uncharted region of the Amazon jungle, an untamed terrain populated by giant spiders, huge scorpions, winged dinosaurs, a lost tribe and King Kong.

Sir Arthur Conan Doyle's classic adventure tale meets *King Kong*, with liberal helpings of television's *Lost* chucked into the brew for good measure. Only Asylum would have the effrontery to plunder *The Lost World* in such a barefaced manner and get away with it. Among the company's usual troupe, Bruce Boxleitner is an ill-tempered Lieutenant Challenger, Jeff Denton plays a rather gormless Ed Malone, Rhett Giles stars as action-man John Roxton

and Sarah Lieving is sweaty and sexy Rita Summerlee (what became of her professor father?). In addition to this rogue's gallery, Asylum stalwart Thomas Downey disappears early on, entangled in a man-eating vine; grizzled Steve Railsback enters the scene as the unbalanced sole survivor of a previous plane disaster, living a hermit-type existence in a cave cluttered with rusting aircraft parts; stewardess Amanda Ward is stripped, as a native girl (exhibiting lesbian traits) fondles her breasts; and the surly Challenger is chatted up by another less-than-nubile native female who coos blissfully into his horrified face, "I fancy you." If all this isn't enough to have the words "infringement of copyright," "plagiarism" and "daylight robbery" buzzing around in our head, the opening few minutes feature a stewardess in a state of undress screaming her head off, a gigantic ape plucking the woman from a treetop. Now where have we seen *that* before? But disregarding the innumerable liberties taken with one of fiction's greatest monster yarns, how does *King of the Lost World* actually rate as a movie per se? Leigh Scott's direction is uneven at times, the continuity suspect in several areas and the soundtrack tends to rise and fall, from a whisper to a deafening racket. Effects-wise, the scorpions come out trumps, the giant spider less so, and as for the mighty Kong himself, well, in most of his short screen time he's a colossal, stomping, roaring blur, warding off flying reptiles and fighter jets in quick undefined motions. The performances overall are a notch above average and the female cast all curvy and delicious as per Asylum's norm. After Kong is nuked at the end, we almost wish the picture would carry on in its own sweet, outrageous style. Whichever way audiences look at it, this is far more entertaining than Fox's 1960 *The Lost World,* which took itself much too seriously and ended up a crashing bore. Boring is what *King of the Lost World* certainly isn't!

Komodo

Scanbox Asia Pacific 1999; 90 minutes; Director: Michael Lantieri; Rating: ☠☠☠

Giant Komodo lizards inhabit the swamplands of Emerald Isle, North Carolina, the result of pollution in the water caused by oil drilling.

Social drama and creature-feature thrills do not always make comfortable bedfellows, which is the case here. Young Kevin Zegers returns to his home on Emerald Isle in the company of a psychologist (Jill Hennessy) and his aunt (Nina Lands). The lad is deeply traumatized following the horrifying demise of his parents, both dragged to their deaths by monster lizards that have bred in the swamps, unmolested for 20 years. When Lands meets the same fate, pulled by her legs through the floorboards, Zegers, Hennessy, ferry owner Michael Edward-Stevens and a couple of company heavies (Billy Burke and Paul Gleeson, acting on orders from unethical oil boss Simon Westaway) find themselves up against the carnivorous reptiles. Deprived of food by the contaminated waters, the reptiles

have taken a liking to human flesh. Shot mostly at night, *Komodo*, admittedly, is unoriginal in concept but does have a lot going for it. The big gray lizards are extraordinarily lifelike (CGI and animatronics) and, what's more important, audiences get to see a great deal of them. Also, although not overly gory, the attacks on Zegers and company are executed in vigorous style. The "delving into Zegers' troubled mind" scenario drags slightly during the initial 20 minutes or so, but by the time the youth plus Hennessy and Burke make it more or less unscathed to the mainland via helicopter, Zegers' head has cleared sufficiently enough for him to appreciate just how tasty his female doctor friend is! Quite frankly, *Komodo* would have made a fairly decent theatrical release. Countless others of its kind have been released that have been much worse, and at least the movie doesn't stint on the monster action. *Komodo* is one of the better "creatures-in-the-swamps" movies.

Komodo vs. Cobra
Cinetel Films 2005; 94 minutes; Director: Jay Andrews (Jim Wynorski); Rating: ☠☠

On a remote Pacific island, geneticists have meddled with animal DNA, producing two giant Komodo dragons and a 50-foot cobra.

Opening with the death of two men—one gets eaten by a massive lizard, the other gobbled up by a gigantic snake—*Komodo vs. Cobra* moves ponderously into sub-*Jurassic Park* territory in its tale of six environmentalists (named "One Planet") chartering a boat from captain Michael Paré to investigate a hush-hush military installation on Isla Darmus. In the meantime, army officer Rod McCary,

after losing one team of commandos on the island, has decided to bomb the place to oblivion, regardless of who's on it. Slackly directed by Wynorski, this unwieldy monster movie is fun to watch for all the wrong reasons. Paré is his usual expressionless self, his features a blank mask, even when chatted up by juicy scientist Michelle Borth. Did this man *ever* attend drama school? Paré isn't the only actor present who will *never* be presented with a Golden Globe. Borth scampers through the jungle in low-cut jeans that threaten to slip below her panty line, her shrill delivery akin to that of Minnie Mouse. The rest of the cast are just as bad, simply going through the motions. The blaring, trumpet-laden music *isn't* easy on the ears but the tropical scenery (although used many times in these under-produced fantasy flicks) is. Why has the swearing been replaced by what sounds like a squawking parrot? The sight of Paré blasting away with a small handgun at a lizard the size of a house, expecting the beast to drop dead, borders on the absurd. What about the creatures themselves? CGI monsters are now starting to appear flat, bland and too similar, lacking the depth, sharpness and color that highlighted, for example, those classic Ray Harryhausen creations of yore. They *look* as though they've been manufactured in a computer, and audiences have become blasé to their visual (or lack of) impact. Having said that, both colossal lizard and mammoth snake make acceptable foes, the much anticipated (well, after sitting through 90 minutes it is!) tussle over and done with in seconds as Paré, Borth and TV reporter Jerri Manthey take off in a chopper, bombs raining down on the island *and* the monsters. The final shot shows a dead marine coming alive—forked tongue, green eyes, eliptical pupils—infected with the Komodo's toxic saliva. Compared to other "mighty animal vs. mighty animal" flicks, *Komodo vs. Cobra* is way down on the list and has a jaded air. Paré's immobile face really speaks volumes and says it all.

Lake Dead
aka: **The Lake of Death**
Alliance Group Entertainment 2007; 90 minutes; Director: George Bessudo; Rating: 🌑🌑🌑

Three sisters inherit a run-down motel from their grandfather, whom they thought died many years ago, not aware that the place hides a terrible family secret involving murder and incest.

The Hills Have Eyes, Wrong Turn, The Texas Chain Saw Massacre and even a few touches gleaned from *Psycho—Lake Dead* dips into these and more, emerging as a fast-paced teen slasher flick containing one extremely harrowing sequence near the beginning. When sisters Kelsey Wedeen, Kelsey Crane and Tara Gerard learn of their unexpected inheritance, Gerard (who swears incessantly in between copious swigging from a whisky bottle) hotfoots it to the Lake Motel to suss the place out and is savagely slaughtered in room 6 by a pair of facially disfigured throwbacks wearing boiler suits. James Caan's leg-bashing treatment at the hands of obsessed Kathy Bates in *Misery* ain't got nothing on this scene. Gerald's legs are tied together as a thin hollow pipe is hammered through both of her ankles with an ax. A chain is threaded through the pipe, then fixed to a concrete block, her comatose body dumped in the lake. Following this gut-thumping murder, the picture settles down into the realms of teen horror (featuring a bevy of toned babes and blaring rock music) as the other two siblings plus friends Alex A. Quinn, Jim Devoti, Vanessa Viola and Malea Richardson converge on the motel, meet long-lost granny Pat McNeely, decide to camp near the lake and are then picked off by the two lank-haired deviants. In comes police officer James C. Burns to the supposed rescue after Quinn, Richardson and Viola have been horribly molested and butchered. Unfortunately Burns is the girls' uncle, in on all the mayhem with McNeely. He wants to carry on the family tradition of incest to produce more members for the family tree and has his perverted eyes on the blonde beauties. Devoti shoots Granny dead and Dan Woods, the real father, turns up at the end, blowing his twisted brother's brains out, unwittingly leaving one badly injured nutcase (Trevor Torseth) hobbling toward the motel in the closing frames, ax in hand, ready to commit further bloody carnage. *Psycho* references? The motel is the obvious pointer, but watch closely in the final 20 minutes when Burns parks outside the motel entrance—McNeely is silhouetted in a window frame, just like Norman Bates' mother. McNeely's wrinkled features even resemble the mummified Mrs. Bates! Watch for an embarrassing continuity error in Gerard's apartment near the start; she rises from the sofa in red panties, walks across her room, turns and is sporting cut-off jeans. Unpleasant at times (incest, cruelty and savage murder are uneasy bedfellows for a lot of people), *Lake Dead* throws in enough shocks and brutality to gratify all hardcore buffs. This is an above-average shocker for the new generation.

A TERROR THAT GETS UNDER YOUR SKIN

Larva
Nu Image 2005; 96 minutes; Director: Tim Cox; Rating: ☠☠☠

In the Missouri town of Host, genetically modified cattle feed causes a species of parasite to mutate within cows, the creatures bursting out of the cows' dead bodies and feasting on the human population.

The first half of *Larva* is marvelous stuff for horror buffs. New veterinarian Vincent Ventresca arrives in Host and straight off is up to his neck in dead cattle, parasitic maggots that multiple when fed on blood and corporate bully David Selby, boss of Host Tender Meats, who holds the townsfolk in the palm of his hand. Selby supplies the feed at cost, the townies sell all their beef to his company and everyone profits. Rod Stewart's ex, Rachel Hunter, turns up as Selby's attorney, trying to steer the inquisitive vet away from the alarming truth that the whole food chain, from feed to meat for the burgers, is contaminated with larvae. And what's more, people are eating the stuff by the truck load, a recipe for disaster. Director Cox involves us from the start as Ventresca slowly unravels the secret behind the parasitic infestation, leading to a gory scene in which a man, having fallen into a stream, lies in a coma in the hospital. A parasite crawls out of his nostril and drops into his mouth, Cox's camera following the creature down the trachea into the stomach where it feeds on the contents, grows huge and evolves quickly into something resembling a giant bat. Then the monster erupts out of the man's stomach in front of his wife and hospital staff (that chest-bursting sequence in *Alien* has much to answer for!). Disappointingly, from that moment on, the movie goes right off the boil, content to let Ventresca, Hunter and farmer William Forsythe run around with guns as Host is overrun by the crawling bat creatures, all the baddies getting their comeuppance before scores of the parasites are lured into a sewer by pumping fertilizer into the drains and dynamiting them to death. For gore fiends, Cox piles on the grisly shocks with aplomb. A courting couple, the sheriff and his deputy, Selby, his wife and young son and a guy in a shower all fall victim to the monsters, either by having ingested the poisoned meat or by being enveloped in a contaminated victim's membranous embrace. If only the second half of *Larva* had matched the first 45 minutes, this could have been a five-star winner. As it is, the picture merely comes across as a well-presented but standard creature-feature.

The Last Sentinel
Gorilla Pictures/Autumn Ent. 2007; 93 minutes; Director: Jesse V. Johnson; Rating: ☠☠

In a post-apocalyptic future, robotic armored police have turned against mankind and plan to eliminate the human race in their quest for world domination.

For aficionados of computer/arcade shoot-'em-up games, *The Last Sentinel* might well be your particular bag. If you're not, then it will leave you as cold as ice. A frail plot, little in the way of character development and not much depth (particularly in the quasi-Isaac Asimov script department) exists. The film has little else going for it, then, except to watch caped Don Wilson, sole survivor of the Elite 700 shock troops movement, and freedom fighter Katee Sackhoff. They extricate themselves from one sticky situation after another on basically one set (a disused power plant) in their attempts to kill as many of

the helmeted, bio-mechanical drone police as possible, by guns or explosives, and ultimately immobilize their communications system. Wilson, in contact with a remote computer that transmits advice via his eye-cam and "hard-wired" implants, finally outwits the drones after countless (and repetitive) shoot-outs. He has a climactic sword fight with a red-suited super drone, slicing him up, the android admitting that his kind cannot, in the long run, control humans. Wilson, Sackhoff and their pet dog are last seen wandering off into the desert wastes to start a new life. The tried and tested "Man's technology turned against him" framework is trotted out yet again, the orange-filtered photography and ashen waste grounds, together with Wilson's taciturn performance and Sackhoff's tousled blonde appeal, about the only reasons to sit through 93 minutes of sci-fi dreariness that is very difficult to relate to or even get worked up about.

The Legend of Lucy Keyes
Moody Street Pictures 2006; 93 minutes; Director: John Stimpson; Rating: ☠☠☠☠

A city couple and their two children move to a rural farming community and become involved in a ghostly tragedy relating to the mysterious disappearance of a young girl in 1755.

Environmentalist Justin Theroux has plans to erect eight wind turbines on land that the townsfolk, and one gray-haired old busybody in particular, have decreed as sacred. Luckily, he has local town planner Brooke Adams on his side to try to win them over. In the meantime, coarse, imbecilic Mark Boone, Junior, the new family's neighbor from hell, is stocking up on foul-smelling pig feed to keep the spooks at bay and blaming *his* new neighbors for the reappearance of the restless spirit. The couple's youngest daughter Lucy (Cassidy Hinkle) hears a woman crying her name in the surrounding woods and wife Julie Delpy sees the specter of an older woman drifting between the trees at night. What does it all mean? Apparently 250 years previously, a child named Lucy ventured into the extensive woodlands and was never seen again, her mother spending the rest of her days hunting for her, slaughtering Indians whom she held responsible and dying a lonely death in the bitter cold. Obviously, as in all good supernatural thrillers of this type, the past events are related to the present. A descendant of Boone Junior and Adams (the two are related) bludgeoned the girl to death with a rock and hid her body in a crypt below a barn that was torched. Hinkle now acts as the catalyst for the phantom mother and daughter. This is all brought to light when the young girl retrieves a tattered parchment from Boone Junior's farm written by the murderer confessing all, admitting he illegally took over the dead family's land, of which Adams is well aware. The curse is finally lifted when the original Lucy's remains are discovered in the ruined crypt, the pig farmer is bumped off by Adams and the evil town planner is done away with by the vengeful wraith of the long-dead mother. The movie sags in the middle section by throwing in too many varying elements at the expense of a cohesive plot, becoming a tad disjointed, its many loose ends remaining unresolved. Nevertheless, for a low-key production, *The Legend of Lucy Keyes* is solid, at times shivery (despite lapses), involving audiences right up to the final few minutes.

Legion of the Dead

Asylum 2005; 90 minutes; Director: Paul Bales; Rating: ☠☠

Two bikers accidentally crash into the tomb of an ancient Egyptian queen, Aneh-Tet. She is reactivated by lightning and sets about resurrecting an army of zombie-mummies to stamp out her enemies.

Legion of the Dead may not be the worst *Mummy* film ever made, but it's a contender. So why does it earn the two-star rating? Two reasons—voluptuous Claudia Lynx plays the foxy queen and the movie is a damn sight more entertaining than Stephen Sommers' big-budget travesties *The Mummy* (1999) and *The Mummy Returns* (2001). Suspend disbelief for a while as we are informed that some Egyptians migrated to America 4,000 years ago, hence the discovery of a tomb near Los Angeles. Banished from her native land for dabbling in sorcery and the black arts, Lynx, her perfectly honed body emerging from bandages like a porn starlet giving an audience the "come-on," has to kill six males in order to reactivate her "army of the dead." Then she must sacrifice a virgin, the blood of which will bring into the world a slimy monster. So one student after another is sucked dry of bodily fluids by Lynx's lethal, electrically charged fingertips, leaving a scorched bloody husk behind. Asylum's very own Man of a Thousand Faces, Rhett Giles, plays the professor of archaeology who, besotted by Lynx, shaves his head and takes on the mantle of the queen's high priest. For aficionados of the Ed Wood school of filmmaking, Bales' directorial

style (or lack of it) will be right up your alley. The action perpetually switches backwards and forwards between the burial chamber and its surrounding woods and the motel and its woods. The movie conjures up memories of Ronnie Ashcroft's legendary *The Astounding She-Monster* in its sheer static settings, especially when the stark-naked Lynx, outlined by a glowing aura, stalks through the trees, draining her teenage victims of their life-force. Heroine Courtney Clonch's sister, Emily Falkenstein, is earmarked for sacrifice after six chanting mummies with a predilection for ripping out spinal chords have embarked on a lurching (and hilarious) rampage. But she is freed when Clonch threatens to blow up the chamber. Then it's time for Clonch's virgin boyfriend (Chad Collins) to die, knifed through the heart, but *he* is resurrected when Falkenstein's blood drips onto his chest following the queen's demise, an ankh plunged into her neck. She crumbles into dust, along with her remaining mummy acolytes. Sloppily made, poorly acted and sporting a muffled soundtrack, it's easy to categorize Asylum's *Mummy* outing as an absolute time waster. But doing so would cause audiences to miss out on Lynx's alluring charms. This is one woman any hot-blooded male would get down on bended knee and pay service to!

The Librarian: Quest for the Spear
TNT/ApolloProScreen/Electric Ent. 2004; 92 minutes; Director: Peter Winther; Rating: ☠☠☠

The oldest student in town is given the job of new librarian at a museum that houses, among its many artifacts, the Ark of the Covenant, Excalibur and Pandora's Box.

A highly diverting, none-too-serious fantasy adventure suitable for all those aged between eight and 80, *The Librarian* gallops along merrily in its own sub-*Indiana Jones* way regardless of absurdities and anachronisms, its plot plundered from every similar movie since film was first projected. Original it is not—fun it most certainly is. Scatterbrained 30-something student Noah Wyle, his head crammed full of every archaeological fact and figure, gets the job of new librarian after a grilling from fearsomely stern interviewer Jane Curtin. New boss Bob Newhart (a wonderfully straight-faced performance from the veteran actor/comedian), after showing Wyle around the cavernous rooms, quickly hands him a consignment that would have lesser mortals running back to the employment queues—the Spear of Destiny has been stolen from the museum! When ultimately reunited with the other two pieces (missing for decades), unheard-of power will be granted to the spear's owner and this could prove dangerous in the wrong hands, in this case Kyle MacLachlan and his gang, members of the Serpent Brotherhood. Can he (Wyle) trace those long-lost pieces? Teaming up with martial arts expert Sonya Walger, Wyle is soon up to his neck in Amazonian savages (friendly, as it turns out), rickety bridges, waterfalls, earthquakes and

a ruined jungle temple complete with death chamber. The final part of the spear is discovered in an Indian temple. The finale takes place back at the museum where a pitched fight between Wyle, Walger and the villains (led by Wyle's former professor) results in MacLachlan squashed under a toppling pyramid apex, after the fabled spear has been restored to its former glory. Olympia Dukakis crops up playing Wyle's interfering mother, eternally on the lookout for a suitable mate to anchor her roving son down. Winther directs in frenetic style as befits the Saturday matinee material. Get the popcorn and cola out, sit down with the kids and indulge in 92 minutes of family entertainment without a single profanity to be heard. Now that *is* a rarity!

The Librarian 2: Return to King Solomon's Mines
TNT/Electric Entertainment 2006; 92 minutes; Director: Jonathan Frakes; Rating: 🎭🎭🎭🎭

An archaeologist teams up with a feisty female and goes in search of King Solomon's fabled treasure, hidden deep beneath a mountain in Africa.

First, did Spielberg nick the idea for *Indiana Jones and the Kingdom of the Crystal Skull* from this frothy, rocket-paced, fun-packed fantasy? The opening sequence has Noah Wyle stealing a crystal skull, originating from Atlantis, right under the noses of a gang of adventurers in Utah's badlands. That energetic appetizer over and done with, Wyle's next assignment, on orders from boss Bob Newhart, is to locate King Solomon's 3,000-year-old treasure and guard the

secret to its whereabouts. En route to Kenya, Wyle is tailed by villainous Erik Avari, meets tomboy Gabrielle Anwar on a Roman dig in Casablanca, and winds up deep underneath twin peaks called The Breasts of Sheba. Anwar fights traitor Robert Foxworth, the man responsible for the death of his father, and a swarm of reactivated wraiths. Do we detect undertones of *Raiders of the Lost Ark* here, as well as Stephen Sommers' two *Mummy* disasters? We do indeed, and Joseph LoDuca's music reeks of Elmer Bernstein and John Williams, but if musicians are going to copy, they may as well copy from the best. All in all, *The Librarian 2* is an enormously enjoyable romp of the old school, more so than the first *Librarian* outing, free from toilet humor and blessed with a truly magnetic partnership between Wyle and Anwar. Their sexual chemistry positively sizzles and these two really do strike sparks off each other in their joint scenes. Fine South African location work, imaginative set design, a great support cast (Newhart again marvelous as the deadpan chief librarian; Olympia Dukakis winning in her brief appearance as Wyle's matchmaking mother) and tons of action all go toward making this a treat for adults and kids alike. A few moments of silliness (the living sword Excalibur taunting Wyle; Hakeem Kae-Kazim throwing chocolate bars to placate marauding hippos) can be forgiven in a production that doesn't lag a second and puts a wide grin on the audience's face afterwards.

Lighthouse
aka: **Dead of Night**
Winchester Films/British Screen Prods. 1999; 95 minutes; Director: Simon Hunter; Rating: ☠☠☠

A multiple killer escapes from a ship transporting inmates to Marshalsea Island Prison, butchers the keepers of the Grenna lighthouse and then proceeds to murder the survivors of a storm that sinks the vessel.

Lighthouse, a gritty British horror outing given a brief theatrical run in 2000, disappeared into the bargain bins on home video. Christopher Adamson plays the homicidal maniac, preying on the survivors of a shipwreck where survivors struggle onto the lighthouse's rocky shores. But they only find the building dark and deserted. Among this disparate group, Rachel Shelley is a criminologist traumatized by the brutal slaughter of her mother at the hands of Adamson years back, and now she studies the monster's psyche as a casebook on criminal behavior (as we witness in the black and white prologue). Also appearing is alcoholic captain Paul Brooke and prisoner James Purefoy, the eventual hero of this rough-and-ready slasher flick. As Adamson, decked out in fetching white shoes, begins a murderous campaign, decapitating his victims, the survivors have to decide on a solution to break free from his clutches. The action culminates (after all but two have met their end) in a drawn-out, uncoordinated climax,  the machete-wielding maniac cornering Shelley and Purefoy at the top of the lighthouse. As they try to escape by shimmying down a rope, the maniac goes to sever their lifeline, gets involved in a protracted fight with Purefoy and winds up a burning corpse hurtling to his death. Muddy color and speech that has an irritating habit of coming and going (was the boom microphone person concentrating at the time?) detracts from a movie of the type that Amicus could have easily knocked out in the 1970s (with far less graphic throat cuttings). There are two genuine moments of pure terror that director Hunter handles superbly. First, Brooke crouches down in a begrimed toilet, sweating profusely, as the psycho prowls the washroom. Second, Christopher Dunne hides in a lifeboat, blood slowly dripping over his panic-stricken face, caused by four severed heads. Yet another variation, in a way, of Agatha Christie's *And Then There Were None* (or *Ten Little Indians*), *Lighthouse* has a claustrophobic feel to it as befits the isolated setting. The movie could have been a whole lot better if the dire soundtrack had been sorted out (the mournful, sonorous music is okay, though). As it stands, this is one nifty horror show that deserved a wider showing than it had at the time of release.

The Living and the Dead
Vita Pictures/Giant Films 2006; 83 minutes; Director: Simon Rumley; Rating: ☠☠☠☠

A rich landowner, down on his luck, has to periodically travel to London to attend to his affairs, leaving his terminally ill wife in the care of his son, who is a paranoid schizophrenic.

Humiliation, degradation, degeneration, drug dependency, tragedy all play a major role in director Simon Rumley's deeply disturbing essay into the effects of mental illness. The director pulls no punches and leaves no stone unturned

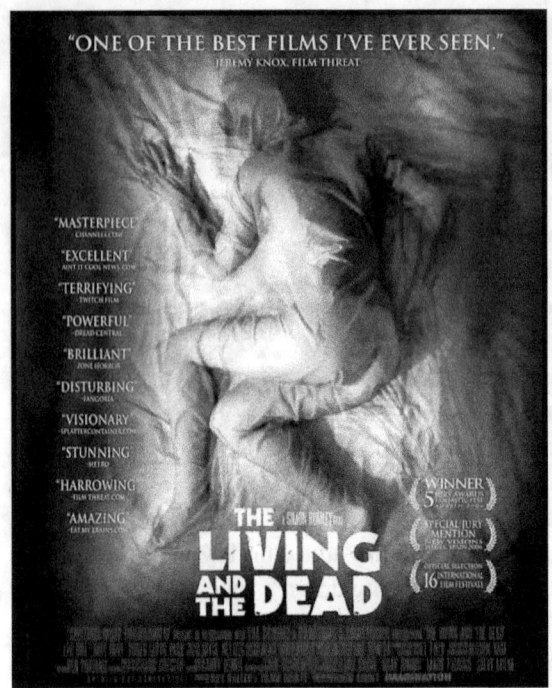

in this Poe-derived descent into madness that makes for uncomfortable viewing. Roger Lloyd-Pack plays the rich lord of the manor, Kate Fahey his sick wife and Leo Bill the psychotic son. The scenario unfolds through the eyes of all three, Rumley utilizing time-lapse photography, speeded-up imaging and overlapping time-frames to present his mental health message on differing levels. If this isn't enough to contend with, the ending's not clear-cut either. This is a movie that's far removed from the standard shocker. Audiences have to concentrate hard and think about the movie long after the finish. The basic plot has Lloyd-Pack leaving for London to sort out his finances, Leo Bill taking on the role of man of the house and attending to his bed-ridden mother, ill with cancer. However, is what we are seeing really happening? Interspersed with the mother and son's fraught relationship are images of a disheveled Lloyd-Pack looking like the brain-dead inmate of an asylum; a hallucinatory episode showing Bill conversing with his deceased parents; and Fahey, fit and well, fighting with her uncontrollable son who stabs her to death. The climactic funeral is shot in a series of short bursts, fading swiftly from one scene to the next. Bill, seeing the spirit of Fahey among the mourners, repeatedly plunges a knife into his own stomach in a fit of guilty rage and expires near his mother's open grave, leading one to ask, has the whole thing been a nightmarish chain of events triggered by Lloyd-Pack's crumbling state of mind? Several moments in this alarming little picture verge on the unwatchable—Bill sticking syringes into his arm, ramming pills down his protesting mother's throat and assisting her after she has soiled the bed sheets. These sequences might not be to everybody's taste. However, *The Living and the Dead* is totally uncompromising fare for the discerning punter, and Bill's turn as the ranting, raving certifiable son, one step away from absolute lunacy, galvanizes in its unflinching intensity. The other bonus here is the vast English Gothic mansion itself, in actuality Tottenham House. The movie's a thought-provoking, albeit highly unsettling, winner all round. What would Sigmund Freud have made of it all?

Loch Ness Terror
aka: **Beyond Loch Ness**
Cinetel Films/Insight Film Studios 2008; 91 minutes; Director: Paul Ziller; Rating: ☠☠☠☠

In 1976, a 12-year-old boy witnesses the savage death of his father and two other men after they anger the Loch Ness monster, pinching one of its eggs. Thirty years later, the now adult boy arrives at a small town on the shores of Canada's Lake Superior to exact revenge on the beast and its offspring.

The monster, or "Nessie" as the British love to call the country's most fabled creature, has managed to arrive in Lake Superior via a network of subterranean tunnels, hard going for a Plesiosaurus when we figure out the vast distances involved. Grizzled old fisherman Donnelly Rhodes believes that something lurks in the lake, even if the locals don't, and pays for his inquisitiveness by being gobbled up by the 40-foot beast, his mangled trunk deposited on a beach. Brian Krause, now a cryptozoologist, cheroot clenched between teeth like Clint Eastwood, turns up with enough surveillance and sonar equipment to support an army and enlists the aid of young Niall Matter to take him out onto the lake in a launch for a spot of "hunt the beastie." From then on in, we are in familiar monster-mayhem territory as Matter's Mum, police officer Carrie Genzel, and a group of kids stranded on Pike Island combat the flesh-eating creature and its frisky infants. However, what distinguishes this movie from similar fare is the diamond-hard outdoor location cinematography (the lake and surrounding woodlands gleam in Canada's cold light), the excellent CGI effects (and you get to see plenty of monsters in this movie), a better-than-average script and fetching performances from the small cast. Moments of gore are few and far between, although the scene where the monster plucks the head off a girl, her torso toppling backwards, blood gushing, will put audiences off their popcorn, and the baby creatures make a real meal (literally) out of one youth's body in the final *Jurassic Park*-style showdown on Pike Island. The waddling, fin-headed Nessie is quite an endearing creation, despite its appetite for humans. What a shame that Krause has to kill it in the end with a lethal injection of cyanide, the infants all shot to death and the remaining eggs destroyed. Ziller doesn't let matters drag, directing with pace and pictorial flare.

Frequent shots of humans seen through the eyes of Nessie (akin to wobbly jelly) impress. Naturally, Krause and Genzel look at one another with just a hint of lust before the final credits role. This Canadian effort is a jolly monster-romp produced in the old tradition, and it's highly enjoyable because of it.

Long Distance
Lascaux Pictures 2005; 90 minutes; Director: Marcus Stern; Rating: ☠☠☠☠

Following a misdialed call, a young woman is plagued by calls from what appears to be a homicidal killer who, disturbingly, appears to know much more about her personal life than seems possible.

In the world of the psychological thriller, no one has been able to pile on the suspense and subtle nuances that Alfred Hitchcock so skillfully managed in his classic movies, so to come across a tight-budget Hitchcockian psychological drama that has real substance is cause for celebration. *Long Distance* keeps it simple—a couple of sets and basically three leading actors. Monica Keena plays a grad student first seen arguing bitterly with her mother over the phone about the break-up with her boyfriend. Then her mobile rings and a caller named Joe makes his presence felt, the conversations turning more and more sinister as he reveals intimate details of her troubled personality. He also appears to be embarking on a killing spree, butchering young women, with Keena marked as an intended victim. Perturbed by the persistent calls, Keena contacts a cop (Ivan Martin)

and, later, an FBI profiler (Tamala Jones), who rig up phone taps in an effort to trace the caller's whereabouts. But why does Keena keep having unsettling visions of death and violence? Why does Jones point out to her the deep-rooted reasons behind her unstable psyche? What's happened to her missing boyfriend? Why does Keena intermittently get the shakes and look so ill? How come she feels instantly attracted to Martin? The myriad of clues leading up to the twist in the tail are all in place, of course, but just like the brilliant *Danika*, this is a movie that viewers have to sit through twice in order to figure out where exactly those clues are and how director Stern has cleverly interwoven them within the film's elaborate framework. We eventually learn that Keena is the killer, the audience experiencing the imaginings of a tortured soul. She stabs her boyfriend to death because of his string of infidelities. Her fevered mind has dreamed up a distorted scenario as far removed from the actual events as possible, Martin in fact becoming a facsimile of the murdered boyfriend and agent Jones actually her psychiatric doctor attempting to encourage Keena out of the shell into which she has withdrawn. The killings (including her own mother's near-demise) become a revengeful illusion created in the dark corridors of the girl's twisted mind. *Long Distance* is a tremendous example of no-frills thriller filmmaking produced by relative unknowns on shoestring finances. Because of its lowly origins, like so many other indie psycho features, mainstream film historians will undoubtedly overlook this gem. That, in a way, is a crying shame.

Long Time Dead
Working Title Films 2002; 94 minutes; Director: Marcus Adams; Rating: ☠☠

For the ultimate buzz, eight teenagers decide to experience firsthand the effects of a Ouija board and inadvertently summon up a bloodthirsty fire jinni that kills them one by one.

Just to prove the Americans don't have a monopoly on teenage horror flicks, Britain came up with this low-budget variation on *Final Destination, I Know What You Did Last Summer* and their ilk, the movie flopping at the box office nonetheless. Kicking off in Morocco in 1979, the eight teens, bored at a party, enter a warehouse, set up a Ouija board and unleash a murderous spirit after Alec Newman, scared as hell, takes his finger off the glass too quickly and the words "ALL DIE" are spelled out. From then on, the youngsters are persecuted by an unseen presence, dying horribly. In a sub-plot, Newman's father was present at the Moroccan shindig when the same jinni was released, crashing his car afterwards, his wife perishing in the blaze. He now resides in a psychiatric clinic, his mind blanking out the memory of that dreadful night. In the final moments, Newman, possessed by the jinni, visits his father and kills him in revenge for his mother's death, for which he holds him accountable. Marcus Adams' directorial debut goes through the horror motions adequately enough, but after 65 minutes, the movie loses its way, becoming curiously rushed and disjointed. The soundtrack jars, a rising crescendo of noise building as the invisible harbinger of death approaches its next victim. The teens' seedy landlord (Tom Bell) apparently is a protector against the jinni's deadly powers; the man's flat is plastered with newspaper cuttings depicting satanic slayings. Joe Absolom (fresh from Britain's popular soap *EastEnders*) shines as a cocky layabout, the first of the group to be possessed by the spirit, (exposing black, slitty pupils). The rest of the cast is simply food for the fire demon, slaughtered in a series of violent vignettes that we all have seen before. Which is the only thing you can say about *Long Time Dead*. Literally it has all been seen, and done, before.

Lost City Raiders
Tandem 2008; 91 minutes; Director: Jean de Segonzac; Rating: ☠☠☠

2048—in a future world inundated with water from rising ocean levels, a treasure hunter and his two sons are approached by the Vatican to locate a biblical scepter that could, it is prophesied, save the planet from further cataclysmic flooding.

Indiana Jones meets *Waterworld* in a colorful effects-laden post-apocalyptic romp that gets sillier and tackier as it moves toward its preposterous conclusion. Grizzled James Brolin and his two deep-sea diving sons (Ian Somerhalder and Jamie Thomas King) are paid a fortune to retrieve a fabled scepter, reputedly possessed with awesome powers, buried inside a Knight Templar's tomb. This religious artifact, once used by Moses to part the Red Sea, can somehow reverse the flooding (known as "The Rising") that is set to engulf the entire planet. Baddie Ben Cross, the villain of the piece, is in pursuit of the scepter for financial purposes, wanting the world totally submerged in order to build floating real estate. In addition, a deranged priest is also on its trail, hoping to prevent all concerned from laying claim to the object, as "The Rising" is (he thinks) a symbol of God's wrath. Brolin, trapped beneath a stone slab, expires early on, leaving it up to his sons and delectable scientist Bettina Zimmermann to avert the impending calamity. After much globetrotting (an excuse to see most of Earth's famous landmarks just above the water line), the holy scepter, in Somerhalder's hands, manages to open up a vast chasm in the seabed into which the waters pour, reducing the flood levels. Humanity is saved from disaster. Imaginative set designs illustrate the world's flooded cities, rooftops poking above the seas. Ingenious shots of the divers entering buildings several fathoms deep are spoiled by an unconvincing script, feeble acting and a daft ending (what is a room filled with cryptic symbols, built over a fiery pit, doing on a remote island?) that suggests a supernatural, not natural, reason for the planet's watery woes. Oddly resembling a *Thunderbirds* movie with live actors, *Lost City Raiders* is one of those action adventures that kicks off promisingly and then deteriorates rapidly in the final half. Okay for the kiddies, perhaps, but for serious buffs, the film's reasonably entertaining but forgettable.

Lost Colony
American World Pictures 2007; 86 minutes; Director: Matt Codd; Rating: ☠☠☠

In 1587, 117 settlers travel from England to colonize an old fort on Roanoke Island in Virginia and are massacred by murderous wraiths inhabiting the surrounding woodlands.

Apparently based on a true mystery, this supernatural horror thriller isn't that bad, considering the meager budget. From the moment the settlers—led by Adrian Paul, wife Frida Farrell and second-in-command Rhett Giles—enter the abandoned fort (the only occupant a desiccated corpse hanging from the rafters with the legend "Save your soul before they take it from you" scrawled in blood on a beam), they are plagued by greenish demons brandishing swords that emerge from the woods and feed off the souls of the living. Pregnant Farrell also has recurring nightmares about her newborn being snatched by these visitors from hell. In the dark forest, trees sprout writhing tentacles that entwine their victims, sucking out bodily fluids. An Indian (Michael Teh), leader of a local tribe, repeatedly warns the newcomers that the place has been cursed for centuries; the creatures are the spirits of long-dead Vikings who tortured and killed a witch. All is not right on this island! Acting and direction-wise, *Lost Colony* is the pits at times, but what can audiences expect from straight-to-DVD fodder like this? One or two shocks (bloody corpses fixed to those flesh-eating trees; the cadaverous wraiths hacking away at the settlers) lead up to a rather confusing climax involving a funeral pyre on a raft, which is used as a lure to destroy the wraiths (who hate water). This gimmick works, but at the expense of the settlers' lives. The Indians take Farrell's baby, adrift in a basket, off the island at the end. A fairly absorbing story is let down by lack of enterprise (and resources), but all in all, this is entertaining fodder.

Madhouse
Redbus Pictures/Madhouse Productions 2004; 91 minutes; Director: William Butler; Rating: ☠☠☠

A fresh-faced student takes up his new post as intern at the Cunningham Mental Hospital. He begins to experience visitations involving a young boy and the inmate of a cell of which nobody else is aware.

This film becomes another variant on a commonplace horror theme—who is and who is *not* insane in this particular nuthouse? Could it be young Joshua Leonard, anxious to please despite the loopy inmates prowling the wards? Is it nurse Jordan Ladd, who Leonard takes a shine to? Maybe it's Lance Henriksen, the bad-tempered boss? What about the head nurse (Dendrie Taylor) who treats any misbehaving patient with a Taser gun? The intern observes lights flickering on and off, weird human shapes drifting around the corridors, and a creepy looking boy coming and going. Leonard also cannot get the occupant of cell 44 to reveal himself. Why is Henriksen reading books about ghosts and hauntings? As we get deeper into the picture, Taylor is tortured to death by electrical voltage to her head, Ladd is revealed to be schizophrenic, a patient is found hanging from a beam and a doctor is murdered.

If audience members have sat through hundreds of horror flicks over a very long period of time, they can see the trick ending coming a mile off. Leonard is the psycho. He's the boy spotted wandering around the passages and he's also the mysterious "Ben" in cell 44. When his cover is blown, Ladd and Henriksen are slain with an ax, as are most of the hospital staff, but the intern lives to fight another day, turning up all spick and span at a new posting. Resembling an Amicus 1970s B movie, *Madhouse* drags in places, the gallery of loony patients tiresome rather than menacing, but the movie is competently directed and the color photography matches the grim exterior of the asylum to a tee. For a low-budget fright show, Butler's effort isn't all that bad.

Mammoth
Castel Film Romania/Union Station Media 2006; 90 minutes; Director: Tim Cox; Rating: ☠☠☠

A meteor containing an alien-transmitting device crashes into a museum, thawing a block of ice containing a 40,000-year-old mammoth. The beast, reanimated, goes on a rampage.

Judging by the amusing opening credits, it's plain to see that *Mammoth* is tongue-in-cheek fantasy/monster fare, with numerous references to other genre movies littering the script. *Alien*'s Tom Skerritt, roped in, plays a grizzled, gray-haired UFO fanatic; his performance complements the tone of a "don't take this too seriously" picture. Vincent Ventresca, head of the museum, has his hands full, not only with his sulky daughter (Summer Glau), her over-sexed feller (Cole Williams) and crusty father (Skerritt), but he must deal with a giant mammoth on the prowl. He must also deal with two government agents jabbering about an alien life-force having landed with the meteor, causing a widespread power blackout. Could this have anything to do with the blue crystal Ventresca extracted from the mammoth prior to its reactivation? As the government wants to annihilate the town in nine hours because of this perceived alien threat, it's up to Ventresca and his gang to capture the beast, freeze it with liquid nitrogen and thus save  the townsfolk from extinction (much like the mammoth itself). After the initial sequence showing the mammoth stomping through the museum and, later in woodlands, killing two cops, it's another 20 minutes plus before we get to see more CGI monster action. When we do it's quite well executed, the shaggy, bellowing creature storming through a teen party, impaling Williams on a tusk, and flattening a car with its two elderly occupants engaged in some over-60 sex. The silly "alien hand" interlude included as a bit of light relief is, however, a regrettable intrusion. The alien-possessed monster is finally frozen at the end and restored to the museum, while Skerritt, also frozen, is retained in an isolated unit, as the authorities believe *him* to be contaminated by an alien presence. More polished than the usual low-budget production and containing a few witty snippets of dialogue, *Mammoth* is entertaining monster fodder for the 10 to 15 age group. Older buffs may find it too lightweight for their tastes.

Man-Thing
Fierce Entertainment/Artisan 2005; 97 minutes; Director: Brett Leonard; Rating: ☠☠

A legendary monster emerges from the swamps to wreak vengeance on oil-drillers who are polluting the waterways.

Nice monster, but it's a shame about the movie. Based on one of *Marvel Comics'* lesser-known entities, *Man-Thing* possesses fine photography (the scenes in the swamps are shot in a greenish tint), creature-perspective views (in sepia), some extremely gruesome killings (one mutilated body has a branch growing *out* of it), and a capable adversary resembling the tree-monster in *From Hell It Came* (complete with red glowing eyes and writhing tendril-like branches sprouting from its back like a woody Medusa). Those are the good points. The bad points are the acting of Sheriff Matthew Le Nevez, teacher Rachel Taylor and the rest of the crew (with the exception of Jack Thompson, playing the roughneck oil refinery boss). The acting of the cast is as wooden as the mangrove trees they continually trek through in search of the person (or monster) responsible for a spate of missing persons. Another flaw is the flat direction. This film patently fails to grip and ends up too formulaic by far. Le Nevez, the new sheriff of Bywater, is thrown into the deep end of the pool on his first day on the job—over a dozen people disappear into the swamps, with the occasional ravaged corpse turning up. Despite a local Indian rambling on about "The Guardian" not being too enamored with the nearby oil refinery, it's not long before Le Nevez is prowling the swamps on the lookout for the murderer who could be (but isn't) a renegade Indian out to cause trouble for the oil men. The final 15 minutes has practically the whole cast wading into

the "Dark Water" area where the creature is believed to be lurking. Thompson meets a grisly end, seized by the monster and pumped full of oil, the liquid gushing out of his mouth like a black fountain. Le Nevez's deputy and Thompson's dim-witted brother also fall victim; and the renegade Indian blows up an oil rig, the tree-being destroyed in the inferno, disintegrating into the murky waters. A cross between Wes Craven's 1982 *Swamp Thing* and the aforementioned *From Hell It Came*, Leonard's hackneyed horror flick would have been more enjoyable if made in the 1950s in black and white. Stick with the Milner Brothers' 1957 schlock classic *From Hell It Came*. At least it's amusing to watch.

The Mangler Reborn
Assembly Line Studio 2005; 84 minutes; Directors: Matt Cunningham and Erik Gardner; Rating: ☠☠☠

A handyman purchases from auction the parts to a giant industrial steam laundry press. Once assembled, the machine possesses him and impels him to feed it live human flesh.

Ten years on from Tobe Hooper's *The Mangler*, we are told of the contraption's violent history in a series of newspaper clippings shown during the credits. For the next 80 minutes, the audience is subjected to one blood-spattered scene after another as hulking handyman Weston Blakesley feeds his wife, daughter, two thieves and two teenage girls to the monstrous press, their bodies sliced, diced, stabbed and, yes, mangled by meat cleavers, extending blades and razor-toothed rollers. It's bleak, it's bloody, it's gross and it's cheap-looking, much like a '70s art-house prohibited horror flick of the type one used to encounter in a London backstreet cinema, a real feast for gore-fanatics everywhere. But anyone else of a squeamish nature may find the unflinching content disturbing to say the least. Nobody escapes dead-eyed, blood-drinking Blakesley in this movie. Abducted Aimee Brooks almost manages it in the end, but not quite, since the maniac's house has bricked-up windows and foolproof locks. The handyman himself is impervious to puncture wounds from a stiletto or a bang on the head with a lump of nailed wood. His injuries simply heal up as he quaffs quantities of blood drawn from the machine's pipes. Between the imagery of Blakesley rendering his victims unconscious with a swift blow of a mallet to the head, bloodstained handprints all over the walls, and minced flesh spewing from the press' waste outlet, this is one outing that might instantly turn any meat-loving person into a vegetarian. But the picture is well directed by Cunningham and Gardner, containing a deliriously gut-churning end sequence guaranteed to put audiences off beef stew for life. Bulky Blakesley is robotically chilling as the possessed loony obeying the telepathic commands of the diabolical machine with a mind of its own.

The Marsh
Norstar Filmed Ent./Sonja Productions 2006; 92 minutes; Director: Jordan Barker; Rating: ☠☠

The nervous author/illustrator of a series of children's spooky books, on medication to curb her violent dreams, takes a convalescence break at Rose Marsh Farm in the rural town of Marshville. There she discovers that a troublesome series of paranormal manifestations is somehow associated with her childhood, which she has repressed for many years.

Ever since *The Sixth Sense*, filmmakers have been trying their utmost to come up with something just that wee bit different on the well-worn topic of the past catching up with the present. *The Marsh*'s climax contains a surprise twist that will leave audiences scratching their heads thinking, "So, *that's* what it was all about." *The Marsh* is no better or worse than dozens of similar pictures. The bottom line is the creative challenge of just how modern-day horror writers/directors can turn out fresh, stimulating entertainment while avoiding all the old repetitious clichés. So, here we have wan-looking Gabrielle Anwar calling on the services of morose occult investigator Forest Whitaker in the hope of solving the mystery behind the mud-spattered, sobbing little girl who keeps appearing in various rooms, sometimes accompanied by a hollow-eyed youth talking gibberish. The woman is also puzzled that her latest illustrated book, aptly named *The Swamp*, seems to mirror her eerie dreams. The film is ruined

by an intrusive soundtrack, and the director throws in every trick in the book, attempting to raise goosebumps, but only partly succeeding. Prominent imagery includes windows slamming in the wind, the mandatory creaking swing, the cold atmosphere, flying cutlery, doors locking themselves, flickering ceiling lights and a misty bog with its guardian scarecrow. One or two serious plot flaws (the 1902 tragedy of the marsh-draining when the small girl and others drowned in the swamp doesn't tie in with what follows—neither does the death of Anwar's parents when she was young) detract from a string of well-staged poltergeist activities, leading up to the revelation that Anwar, as a child, was the sister of the phantom girl (Niamh Wilson). One day in 1982, a gang looking for sexual kicks lured the girls into the farmhouse. Wilson was molested (raped?) by teenager Ryan Giesen in a bedroom and died. Horror-struck by the act, Anwar, as small as she was, picked up a Derringer pistol and shot Giesen dead. Both bodies were interred in the marsh, the incident kept hushed-up (even by the town's future newspaper editor, Justin Louis). Then the haunting began and Anwar subconsciously blotted out the frightening episode from her mind. By smashing a stained glass window, the portal to a netherworld, Anwar succeeds in overcoming Giesen's spirit, at the same time bringing peace to Wilson's wandering soul. Saddled with a weak script, Anwar (so good in *The Librarian 2*) drifts through the "wide-eyed, mouth agape" frightened cat motions without too much conviction, while the normally excellent Whitaker wears the demeanor of someone who wishes he was somewhere else, mumbling his lines to himself. A lively *Exorcist*-type climax is small change in a predictable thriller that, despite the odd shudder, brings nothing new to this particular genre of horror cinema. Frankly, the movie reflects a tired sameness.

Mega Shark vs. Giant Octopus

Asylum 2009; 90 minutes; Director: Ace Hannah; Rating: 💀💀

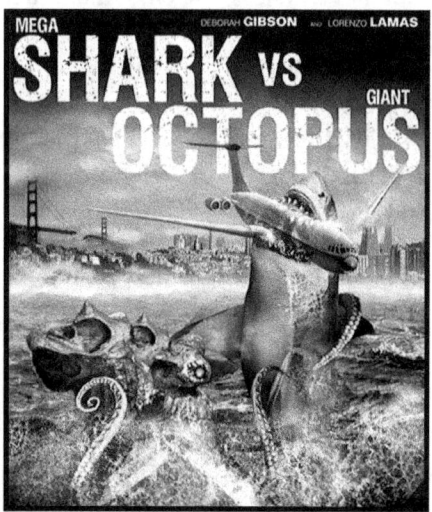

Locked inside an Alaskan glacier for millions of years, a gigantic octopus and a colossal shark are unleashed on the world when the ice melts.

In the great tradition of *King Kong vs. Godzilla* comes one of Asylum's most recent offerings (their first to get a theatrical release), starring one-time '80s pop starlet Debbie Gibson as an oceanographer who, together with scientist Sean Lawlor, marine biologist Vic Chao and submarine commander Lorenzo Lamas, is charged with ridding the planet of these two titanic terrors of the deep. After a Japanese oil rig, an airliner, a helicopter, two U.S. destroyers and even San Francisco's Golden Gate Bridge have been attacked by either the octopus or (as Lamas puts it) "Sharkzilla," the authorities decide to nuke the monsters. However, Gibson has a brainstorm, resolving to lure both creatures to the same area by dropping large quantities of pheromone into the Arctic waters where, she opines, they will engage in mortal combat with each other. Her plan succeeds. After destroying a couple of subs, the behemoths fight to the death, both bodies disappearing into the murky waters. That's the plot in a nutshell, but how has this potentially juicy, monster-laden material been executed? With a great deal of ineptitude, it must be said. It resembles a typical '60s Toho production (the pristine cinematography is the one bonus). Gibson, based on this showing, is way out of her depth as the female lead, her nasal drawl rendering most of her lines unintelligible. Lamas mouths dialogue of such incredible banality ("When we find the beast, we're sending it to hell.") that one would have thought the script had been written by a 10 year old. Also, why are armed soldiers standing around on set doing absolutely nothing in latter sequences? And if Nu Image can come up with a fairly impressive prehistoric Megalodon shark in *Shark Attack 3*, why can't Asylum, seven years down the line, manage the same? The scene of the shark leaping from the ocean into the skies and devouring an airplane has to be seen to be believed, as does the sequence where the predator takes a chunk out of the Golden Gate Bridge. It's probably best not to dwell on that big plastic fin (looking like an inverted rudder) coasting toward a miniature destroyer. Gibson gets to have some s-exercise in a broom closet with Vic Chao as the two little-seen giants are causing havoc, and the couple are last seen on a California beach gazing into the sunset. Audiences can pick holes in this chunk of schlocky hokum. Yes, it could and should have been much better, particularly in the effects department. But, nevertheless, the enjoyment factor is still there for those of us brought up on the Japanese monster movies of the 1960s.

Meltdown
aka: **Meltdown: Days of Destruction**
Porchlight/Front Street Pictures 2006; 90 minutes; Director: John Murkowski; Rating: ☠☠

As a media stunt, a TV company detonates a 10-megaton bomb on an asteroid heading for Earth, splitting it into three segments. The largest piece (the size of Iceland) skims the Earth's atmosphere, dragging the planet out of orbit into the direction of the sun that, as a result, causes global climate change.

Square-jawed Casper Van Dien plays a cop romancing news reporter Stefanie von Pfetten. Her brother Vincent Sale works for the same TV company and tries to warn his arrogant boss, to no avail, about the consequences of blowing up a colossal asteroid to boost ratings. It's quite apparent in *Meltdown* that all the money, resources and talent (?) were expended on the opening 10 minutes of special effects. From there on, this is one almighty disaster of a disaster movie. World temperatures rocket, water disappears, forests blaze, looters roam the streets, cars explode, buildings catch fire and both hospitals and streets are packed with blistered corpses. Van Dien's police squad is disbanded so the hunky one, together with von Pfetten, his ex-partner (Venus Terzo) and daughter, the daughter's punk boyfriend and Sale all head for the airport through the cleanest sewers we will ever see in a motion picture. Their aim is to fly north to colder regions. En route, a rogue cop joins them after gunning down three disfigured psychos. The rogue cop leads them to a trap (he's  also a deranged looter) and abducts Sale with the assistance of a bunch of heavies, culminating in Van Dien and company storming an aircraft hangar in a refrigerated truck, rescuing the TV man after a gun battle. Much to von Pfetten's dismay, her cop boyfriend falls back into the arms of his ex (it's happy family times, you see) as it starts to rain, prompting Van Dien to utter the immortal line: "It's over—we all get a second chance." Ideas from *The Day the Earth Caught Fire* and *Panic in Year Zero* are buried in the mix, and unsurprisingly, the "asteroid experimentation" program is entitled *Deep Impact*. But this tired-looking sci-fi disaster flick will sorely test the patience of even those indefatigable lovers of the awful. Audiences will be fidgeting in their seats long before this unlikeable group stand under a pink sky at the end, the cooling rain raising their spirits, if not ours.

The Messengers
Ghost House Pictures 2007; 91 minutes; Directors: Danny and Oxide Pang; Rating: ☠☠

A family moves from Chicago to an isolated run-down farmhouse in the Midwest. Almost immediately the teenage daughter and her baby brother begin to sense abnormal phenomena around them.

It's all been done before, of course, in countless other movies, most recently Asian horror flicks. So, did the Pang Brothers, on their first American picture,

bring anything new to this tried and tested "spooky house" formula? Well, the movie boasts atmospheric color photography and a high percentage of eerie scenes. Kristen Stewart (she was responsible for her brother's loss of speech) and little Evan Turner observe strange forms lurking in the shadows—a pallid, malformed human scuttles across the ceiling; a wraith-like figure manifests itself behind the locked cellar door, as do decomposed arms; vague shapes stir the dust motes; queer scratch marks on the floorboards appear; a black ooze bubbles up from beneath the cellar floors; and huge crows settle menacingly in large numbers on the building's weed-infested façade.

Father (Dylan McDermott) hires drifter John Corbett to help harvest sunflowers, while his wife (Penelope Ann Miller) is at a loss as to how to cope with her daughter's assertions that there is something horribly wrong with their new home, until mother observes a gray corpse materializing from a patch on a wall! After 80 minutes of lively supernatural mayhem, with a few shocks thrown in for good measure (including that already mentioned sequence involving hundreds of crows as homage to Hitchcock's *The Birds*), the payoff is something of a disappointment. Corbett turns out to be the former farm owner who defaulted on payments and, because of this and a bad harvest, lost his mind, changing into "Jack Nicholson" mode from *The Shining* and going berserk, slaughtering his entire family with a pitchfork. After nearly doing the same to McDermott and *his* family, he is seized by phantoms in the cellar and dragged underground to his death. The final sunlit shot (as opposed to all those gloomy interior shots) shows husband, wife and kids together again, Turner's speech restored. Denied a general release in the United Kingdom, *The Messengers* is guaranteed, at times, to bring on the goose bumps and is tautly directed, the Pang brothers having a genuine feel for this type of horror fare. The conclusion, though, really does the picture no favors at all.

Minotaur

First Look Intl./Scion Pictures 2006; 93 minutes; Director: Jonathan English; Rating: ☠☠☠

During the Iron Age eight youths are taken from the village of Thena every three years, sacrificed to the Bull God as revenge for the death of a prince.

Commencing with a gory Cesarean birth using a ceremonial dagger on a woman who has mated with a bull (and endured a 13-month pregnancy), we might mistakenly be of the belief that we are back in 1961, the heyday of the Italian sword-and-sandal epics. But no, those movies didn't feature a CGI monster (men-in-suit monsters, yes. CGI, no!) that inhabits a gloomy labyrinth, skewering victims on its horns and ripping them apart with slobbering jaws. It's in the direction of this labyrinth that Tom Hardy travels with a group of would-be sacrificial lambs. The young shepherd has had repeated visions of his lost love, taken by soldiers three years ago. She survived and lives in the network of galleries that the Minotaur inhabits, and now he wants to rescue her *and* kill the monster. Tony Todd hams it up as the bald, incestuous High Priest, presiding over a gated shaft leading to the Minotaur's lair. He constantly inhales a gas that leaves him in a permanent objectionable mood. Michelle Van Der Water plays his sister, an exotic High Priestess-cum-Queen, sympathizing with Hardy (the shepherd) and his companions as they are fed to the giant, roaring, foot-stomping beast. Most of the action is taken up with Hardy and company trying their level best to evade the monster, Van Der Water joining them (anything to get away from the repulsive Todd), hopefully, to lead them to safety. Any pretense at technical expertise is swiftly thrown out the window as, one by one, the chosen victims are charged at, spiked and eaten, Hardy's former sweetheart appearing as a delicate bloom for all of a minute before changing into a withered corpse. In the end, the creature is defeated, both by fire and by Hardy, plunging a broken-off tusk into the beast's throat. Van Der Water suffocates Todd, now a broken man because his beloved god has been vanquished, in the ruins of his palace, and Hardy is last seen gazing out over a golden sea. All this slice of entertaining baloney needed was Steve Reeves to appear in a loincloth, sword in one hand, ball and chain in another, to wrap things up in

a production that reeks of all those badly dubbed Italian potboilers that filled cinema screens between 1959 and 1964. But that's not a bad thing. This slightly different (and camp) creature-feature is a real barrel of fun for all the right reasons.

Monster
Asylum 2007; 82 minutes; Director: Erik Estenberg; Rating: ☠

In 2007, video footage on a camcorder discovered in the ruins of Tokyo proves to the world that the city wasn't destroyed by an earthquake in 2003, as was stated by the authorities. Instead, a gigantic octopus rising from underneath the city was responsible for the devastation.

The trouble is, in an 82-minute movie, this octopus, or its red tentacles, is only glimpsed for around 15 seconds total. As cleverly pieced together as *Monster* may be, what is the point of it all if there's no monster on display? *Monster* draws the viewer into the events as Paramount managed to do so effectively in *Cloverfield*—shaky images breaking up into pixels, sudden breaks in the recording, crowds of people on the run, explosions, buildings collapsing, bloodied human beings, aircraft screaming overhead. And if this colossal octopus is rooted in one spot, why can't the two young posing female filmmakers (Sarah Lynch and Erin Sullivan) escape Tokyo instead of wandering around in a daze, sobbing hysterically? Without a shadow of a doubt, *Monster* is one almighty fraud, especially as the inexcusably misleading promotional poster is such a work of art—82 minutes isn't important in the normal run of things, but there are much better ways to spend your precious time than watching Asylum's bargain-basement monster-that-*isn't*-on-the-loose calamity.

Mortuary
Echo Bridge Entertainment 2005; 94 minutes; Director: Tobe Hooper; Rating: ☠☠☠

A woman takes up the position of mortician at a run-down mortuary with a dubious reputation, which includes a crazed, disfigured freak who, the locals say, still lurks under the building.

For the first 60-odd minutes, *Mortuary* is splendid stuff, Hooper setting out his stall to perfection. Mum Denise Crosby, teenage son Dan Byrd and young daughter Stephanie Patton arrive at the mortuary from hell, situated near a construction site. It's a dilapidated building whose dark moldy rooms are in dire need of redecoration—with an overflowing septic tank, a graveyard standing in a sea of mud and brown water flowing from taps. Nearby, the state's most dangerous highway provides the mortuary with a steady supply of mangled bodies. All this, and a local legend tells of an abused, deformed mutant still alive in the area. Anybody in their right frame of mind would immediately turn heel and run for it. But no,
Mum and kids move in, exploring each grim, filthy room with barred windows, empty coffins and, in an upper room, the inscription "Bobby F" gouged into the woodwork. Where does that small metal door lead? Why are there cartons of rock salt stacked in the embalming room? An unusual key fits the lock to a door at the end of a sloping passageway under the mausoleum. What lies in wait behind that door? And what are those fungus-like tendrils spread over parts of the walls and floors? Careful pacing, expert direction, thoughtful script and believable acting are all set firmly in place until the moment when Crosby makes a mess of things when embalming a grotesque corpse. Blood and embalming fluid spill onto the floor, the stitched-up corpse comes alive and we quickly descend into horror farce. Everything that has gone before is swept aside in a tidal wave of frenetic absurdity. Crosby, a trio of obnoxious teens, the sheriff and several corpses are zombified, spewing blood and chasing Byrd, his girlfriend Alexandra Adi and the gang through passages and secret tunnels. Price Carson (as Bobby Fowler), looking like a cheap reject from a second-rate *Frankenstein* flick, joins in on the scream-filled chase which culminates in virtually the entire cast poised over a deep walled shaft, home to a mass of black writhing tentacles. Throwing salt over the monster and the zombies apparently reduces them to dust, although in the final few seconds, Byrd is dragged to regions unknown by another set of fungus tendrils while Crosby, as mad as a hatter, swoops on the surprised Adi and Patton. Cast-wise, Patton stands out as the 10-year-old, a child actress who amazingly, for once, turns in a grabbing performance that is definitely non-cutesy, and Byrd is also fine in his role of the awkward teen. *Mortuary* is good. It could have been brilliant if it had stuck to the opening set-up instead of pandering to those zombie/thrill-a-minute buffs who demand Hooper's normal quota of slam-bang shocks found in his other works.

MosquitoMan
aka: **Mansquito**
Nu Image 2005; 92 minutes; Director: Tibor Takacs; Rating: ☠☠☠☠

Exposed to a blast of radiation and plastered with an experimental vaccine created to combat the West Nile virus, a mass murderer's DNA is altered and he mutates into a hellish half-man, half-insect monster, embarking on a reign of terror.

Fast-moving and grisly, *MosquitoMan* features a formidable blood-sucking monster in the shape of convict Matt Jordan, looking rather like the creature in David Cronenberg's *The Fly* in the closing stages of metamorphosis, but he's a great deal bulkier. In fact, quite a few references to Cronenberg's movie appear in this gore-laden horror outing. Taken to a laboratory as a guinea pig, to be treated with a serum concocted to defeat a virulent disease caused by plagues of mosquitoes, convicted killer Jordan escapes from his guards and becomes

contaminated with the serum when the lab blows up after a gun battle. With it goes most of the plot. The monster is on the loose, so who needs a story to complicate matters! The creature first slakes its thirst for blood by spearing his (Jordan's) former girlfriend with its proboscis, and then hunts down the doctor (Musetta Vander) whose arm was splashed by the serum in her lab and is now displaying worrying symptoms herself (red eyes, a taste for blood, ugly markings on her flesh). She could be good breeding material! Also on Vander's trail is cop boyfriend Corin Nemec, unaware that his girl might transform at any moment into an insect-woman (she almost does when they make love). In a lengthy, deliriously gruesome

sequence of explicit carnage, the mosquito-monster decimates an entire squad of police officers *and* a S.W.A.T. team in a hospital, dismembered arms and legs scattered over the floor in pools of blood. The thing then helps itself to the contents of a blood bank. Vander, looking less human by the minute, eventually electrocutes both herself and Jordan on scaffolding in an abandoned tunnel, the virus finally contained by releasing clouds of treated mosquitoes into the air. If afforded a cinema release, this classy made-for-DVD flick, incisively directed by Takacs, might well have given 1986's *The Fly* and even *Mimic* (which in part it resembles) a run for their money. It's certainly far superior to *The Fly II* in all aspects, becoming one of Nu Image's worthier releases, and the monster is an absolute cracker.

Never Cry Werewolf
Red Duck Pictures/Peace Arch 2008; 87 minutes; Director: Brenton Spencer; Rating: ☠☠☠

A teenage girl is alarmed to discover that her hunky, motorcycle-riding new neighbor could be a werewolf responsible for a spate of grisly killings in the area.

Twenty years on from 1985's camp classic *Fright Night*, we have virtually the same plot and treatment, only this time around a werewolf is substituted for a vampire. *Never Cry Werewolf* in fact resembles a typical mid-'80s horror movie in looks, dialogue and effects, but an over-loud soundtrack (which really should have been turned down a bit) ruins the mood. When newcomer Peter Stebbings turns up next door with his low-slung motorbike and large black dog, teenager Spencer Van Wyck is immediately struck by a severe dose of hero-worship, but his kid sister (Nina Dobrev), spying on Stebbings through a telescope, quickly has her doubts. Why does the guy shave his palms? Why do his eyes glow in the dark? Why does he visibly jump when a lighter is struck? And news of a missing prostitute coincides with the woman last seen entering the man's house. After a local sex-offender is brutally slain, we are in familiar horror territory. Dobrev just *has* to break into the house to gain proof of  Stebbings' activities, uncovering an eyeball simmering in a vomit-inducing red soup. The local cops refuse to believe her far-fetched lycanthrope theories, so has-been hunter Kevin Sorbo is enlisted by the teen to get rid of the wolf man. Commencing splendidly with a mist swirling creepily down a darkened street at night and coming to rest at the sex-offender's home, followed by the slashing of the pervert's throat, *Never Cry Werewolf* loses its way slightly, treading a thin line between outright horror (the savage murder of Dobrev's girlfriend, caught by the monster while she has sex in a car) and semi-comic parody (Sean O'Neill, besotted with Dobrev, is bitten by the beast, becoming half-man, half-werewolf, his face resembling a badly constructed Halloween mask). Transformation-wise, this is strictly sub-*Howling* stuff, but in the context of the rest of the picture, it suffices. Naturally, Stebbings is defeated at the end by Dobrev and Sorbo, a silver-plated gun barrel fired into his open mouth. One truly bizarre sequence occurs in which the wolf man's dog is shot by silver bullets in a hardware store, the creature losing its fur, changing into a pink-skinned, clawed mutation, much to the consternation of the terrified shoppers. In-your-face werewolf thrills with no frills, Spencer's offering would have warranted a cinema run years ago. It's one of the better indie werewolf flicks available at the moment, a little-seen nugget for lycanthrope fans everywhere.

Nightmare at the End of the Hall
Insight Film Studios 2008; 92 minutes; Director: George Mendeluk; Rating: ☠☠☠

A writer takes up the post of Artist in Residence at the Douglas Academy Boarding School, which she attended 17 years ago as a pupil. There the tortured spirit of her best friend, who supposedly hanged herself in a storage room, haunts her.

Merging present scenes with the past almost continually, director Mendeluk, give him credit, does a far more professional job with this fairly derivative material than he accomplished with the embarrassing *Swarm*. Sara Rue plays the grown-up Courtney, author of the best-selling *My Dead Friend*, a thinly veiled exposé on life at the school when she was a pupil (Amber Borycki), detailing her stormy relationship with Jane (Jacqueline MacInnes Wood). Jane was in love with Brett (Sebastian Gacki), but he in turn fancied Courtney. This teenage *ménage a trois* ended with Jane hanging herself from the rafters. Now currently back at the school, a girl called Laurel (again played by Wood) is bunking down in the converted storage room; she is obviously a reincarnation of the long-dead Jane. Spooky ghostly sequences occur. And what precisely does that creepy headmaster (Duncan Regehr) have to do with any of this? It's a very familiar scenario and the payoff has been seen many, many times before over the years. Jane had a baby (Laurel) by Brett, and the baby was stolen from her by Regehr and given to the family funding the school. The head teacher strangled Jane and made the crime appear like suicide, and Laurel now finds herself in imminent danger from Regehr who, the truth now out, needs to do away with her. So it's all down to presentation. Rue and Wood are excellent and Mendeluk directs in customary "spooky house" fashion, injecting some life into a jaded format (thunder and lightning, whispers, heavy breathing, an out-of-frame ghostly face) to present a passable story of the supernatural, scotched by a rather ineffectual climax (Wood is saved from strangulation, the police take Regehr, and Rue is back in the arms of the adult Brett, Kavan Smith) that demotes it to the also-rans.

No Such Thing
American Zoetrope/Icelandic Film Corp. 2001; 102 minutes; Director: Hal Hartley; Rating: ☠☠

A young TV journalist travels to Iceland to investigate the disappearance of her cameraman fiancé and his news crew, only to meet up with a near-immortal humanoid monster that craves peace through death.

What do we make of Hal Hartley's variation on the *Beauty and the Beast* legend? Well, it's a fantasy movie audiences will either love or loathe, falling, as it does, between two stools—a kid's picture and one for the grown-ups. It's neither too serious nor too humorous, thereby shooting itself in its over-ambitious foot and falling flat on its face long before the 102-minute running time is up. Sarah Polley is fine in the role of the naïve innocent sent to Iceland by bossy corporate news chief Helen Mirren. Polley befriends man-monster Robert John Burke in his hideaway on a storm-lashed Icelandic island. The creature reacts to human interference using violence, and swears and drinks continuously, resembling Ron Perlman's *Hellboy* in facial design and temperament. Taken to New York, examined by doctors and made fun of, the beast becomes the center of a media circus run by the haughty Mirren. At this stage the picture degenerates into travesty. Mirren hams up her "nasty boss" image to the hilt, Burke staggers around drunk in an ill-fitting suit and the up-to-then demure Polley indulges in an all-night, totally out-

of-character sex romp with a dumb hunk. She is now a fully qualified nymphet! Escaping back to Iceland, Polley and Burke find doctor Baltasar Kormakur holed up in the monster's retreat, complete with a lavishly equipped laboratory (how did it get there?). The final shot of the beast undergoing more weird and wonderful tests, the camera closing in on his troubled features, resolves nothing. Julie Christie is on hand as a foil to Polley's *Wizard of Oz*-type Dorothy persona, but her gifts are wasted as a sympathetic nurse. What is the relevance of the "punk girl at the airport" sequence, and why is Polley's operation scene (she's the sole survivor of a plane crash, fished out of the sea near Reykjavik) dragged out to almost 10 minutes? The picture flies off into too many tangents and tries to be too many things. Perhaps the movie would have worked if treated in a less frivolous manner. *No Such Thing* becomes a disappointing fantasy that made absolutely no impact in the United Kingdom, and the movie was only recently issued on DVD.

Octopus

Nu Image 2000; 100 minutes; Director: John Eyres; Rating: ☠☠☠

A U.S. submarine transporting a notorious terrorist from Europe to America for trial falls foul of a gigantic mutated octopus.

For the first quarter of an hour of *Octopus*, audiences would be forgiven for thinking that what they were watching was a *James Bond*-type espionage thriller, with its accent on bombings (the U.S. Embassy in Sofia, Bulgaria) and CIA agent Jay Harrington chasing after, and capturing, mad terrorist Ravil Isyanov. How does all this tie in with what should be a monster movie? But once on board submarine S.S. Roosevelt commanded by David Beecroft, all becomes clear. Ditzy oceanographer Carolyn Lowery reckons something horrible lurks in an area of the ocean known as "The Devil's Eye" (which the sub has to cross) and that this "something" is responsible for the loss of 27 ships. [The pre-credits sequence shows a U.S.S.R. sub loaded with anthrax torpedoed in 1962 during the Cuban missile crisis, the chemical seeping into the ocean depths, mutating the DNA makeup of said cephalopod.] However, unbeknown to Beecroft and his crew, a passenger liner commanded by Russian terrorists is on his trail, hoping to rescue Isyanov and then sink the ship. The plot done and dusted, *Octopus* subsequently develops along *Deep Rising* lines, with the beast's tentacles playing havoc with the stricken sub and then, in the final segment, the monster attacking the liner full-on *and* a helicopter that tries in vain to rescue the bomber. Harrington saves the day by guiding a mini-sub loaded with explosives into the creature's immense jaws, and Lowery falls into Beecroft's hunky arms after the octopus is blown to bits. In true indie style, the effects come into their own during the last 10 minutes, but they don't disappoint. Lowery flashes her ample charms at every male cast member, while Harrington and Beecroft vie with each other in the "wooden acting" stakes, Harrington perhaps coming out on top as the wimpy agent. All said and done, *Octopus* is good old corny fun with an impressive monster, and maybe it's just a tad more enjoyable than the far more expensive *Deep Rising*, on which it appears to be modeled.

Octopus 2: River of Fear
Nu Image 2001; 91 minutes; Director: Yossi Wein; Rating: ☠☠

As the Millennium July 4 celebrations approach, a gigantic octopus lurking in New York's East River decides to spoil things for the mayor's tourist office by embarking on a killing spree.

Not really a sequel to 2000's *Octopus*, *Octopus 2*, even by discount movie standards, is terribly unoriginal in all departments. Cardboard characters acting out cardboard situations abound—two cop-diver buddies (Fredric Lane and Michael Reilly Burke) encounter the mighty cephalopod in the harbor, one (Lane) dragged unconscious beneath the murky waters; the other sets out to avenge his death; their boss refuses to believe them; a drunk rambles on about a sea-monster; the mayor turns a blind eye to the truth, scared stiff that his million-dollar celebrations will go up in smoke if there is an outbreak of public hysteria; and sassy Meredith Morton from the mayor's office falls for Burke after witnessing the monster herself in a treatment plant's storm tunnels. The special effects are below par. Extensive stock footage from the first picture is used, and the remainder of the effects has the cast wrestling with thick rubber tentacles as the creature looks on with one large yellow eye. Overall, the CGI work is second-rate. The only worthwhile pieces of monster action are of the beast rearing up out of the river and yanking the head off the Statue of Liberty (but that only occurs in Burke's dream sequence!) and a night attack on a tugboat. Added to this is the farcical climax in which, after 76 minutes, Burke plants a depth charge on the monster and blows it to bits. Is this the end of the movie? No! The remaining quarter of an hour plunges into *Daylight* territory (it only needs Sylvester Stallone to wander on set to complete the picture) as Morton and a bus full of kids, trapped in a collapsing road tunnel, are rescued by Burke in the nick of time before the roof caves in amid a barrage of explosions. Burke and his new buddy then blast the octopus to pieces *again* with explosive bullets after it has miraculously survived the first explosion! The gore quota is strangely absent from *Octopus 2*, even when the police divers are being hauled into the monster's gaping jaws. What we are left with is a very average creature-feature for youngsters to enjoy, but adult horror buffs who enjoy the much stronger stuff will find the production too distilled for their tastes.

Office Killer
Good Fear Films/Kardana-Swinsky Films 1997; 82 minutes; Director: Cindy Sherman; Rating: ☠☠☠

Ridiculed and sneered at behind her back, the office mouse, working at a high-profile magazine, exacts revenge by murdering all those who have poked fun at her.

Part sit com, part comedy, part horror, this cheapo direct-to-DVD movie takes the rise out of office politics (and office bitchiness) with a fair degree of wit, and Carol Kane as the butt of everyone's jokes is perfect in the role of a downtrodden proofreader. When a memo is circulated informing the staff that working hours are to be reduced and it might be a good idea to take work home, Kane decides to act on that memo literally by taking her tormentors home. She does away with the office manager (Barbara Sukowa), her assistant (Jeanne Tripplehorn), the assistant's boyfriend (Michael

Imperioli) and sundry other personnel, keeping their putrefying corpses in her living room. Why is the frumpy lass with the Minnie Mouse voice behaving like this? It may have something to do with her father's perverted habit of rubbing his hands over her legs when she was a teenager. He died in a car crash, leaving her to look after her housebound mother. Apart from the brutal killings and scenes of Kane playing with severed, decomposed hands, cleaning up one revolting liquefied corpse and talking to her victims, her cat licking at bloody digits (dig those rotting fingers stuck on the hands of a wall clock), not a great deal happens in this bizarre little picture, Sherman's static direction is content to let Kane ham it up playing the loopy, 30-something virgin with the soul of a psycho. After eliminating half-a-dozen office staff without anybody noticing (plus two young girls and a tramp), a glammed-up Kane sets fire to her house (following the death of her mother) and is last seen driving off for a job interview as an office manger, a decapitated head and chopped-off hand nestling in a bag on her car's passenger seat. Roger Corman's *A Bucket of Blood* and *The Little Shop of Horrors* spring to mind when viewing this freaky black farce that, despite its obvious shoestring budget, enthralls *because* of its complete lack of cinematic finesse and star quality. Kane, really, is the main reason to catch it.

100 Feet
Blue Rider Pictures/Grand Illusion Entertainment 2008; 98 minutes; Director: Eric Red; Rating: ☠☠☠☠

After serving seven years in prison for the murder of her abusive policeman husband, a woman is placed under house arrest for the remainder of her sentence, forced to wear an electronic tag limiting her movements to a radius of 100 feet. This proves to be a real handicap when the violent spirit of the dead husband reappears to terrorize her.

This stylish supernatural shocker from Eric Red is bolstered by a totally believable performance from Famke Janssen, playing the harassed wife who is pestered not only by Bobby Cannavale (the embittered partner of Janssen's dead hubby) but by Michael Paré, the phantom husband himself. He's a cadaverous Michael Myers look-alike, coal-black eyes staring from blood-soaked features. Yes, this has all been done before a thousand times over. The lights flicker, candles are snuffed out, bloodstains appear on the walls, echoing footsteps ramp up the tension, crockery and furniture fly throughout the house, the cat senses all is not right and kids won't go near the place (not even on Halloween night). Eric Red makes excellent use of the interior light and shade in the spacious rooms, piling on the spine-tingling set pieces carefully with (thank goodness) the minimum of music. Janssen, unable to escape the confines of the building without bringing every cop in the neighborhood banging on her door, is physically assaulted by the vengeful wraith, even though it transpires that she stabbed her bullying husband in self-defense. The scene in which Paré savagely beats the young grocery boy (who is caught in a sexual fling with Janssen) to a twisted pulp is way, way too sickening for the faint-hearted (the movie was rated "15" in Britain). The climax, unfortunately, resorts to standard "let's get out of the basement before the place burns down" tactics, the evil apparition having been vanquished by the potency of Janssen's wedding ring. But just how original *can* you make these endings nowadays? All things considered, *100 Feet* is a surprisingly neat little horror show that leaves a lot of other similar big-budgeted fare (*1408* is a prime example) trailing in its tension-fueled wake.

100 Million BC
Asylum 2008; 93 minutes; Director: Louis Myman; Rating: ☠☠

Two cavers chance upon a cryptic message scrawled on a remote cavern wall ("Frank, It Wasn't Your Fault"), alongside paintings of prehistoric animals. When the authorities are informed, a team of navy SEALS is sent back 70 million years through a time portal to ascertain whether or not a scientist and his colleagues who vanished in 1949 while experimenting with wormholes are still alive in the Cretaceous period.

One of Asylum's more ambitious efforts (issued directly to DVD, unable to compete with Roland Emmerich's *10,000 B.C.* in theaters) is burdened with some truly awful grade Z CGI effects. They would have looked okay in 1965 but not in 2008. Michael Gross, the inventor of

Project Rainbow, is the group leader, landing in rocky, decidedly non-primeval-looking, terrain. Almost immediately he comes under attack from briefly spotted dinosaurs (a creature in a lake, a Brontosaurus, Velociraptors and flying reptiles) and plants that spit out a blinding fluid. Four survivors from the 1949 expedition are located in caves, including Gross' brother, Christopher Atkins. Together with the remaining members of the squad, they all return to the present day via the portal (except for Gross, who elects to stay behind to close the wormhole). Unfortunately, a T-Rex comes back to the present with them. Crashing through the hangar, the monster proceeds to run rampant through the oddly deserted Los Angeles suburbs until Gross turns up as a young man and throws a wormhole device into the predator's mouth, whereupon it disappears in a flash of dazzling blue light. The idea behind this monster/adventure programmer is disappointingly familiar, and the monster that looks great on its first appearance in the hangar soon resembles a cartoon-type puppet when stomping through those empty streets tailed by helicopters and the frantic cast. One neat touch—the movie's environment shakes every time the Tyrannosaurus approaches. Acting, direction and photography are adequate, but this is sci-fi for the 10 year olds, despite the "15" rating received in Britain. Other minds will probably wander back to the days of Hammer's *One Million Years B.C.* and Universal's *The Land Unknown* and give this a miss.

Out for Blood
aka: **Vampires: Out for Blood**
Brandes Productions/Future Films 2004; 95 minutes; Director: Richard Brandes; Rating: 🐾🐾🐾

A detective held in police custody over the disappearance of his wife claims that she is a vampire.

This is a smart little vampire tale that possesses good pace, weighty performances and quite a few scares along the way. The vampire make-up is a bit obvious, though, bearing an uncanny resemblance to Hammer's make-up on Jacqueline Pearce in 1966's *The Reptile*. Violent-tempered cop Kevin Dillon is on the trail of a missing woman, Jodi Lyn O'Keefe. It turns out that she's become involved with a vampire sect that inhabits an abandoned hospital during daylight hours, and she is one of the undead. O'Keefe also takes a shine to Dillon when he catches up with her, nipping him in the neck as they share a frenzied bout of lovemaking. Dillon's estranged wife (Vanessa Angel), a horror writer, gets a little *too* inquisitive when she learns about her husband's alarming discovery and soon the pair of them are up to their necks (no pun intended) in bloodsuckers. The showdown with the vampire leader (who resembles a weird fusion between *Nosferatu* and Yoda from *Star Wars*) results in the creature's death after it has infected Angel with its tainted blood. Dillon, incarcerated in a hospital cell and displaying vampiric tendencies, is visited by his now-vampire wife and he plunges a chair-leg through her heart. As Dillon lies on his bed, sedated and thought to be insane, his chief (Lance Henriksen) looks under the bed—bad mistake. Angel, red-eyed and fanged, is still alive and kicking. A bit lightweight in parts, this lively chiller is a treat for all horror fans, with plenty of gruesome shocks and transformation-into-vampire scenes in all the right places. Plus the movie features an overwrought turn from Dillon as the distraught husband that no one believes.

Pavement
ApolloProMedia/MPC 2002; 93 minutes; Director: Darrell James Roodt; Rating: ☠☠☠

A psychotic killer stalks the streets of San Francisco, targeting those in the medical profession and leaving corpses covered in syringes.

Cape Town stands in for San Francisco, would you believe. Artful cropping employed in this South African-made thriller leads one to believe that the action takes place in the city made famous by Michael Douglas, Karl Malden and Tony Bennett, but it doesn't succeed in fulfilling that illusion. Dour Alaskan tracker Robert Patrick arrives unannounced in the city after the body of his sister, a nurse, has been discovered in her apartment, a forest of syringes plunged into her body. Viewed with a certain degree of hostility by the police (especially chief Barry Shabaka Henley), Patrick's expert tracking skills are quickly put to good use when he picks up signs at the crime scene that the investigators have missed. Patrick states confidently

that the psycho cornered by the FBI, dressed in S&M bondage gear and holed up in a warehouse with a roomful of dolls, is *not* the psycho the cops should be seeking. Meanwhile, lurking menacingly in the shadows, a malevolent hooded figure with pale features, wearing night vision goggles and limping heavily (his right leg is in a calliper), has homed in on another nurse, murdering the woman in the same fashion as Patrick's sister. The stone-faced lonesome tracker has a one-night stand with blonde streetwise ("I like to be in charge") cop Lauren Holly before the *Psycho*-type climax reveals that the killer (Alex Duncan) was a premature baby who, against all odds, survived, albeit with severe mental and physical deformities. Kept isolated by his doting mother, a religious fanatic who hates the medical fraternity, he breaks out of his room occasionally to slay those who attended his difficult birth (pictured in the opening sequence). It sounds and looks like one of those Amicus horror flicks that proliferated from the mid-1960s onwards. Capably directed and reasonably acted, Duncan's creep resembles a wild-haired, blank-eyed albino. *Pavement* could have upped the gore quota a tad more, but it is an all right addition to the continuing cycle of serial killer flicks.

The Picture of Dorian Gray
American World Pictures 2004; 90 minutes; Director: David Rosenbaum; Rating: ☠☠

Oscar Wilde's novel managed to shock Victorian England, concerning a beautiful young man whose portrait ages while he remains forever young.

Rosenbaum's directorial version uses color effectively, as well as including stunning Bulgarian locations, a decent score and a script containing actual passages and quotes from Wilde's prose. But it does have a major weakness—Josh Duhamel as Dorian resembles the type of blonde-haired hunk seen preening on a California beach. The cynical Harry, in the hands of Branden Waugh, is a charmless bore. It's hard to believe when watching this pretty but lifeless production that Wilde's morality novel had such a shattering effect on English society over a century ago. In this production the time span as everyone ages (but not Huhamel) seems all wrong and out of sync. The one bright spot in a sea of mediocrity is actress Rainer Judd, who paints the infamous portrait. Hers is a spirited performance that at least gets under the skin of the character, as opposed to the lethargy

displayed elsewhere; she's a woman in love with the ever-youthful Dorian yet she marries the priggish Harry. The less-than-thrilling climax sees Duhamel killing himself and subsequently being transformed into a shriveled-up version of his own grandfather, the portrait again depicting the blonde beefcake posing on rocks by the sea. Amazingly, 60 years on, MGM's 1945 classic still remains the best-ever adaptation of this particular novel, despite so-called advances in film production.

Post Impact
aka: **PI: Post Impact**
UFO/Tandem 2004; 90 minutes; Director: Christoph Schrewe; Rating: ☠☠☠

A comet that appears every 350,000 years collides with an asteroid and hits Northern Europe, creating a new ice age. UFO's German-produced fantasy *can* be entertaining fare if audiences are in the right frame of mind and take the film in the proper context. No giant studio is spending millions of dollars on effects and star names here, so in essence this is not another *Deep Impact* or *The Day After Tomorrow*. But elements from these mainstream movies crop up. Security officer Dean Cain and his dog struggle to reach an ice-bound Berlin to reunite with his wife and daughter three years after the comet turned the world's climate topsy-turvy. Accompanying him are two armored vehicles of militia and scientist Bettina Zimmermann. Solstar 2, a space satellite, is being manipulated by a rebellious force in the German capital that plans to dominate the Earth using its microwave beam, invented by Zimmermann's father. She reckons the satellite could kick-start the planet's weather patterns, restoring everything to normal. Grainy yet plausible effects depict snowbound Morocco, Paris in ruins, ice cracking up under the vehicles and Berlin submerged beneath vast banks of snow. When the team reaches its goal, they meet up with resistance fighters in the city's subway tunnels, locate Zimmermann's father in a giant eco-dome and overthrow the long-haired jerk manning the satellite, directing its beam into the frozen north and allowing sunlight to filter through the clouds. Cain has to contend with (and defeat) crazed former-SAS soldier Joanna Clark, who has her own devious designs on Solstar 2, wanting to annihilate the Arab States and negotiate worldwide for their oil reserves in her control. Cain then locates the bodies of his wife and daughter, but not to worry. The gamine charms of Zimmermann are waiting for him when he recovers from his loss. Apart from Zimmermann, the acting leaves a lot to be desired, but *Post Impact* moves efficiently through the action set pieces, looks just fine and really is no worse than many other similar "end-of-mankind" features produced in the 1960s. In the domain of economical sci-fi fantasy, it comes off with a fair degree of respectability.

Prey
Odyssey/Distant Horizon 2007; 92 minutes; Director: Darrell James Roodt; Rating: ☠☠

Hydraulic engineer Peter Weller's family drives off into the African bush for a mini-safari and find themselves at the mercy of a pride of savage lions.

In *Prey*, we have the statutory dysfunctional family—new, younger, wife (Bridget Moynahan), obnoxious, new-wife-hating daughter (Carly Schroeder), and new-wife-loving young son (Connor Dowds). Off they drive (without Weller) into the bush, the driver deciding to take an off-the-beaten-track route and then needing to answer the call of nature. When the ranger steps out of the Jeep to keep an eye on the youngster, a ferocious lion mauls the ranger to death, the vehicle's keys lying near his mangled body. The woman and her two step-kids are now marooned inside the Jeep, a group of very large big cats studying them greedily. It's then a case of whether or not Moynahan can retrieve the keys. She does, drives off for a mile or so and crashes, the lions in hot pursuit. A couple of dodgy poachers appear out of nowhere, one lion is shot, both poachers fall victim to the man-eaters while Weller is enlisting the aid of a dubious hunter (Jamie Bartlett) to help track his family down. Naturally, everything ends happily ever after. Weller comes to the rescue, the hunter is eaten piecemeal, the Jeep is set alight with the most aggressive lion inside and Schroeder finally bonds with her new mom. Stunning, well-photographed African bush scenery, some authentically vicious lion attacks and a few moments of human butchery go a little way into slightly raising the interest levels. But otherwise, this overworked angle on a theme as old as cinema itself offers nothing that hasn't been seen many times before, albeit in less violent form.

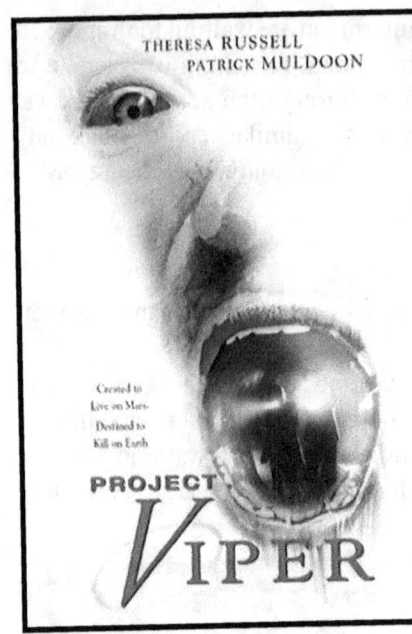

Project Viper

Cinetel Films/Crystal Sky Worldwide 2002; 85 minutes; Director: Jim Wynorski; Rating: ☠☠

A being created on Mars and one that can survive in space has a double contained in a canister on Earth. Falling into the wrong hands, the creature escapes from the canister, rapidly increases in size and terrorizes a New Mexican town.

Project Viper's opening 10 minutes is fantastic *Quatermass*-type science fiction. The crew of the space shuttle Olympus has an unwelcome visitor, the Viper prototype, which breaks out of its canister and decimates all three men. On Earth, a second prototype is stolen by aliens replicating humans (this particular plot thread is left hanging in the air) and, after a high-speed car chase (cops vs. replicate woman), escapes from its confines, using the waterways to navigate, homing in on a local uranium mine to feed on the rich ore deposits. One of those movies that starts well and then slumps into a decline, *Project Viper* simply runs out of gas once back on Earth, relying on tired old sci-fi chestnuts in both story development and dialogue. Every monster/alien movie since time began is plundered here. We have the *Alien*-like music, the *Quatermass*-styled scenario, the government cover-up of the facts, the tentacled monster in mine workings, the beeping tracking device, a slimy trail, the disbelieving police officer (Tim Thomerson), the hunt for the alien inside the sewers, the heroic agent (Patrick Muldoon) and the sassy female lead (ex-siren Theresa Russell, still looking good). Muldoon finishes the thing off by throwing a case containing a bomb into its gaping jaws. How many times have we seen that before? A sub-plot, eventually abandoned, concerns the town's residents contracting cancer through the water supply. By the time we enter into the film's final stages, we are firmly rooted in monster cliché land ("Let's get this show on the road," yells Muldoon to no one in particular). The CGI-created alien itself saves this flick from a one star rating, a metallic gray blob that sprouts writhing tentacles and sports a hooded head armed with silvery fangs. The "all is not well" ending has the pilot-less shuttle crashing into the ocean with the original prototype still on board, ready to multiply in the water. A couple of moments of gory suspense raise the interest levels slightly, but overall, this is vacuous stuff. The chief reason to sit through this picture is to feast one's eyes on Russell, who has most definitely improved with age.

Pterodactyl

American World Pictures 2005; 89 minutes; Director: Mark L. Lester; Rating: ☠☠☠

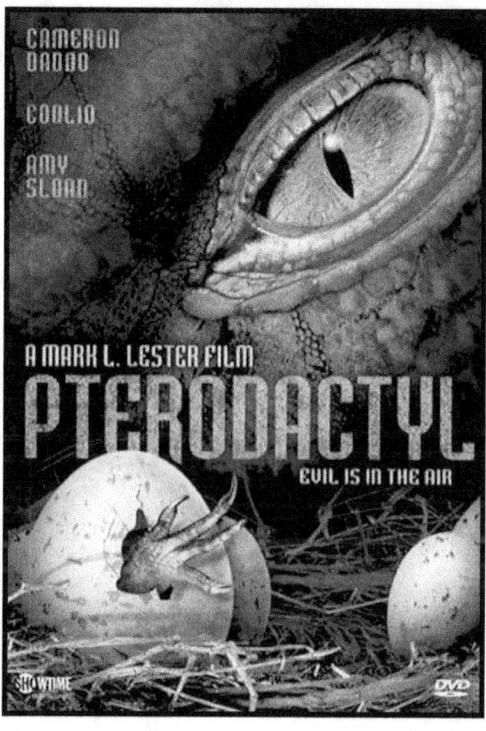

Mount Ararat, a dormant volcano in Turkey, is home to a nest of carnivorous prehistoric flying reptiles.

From the opening shot of three hunters wiped out by a Pterodactyl in true cheapo gory fashion (one man is ripped in two), to the closing image of a T-Rex roaring its head deep within the volcano, Lester's "man vs. Pterodactyls" outing is a lively horror thriller. It features some truly stomach-churning scenes of slaughter that make amends for the half-baked cast, especially Mircea Monroe as an eye-rolling self-obsessed teen. Thankfully, her left arm is separated from her body midway into the action and she expires. Ex-rapper Coolio plays the head of a Special Forces team sent into the forests to capture a bandit chief. Coolio's squad, after successfully seizing the leader, meet up with professor Cameron Daddo's bunch of nerdy students who are on a fossil-hunting expedition in the area. Both groups immediately come under attack from a pack of Pterodactyls that either eat their targets on the spot or carry them back to the main nest inside the volcano. Cue for bucket-loads of butchery as arms and legs are ripped off, soldiers decapitated and torn in half, a female soldier savaged to death, body parts scattered over the terrain, bones broken and, to cap it all, hatchlings feast on entrails. Amy Sloan, Daddo's requisite love-interest, is carried off to the inaccessible nest but eventually rescued. A sheep with a rope tied around it is used as bait, after which a fatally injured soldier triggers an explosive device buried inside the entrails of a victim, blowing up the nest, the baby and adult Pterodactyls. But don't forget that T-Rex lurking in the depths! For a low-budget production, *Pterodactyl*'s CGI effects are pretty good (the winged predators easily equal those in *Jurassic Park 3*). The "creature-perspective shots" (in distorted green), the monsters flying over and homing in on their prey and one larger specimen battering its way into a cabin are decently executed. Okay, this isn't high art, but for '50s B movie junkies, *Pterodactyl* represents 89 minutes of fast-moving monster mayhem of a bloodier variety.

P2

aka: **No Exit**

Summit Entertainment 2007; 98 minutes; Director: Franck Khalfoun; Rating: ☠☠

On Christmas Eve, a young businesswoman works later than usual. When she goes to leave the deserted office, she finds herself targeted by a mad security officer.

P2 becomes *Psycho* in a concrete setting as blonde Rachel Nichols is first befriended and then subjected to a series of harrowing assaults by guard Wes Bentley in basically one set, an underground parking lot. Another "woman in peril" flick that uses every cliché in the cinematic book—cars that refuse to start; Nichols monitored on CCTV; nutcase Bentley dressed as Santa; Bentley stabbed with a fork and a spike in the eye; a rabid Rottweiler; Nichols trapped in a flooding elevator; and finally the bruised and battered heroine torching Bentley's car and him with it. Midway through *P2*, older fans might be tempted to throw in the towel. The only thing to keep them glued is the sight of Nichols' magnificent breasts defying the laws of gravity by refusing to tumble out of her soiled slip, despite all that Bentley puts her through. Bentley attempts an Anthony Perkins but fails miserably. Even his deep-set eyes can't make allowances for his hysterically inept performance. Nichols takes all that is chucked at her with aplomb, but this now older-than-old concept needs a new approach to maintain the horror buff's interest. Despite imaginative direction by Khalfoun, *P2* is just one more loony-on-a-rampage offering that we have all experienced before.

Pumpkinhead 2: Blood Wings

Live Entertainment 1994; 88 minutes; Director: Jeff Burr; Rating: ☠☠

In the small town of Ferren Woods, five teenagers resurrect the soul of a deformed boy who was beaten, knifed and dropped into a mineshaft in 1958. Unfortunately for them, the boy's soul assumes the form of an avenging demon.

This is a straight to home video sequel to Stan Winston's 1988 *Pumpkinhead* that never saw the light of day in Britain. *Pumpkinhead 2* follows the formulaic "teenagers vs. boogeyman" route figured so prominently in umpteen movies from the mid-'80s onwards, so we know just what to expect. Three geeks and two bimbos (one, Ami Dolenz, the sheriff's willful daughter) run for their lives from a hideous monster in backwoods U.S.A., while the townsfolk ignore the new law officer (Andy Robinson) and form a posse of their own to hunt the creature down. A *Waltons*-type rural setting, backed by a running harmonica score, completes the redneck community canvas. The picture's sole redeeming feature is the demon itself, a leprous, seven-foot tall skeletal, bug-eyed goblin with teeth like steak knives and long, clawed talons. The pre-credits sequence, shot in monochrome, relates the story of how the disfigured youngster came to meet

his brutal end. Up to the moment obnoxious hot-rodder J. Trevor Edmond digs up the corpse, reads a spell and splashes blood over the remains; all is fairly interesting. Once the monster is revived, with the blind witch mother in the hospital, it's simply a case of adding up the body count until nine victims are horribly slaughtered, Dolenz escaping from the thing's clutches on the pleadings of Robinson who, as a youngster, had a friendly encounter with the boy himself. Then the vigilantes turn up, letting fly with rifles, the demon's broken body once more falling into the mine shaft, followed by a talisman given to the sheriff by the creature's mother. Director Burr throws in plenty of red-distorted viewpoint scenes to generate some tension as the demon approaches its victims, and Robinson is the only cast member on show to throw any weight behind his performance. But the real star is that well designed eye-opener of a monster. Without it, *Pumpkinhead 2* would be instantly forgettable teen horror fodder.

Puppet Master vs. Demonic Toys
Sci Fi Pictures/ApolloProScreen Films 2004; 88 minutes; Director: Ted Nikolaou; Rating: ☠☠☠☠

At Christmas, the power-mad female head of Sharpe Toys is flooding the market with lethal dolls ("Christmas Pals"). Her objective is to murder millions of people and take over the world, at the same time planning to steal the living puppets and life-giving formula from rival Robert Toulon, the man who runs the Toulon Doll Company Hospital.

A long, long way down the line from Full Moon's 1989 *Puppet Master*, this, the ninth in the series, can be viewed as either polished high camp, a darkly twisted Christmas movie parody or 88 minutes of light-hearted nonsense. It's easily acceptable as a one off, divorced from all the others in the *Puppet Master* saga. With Corey Feldman playing the scatterbrained great grandnephew of the original puppeteer/alchemist and Vanessa Angel's pantomime-like Cruella De Vil impersonation delivered through Botox-enhanced lips, it's almost impossible to take this comedy horror picture seriously. But perhaps that's the point. Angel wants to lay her hands on Feldman's four puppets—Blade, Six-Shooter, Pinhead and Jester—and the magic potion (virgin's blood mixed with a blue liquid) that's injected into them. She employs the aid of her own three little horrors—malevolent, green-eyed (and very windy!) Baby Oopsy, a killer clown jack-in-the-box and a feral monkey—for this purpose.

She enters into a mutual pact with a demon summoned from a fiery pit by (yes, you've guessed it) the blood of a virgin. Also in on the madcap action is Feldman's elfin daughter Danielle Keaton, Angel's dour Eastern European assistant (Nikolai Sotirov), and a female cop (Silvia Suvadova) who unaccountably falls for Feldman's goofy charms. We half expect Mike Myers in *Austin Powers* mode to leap on set at any moment as Feldman's puppets, turned into mini-cyborgs, take on Angel's trio of terrors, a couple of heavies and the demon, Keaton trapped inside a "Blood Extractor" and screeching her head off. The final reel has the thwarted demon jumping back into the pit with Angel and Feldman, reunited with his daughter and puppets while rolling his eyes at Suvadova. But wait—gravel-voiced profanity-spouting Baby Oopsy is alive and well, wishing the audience a "Merry Christmas and a crappy New Year." The musical accompaniment to this colorful alternative to the usual saccharine-coated yuletide family fare is none other than "Jingle Bells," which will no doubt have some kind of malicious appeal to the more "bah-humbug" minded punter not overly keen on this particular time of the year. Directed with pace and imagination, hammed up to the hilt by the entire cast and very '60s in looks and set design, *Puppet Master vs. Demonic Toys* is a freaky treat to savor, outlandish enough to become a cult favorite in years to come. *White Christmas* it certainly isn't!

The Rage: Carrie 2

Red Bank Films 1999; 104 minutes; Director: Katt Shea; Rating: ☠☠

Teased and ridiculed by both the high school jocks and her classmates, a student gets revenge by unleashing, during a party, awesome telekinetic powers on all those who have made her life a misery.

Twenty-three years on from Brian de Palma's classic *Carrie*, this belated low-budget sequel sunk without a trace in the United Kingdom and has rarely been seen, basically because it's simply *Carrie* all over again but presented less competently. Repressed teen Emily Bergl is taunted by the most disagreeable bunch of sex-obsessed male students ever to hit the horror screen, while her so-called best pals scheme behind her back with the ultimate aim of mocking her at Dylan Bruno's bash at his swank home. In the meantime, teacher Amy Irving (reprised from the original film) is in contact with Bergl's sick-in-the-head mother (J. Smith-Cameron), incarcerated in an institution, and tries to reason with the woman and warn her of the powers that have been passed on to her daughter.  When Bergl's close friend leaps to her death from the college roof after being casually rejected by chauvinist Zachery Ty Bryan, Bergl withdraws into a shell, only consenting to attend Bruno's party if local hero Jason London goes with her. The scene is then set for the inevitable showdown. Bergl, maliciously handed a notebook containing girls' names (hers included) that list scores (from one to 10) for sexual performance, a list compiled by the abominable Bryan and company, releases her pent-up fury, wiping out everybody and everything in sight. During several minutes of well-staged bloody mayhem, Bergl is crushed beneath a roof collapse, leaving London the sole survivor, who is haunted in the end by her faded spirit. Like a '70s horror flick transported into the 1990s and played slightly more graphically (compact discs slicing into bodies; a spear gun fired into Bryan's genitals; Bruno drowned under a pool cover; a head decapitated), the film contains several brief flashbacks to *Carrie*. Director Shea's effort is so-so regurgitated teen horror offering nothing new or special, although one can gain a certain amount of grim satisfaction from watching all those detestable male students getting their just deserts.

The Raven

Shadow Factory/Hollywood House of Horror 2006; 81 minutes; Director: Ulli Lommel; Rating: ☠

A homicidal maniac, who is stalking and murdering members of an all-girl group, focuses upon one of the band members obsessed by the works of Edgar Allan Poe.

When she was 10 years old, orphan Lenore's (Nicole Cooke) adopted grandfather read her stories written by Poe. Fifteen years later, the singer/songwriter (Jillian Swanson) is shadowed by a bald, bloodstained figure that *might* be the vengeful ghost of a man Swanson electrocuted in a bathtub after he raped her. Or he *could* be the figment of her fevered imagination. Who knows, and who really cares? Never has 81 minutes seemed so long. German director Lommel's experimental/artsy-fartsy approach to Poe's hallowed prose bombards the viewer with random images intended only to confuse—black candles, overhead electricity lines (filmed in monochrome), telegraph poles, black roses scattered across Swanson's bed, ravens wheeling in the sky, black clawed hands on a steering wheel, savage knife slayings, an eyeball dug from a victim's face, a mysterious man with a curved dagger hovering in the background, another weird person lurking on the moorland, spiders, ghosts and a cartoon Frankenstein monster. Heavy breathing, red writing on the screen and a bevy of serious-looking nuns complete the confusion. Did anyone connected with *The Raven* have the slightest inkling as to what this incomprehensible digitally shot moonshine was meant to convey?

Two protracted scenes (at the poolside and the dentist's surgery) occur that will test the endurance of even the most fanatical lover of the awful. Swanson, like the rest of the cast, doesn't act. She's content to stare mournfully at the camera or move around like a punk rag doll. Enigmatic-ridden cheapjacks such as this only serve to exasperate one and make you wonder what was going on through the minds of those involved during production. There have been plenty of worthwhile movies based on Poe's famous poem, Universal's 1935 Karloff/Lugosi classic and Corman's 1963 opus being two brilliant examples, but audiences can easily run out of adjectives in describing just how god-dammed dreadful this latest adaptation is.

Reeker

Primal 2005; 91 minutes; Director: David Payne; Rating: ☠☠☠

A group of college students on vacation find themselves trapped at a deserted diner in the middle of the desert, preyed upon by a ghostly, cloaked phantom.

The familiar "they're all dead" scenario is given another airing in what in many ways is a somewhat peculiar chiller. Following the gruesome pre-credit sequence of a man staggering toward his car with half his skull missing, we're off down that same road with three guys (one is blind) and two girls. When stopping for a break, a small tremor is felt. Police sirens are heard, no signals can be found on their mobiles and, when they set off, an overturned vehicle uncannily resembling their own is passed. Stopping at a deserted motel, the group finds corpses of rotting animals in one room. Scribbles on a wall relate to violent deaths and the hereafter. Mutilated people are glimpsed; a trucker arrives on the scene, looking for his wife, only to drop dead from a heart attack. An angry drug dealer is also on their tail but doesn't seem to be aware of their presence. When a gray hooded figure with a decomposed face appears, determined to kill them all, emitting a foul odor, audiences can probably twig where all this is heading. It's fun to see the intricacies of the story unfolding anyway. Two of the guys and one of the girls die horribly at the hands of the visitation and experience flashbacks of their lives as they expire. Tina Illman and the blind

Devon Gummersall speed off in the car that skids off the road and crashes as they try to get rid of the creature perched on the roof, and then all is made clear. Three of the kids died in a pile-up at the start of their journey, caused by the truck driver smashing into them when they took that break, the driver struck suddenly by a heart seizure. The dealer pulled Illman and Gummersall from the wreck and saved their lives; the Grim Reaper, or "Reeker" as the phantom is known, didn't claim them. An offbeat, eerie little horror/mystery picture,

Reeker provides entertaining supernatural fare with a surprise ending that for once will not leave audiences feeling deflated.

Reptilicant
Cine Excel 2006; 91 minutes; Director: Desi Singh; Rating: ☠

A team of treasure hunters investigating $20 million in diamonds stashed away on Alcatraz Island encounters a deadly, shape-changing alien.

Why would a supposedly intelligent being from another world travel millions of miles across deep space only to hole itself up in a disused prison in the middle of San Francisco Bay and then act like an unintelligible, psychopathic maniac? After the opening (and rather splendidly scenic) credit shots of a space capsule resembling a seed pod endlessly drifting through our solar system, we are plunged into gray, dingy looking, shaky camcorder territory as the squabbling group of stereotypes breaks into Alcatraz, led by Tina-Desiree Berg sporting a cherry-red rinse. The rubber-suited alien that resembles a cross between a muscular gorilla and *The Monster of Piedras Blancas* picks them off. This fanged creature also possesses the ability to take on the appearance of its victims and ape (rather irritatingly) human gestures. Tough guy Gary Daniels (who has unknowingly been interviewing the monster all along in the guise of Berg, as most of the action is told in flashback) ends up the lone survivor. Daniels rips the thing's skin to ribbons with a diamond-encrusted fist in a drawn-out fight, and then the alien is fried between electrodes like *The Thing from Another World*. Daniels, dazed from his efforts to eliminate the monster, then stumbles across a batch of alien eggs in a conduit (take a bow, *Alien*) and, in the final shot, Daniels stares at the FBI agents with green eyes, having been taken over by the alien presence. Every sci-fi fan appreciates a dose of guilty pleasure on occasion, but *Reptilicant* really does plumb the depths in all departments, despite moments of gore (a grisly decapitation; the monster leaking green blood). Even Ed Wood could have made a better job of this material. A clumsily edited, badly scripted, terribly photographed farrago that might not even appeal to fans of the truly awful.

The Resurrected
Scotti Brothers Pictures/Border/Raich 1992; 108 minutes; Director: Dan O'Bannon; Rating: ☠☠

A doctor uncovers a 250-year-old journal written by an infamous necromancer that holds the secret to reviving the dead, and he is soon up to his eyeballs in sorcery.

The wild, almost impenetrable, imaginings of H.P. Lovecraft do not always transfer well onto the big screen. They are far less successful, in fact, than translating Poe's works. *The Resurrected* is just one of a number of movies that tries, and fails, to capture the atmosphere of eccentric terror contained within

the author's verbose texts. Based on *The Case of Charles Dexter Ward* (one of Lovecraft's few novellas), the ingredients are all here for a great horror yarn, told in flashback by investigator John Terry. Jane Sibbett, the wife of Dr. Ward (Chris Sarandon), visits Terry. Ward has disappeared after meddling around with experiments of a devilish kind in the family carriage house. Terry tracks his last whereabouts to a dilapidated farmhouse that emits a foul odor for miles around, the rooms stacked with the cremated remains of scholars and wizards. The journal of Joseph Curwen (also played by Sarandon) details ungodly procedures for bringing back the dead, or even parts of the dead (a strange elixir, poured over a fleshy inert blob on a table, imbues the object with a blue light and transforms it into a living hand). The main dramatic thrust of the picture is in the strung-out sequence showing Terry, Sibbett and colleague Robert Romanus creeping through dark, vaulted chambers and galleries beneath the old house where the "mistakes" from Sarandon's experiments grovel wretchedly in pits like moth-eaten skeletons, one hideous monstrosity grabbing Romanus to feed on his flesh. After which Terry and Sibbett escape from the catacombs and trigger bombs planted during their flight, demolishing the house. There has to be a trick ending, naturally. The doctor is now Curwen himself, incarcerated in an asylum. Visited by the investigator, Curwen's collection of yellowing bones in a suitcase spills onto the floor in a confrontation between the two and a male nurse. The nurse's head is ripped off, the life-giving potion splashes over the remains and a stop-motion skeleton emerges, draining the flesh from the necromancer as Terry hurriedly leaves the room. The 1990s was an unrewarding period for horror films per se. O'Bannon's effort (rarely shown in
England) now appears both terribly dated and heavy-handed, Richard Band's noisy score an intrusion rather than a bonus. Faithful to the novel it may be, the movie's still indigestible fare, vaguely unsatisfying without doing too much wrong. Perhaps one day some enterprising filmmaker will tackle Lovecraft's other great novella, *At the Mountains of Madness*. Written in 1931 and set in the Antarctic wastes, this masterpiece of horror literature ranks as one of the elusive author's most spellbinding macabre tales, incorporating in its framework his favored Cthulhu Mythos themes, little of which is in evidence in this movie.

Rise of the Gargoyles
RHI Ent./MediaProPictures 2009; 91 minutes; Director: Bill Corcoran; Rating: ☠☠☠

A living gargoyle emerges from the bowels of an ancient church in Paris and begins a reign of terror in Paris.

Rise of the Gargoyles, not to be confused with *Gargoyle* (2004), has a paper-thin plot to say the least, with Bucharest standing in for Paris. An unseen creature kills two workmen on the lookout for valuable artifacts in the gloomy crypts of an old church. Architectural historian Eric Balfour and girlfriend Tanya Clarke, exploring the church, stumble across the caged gargoyle and its glowing red eggs. Clarke is slaughtered early on, as punishment for stealing an egg. Balfour enlists the aid of TV reporter Caroline Néron and cameraman Justin Salinger to convince the authorities of the monster's existence. A mad priest (Nick Mancuso), the thing's guardian, is thrown into the mix as per the norm (where would these films be without a deranged priest?). First, we have good news. The intensely irritating Clarke, who spends all of her limited screen time mugging furiously at the camera like a diva in heat, is polished off in half an hour. The huge gargoyle is an impressive creation, and the final 15 minutes, mostly set in dust-filled passages as the creature goes on the attack, are intense and claustrophobic. We also have bad news. Lanky Balfour looks (and acts) as though he's just stepped out of an Armani advert, the dialogue is lame in parts, and audiences don't see nearly enough of the winged protagonist. Included are a couple of well-staged night assaults by the gargoyle on the terrified local citizens and a few effective moments of gore (entrails splattered all over an alley wall). The climax has the monster turning back to stone when caught in strobe lighting, but coming alive and pouncing on Mancuso, who has wired himself up with explosives. He hits the detonator button and blows himself, the monster, the smashed eggs and the church sky-high. Nice clear color photography and speedy direction make this a low-budget, undemanding treat for monster movie lovers. It's nothing new, but the movie is relatively entertaining all the same.

Ritual
RKO Pictures/Silver Pictures 2002; 99 minutes; Director: Avi Nesher ; Rating: 💀

After she is suspended from her post at a New York hospital, a nurse takes up an assignment in Jamaica on a rambling estate, offering supportive care to a man who claims to be a zombie.

A lame rehash of Jacques Tourneur's classic *I Walked With a Zombie* (hence the RKO connection), *Ritual* is a hard film to like. Clumsily directed, unsympathetic performances, a couple of shock-horror moments plus a silly ending all contribute to a tired zombie outing that is about as riveting as United Artists' 1960 schlock effort *Macumba Love*, which isn't saying a lot. Jennifer Grey stars as a nurse traveling to Jamaica to care for Daniel Lapaine, a sweaty looking individual who is convinced he is under a voodoo curse. Black beauty (and highly sexed) Kristen Wilson takes Grey under her wing because Lapaine's oily brother (Craig Sheffer) appears to be up to no good, being in cahoots with the mountainous local law officer (Ron Taylor) involving the underhanded sale of the estate. The director bombards us with repeated visions (from Lapaine's fevered mind) of voodoo rituals, beating drums, fierce painted faces, Grey's nightmares involving spiders and gruesome slayings, a carved-up female corpse and Tim Curry playing a scruffy doctor who doesn't do a great deal. The movie simply refuses to get into gear and involve its audience. Not even the unsurprising climax helps, showing another drum-thumping ceremony as Wilson turns out to be a voodoo high priestess and the half-sister of Sheffer who, it is revealed, has been trying to send his brother mad (claiming his sibling's share of the inheritance and selling the estate at a huge profit). In  revenge for the death of her mother at the hands of Sheffer's father (keep up, please!), the conniving brother is stabbed to death. However, Lapaine, now cured of his virus-induced zombie state by an antidote concocted by Grey, turns the tables and blows a magic smoke into the priestess' face, thus turning *her* into a zombie. That risible final scene shows Lapaine and Grey getting hitched, swiftly cutting to zombie Wilson, wearing both a wedding dress *and* a blank expression, being plonked on a bridal bed by her new, overweight Police Chief husband who has fancied her from reel one. If audiences take everything on board with a pinch of salt, they might derive some pleasure from seeing how badly constructed this horror potpourri is. On the other hand, audiences will fully appreciate why *Ritual* vanished off the circuits in 2001 and was subsequently issued on DVD five years later.

Road Rage
aka: **A Friday Night Date**
GFT Ent./Hilltop Ent. 2000; 96 minutes; Director: Sidney J. Furie; Rating: ☠☠☠

Rescuing a college girl on campus from her jealous and fist-happy ex-boyfriend, a young man offers to drive the damsel in distress home. Soon they are running for their lives, pursued by a giant truck whose unseen driver is intent on killing the pair of them.

Road Rage is included here because of its *Duel*-type leanings, with strong hints of psychotic behavior chucked in for good measure. For virtually the whole length of the film, a big black Dodge truck relentlessly chases Casper Van Dien and Danielle Brett, the psycho driver invisible behind a tinted windscreen. Thundering down freeways, swerving to avoid collisions, driving the wrong way up traffic-congested roads, smashing into police vehicles, running a forest ranger over, and so on, this is one angry, aggressive driver. Of course, we all know the driver of the Dodge to be the ex-boyfriend Joseph Griffin, partnered by Chuck Byrn and Anthone Tullo, but even these two take exception to the maniacal Griffin using a gun on Brett, as well as trying to ram Van Dien's car off the road at regular intervals. The real man behind the wheel, so to speak, is veteran director Sidney J. Furie and he does a great job at providing some nerve-shattering thrills and spills in the bruising manner of *Duel* and *Speed*. Trying to inject some chemistry (and humor) into the pairing of feisty Brett and what-a-great-haircut-I've-got Van Dien is a little bit more difficult, though. Brett rants and raves while laying on the sexual tease with a trowel, but Van Dien remains impervious to her gamine charms, or to *anything*, come to that. Griffin and the battered Dodge are engulfed in a fireball at the end, leaving Van Dien and Brett to get better acquainted by mooching off to the nearest motel.

Road Rage is an indie thrill ride that is a bit of an adrenalin rush all round. Just try to ignore the forced banter between the two leads.

Romasanta: The Werewolf Hunt
aka: **Werewolf Hunter**
Filmax Intl./Future Films 2004; 90 minutes; Director: Paco Plaza; Rating: ☠☠☠☠

In a rural area of Spain in 1851, the local villagers and townsfolk attribute an escalating number of savage murders to be the work of either a madman or a werewolf.

The incidents depicted in this well-staged Spanish horror movie actually took place, the director embellishing the yarn with the lycanthrope legend to create a complex thriller that resembles a hybrid cross between a Hammer 1960s feature and a continental horror outing from the same period. The result is a stimulating departure from the norm, possessing standout color photography and believable performances. Lanky Julian Sands is traveling vendor Manuel Blanco Romasanta, whose specialty is involving himself in the lives of lonely women, writing letters on their behalf to another member of their family and then butchering that member, stripping their corpses of fat which he uses to make bars of soap. Why he carries out this *modus operandi* is not made clear. Is it because he's the ninth son in his family (regarded with superstition by the Spaniards at that time), is he simply insane or is he in fact a werewolf? Whatever the reason, burly John Sharian, his ex-partner, is after him with a musket filled with silver bullets. Elsa Pataky is also on his trail, wanting revenge for the slaughter of her sister and young niece. Bloody, shredded bodies turn up, the police and a forensic professor are baffled, wolves are snared and shot and all the while Sands drifts from one family to the next on his killing spree. The one transformation scene comes as a sudden shock and is a hair-raiser. In the forest at night, rain pelts down on a recumbent wolf. The fur sloughs off, the torso swells in blue blisters, limbs and facial features contort painfully into human shape and Sands emerges naked out of a sticky cocoon looking like a loathsome pupa that has just hatched. Sands is finally captured working as a laborer in a cornfield

and charged on a count of 15 murders (he claims to have killed more). The professor believes that he can eventually be cured of his affliction, so he is not sentenced. Incensed at this piece of injustice, Pataky enters Sands' cell and stabs him to death with a silver knife, thus giving rise to the legend of The Wolf Man of Allariz. It's always been the case that the continentals have the knack for producing highly imaginative horror dramas, and *Romasanta* is no exception to the rule. This is a werewolf flick with a different slant, enriching and fruitful, an unexpected treat that really deserves to be sought out by all aficionados of Spanish/Italian/French horror fare.

Rottweiler
Filmax Intl./Future Films 2004; 95 minutes; Director: Brian Yuzna; Rating: ☠☠

In 2018 a determined robotic Rottweiler tracks a fugitive on the run from an immigration camp in Southern Spain.

The Rottweiler's fearsome reputation as an animal not to be tampered with gets the full-blown horror treatment in this lurid Spanish gore-fest whose blood-spattered effects are ruined by a wimpy hero (William Miller), a vapid script and a none-too-interesting plot. Miller escapes into the mountains after his partner, shackled to him, has his arm torn off by the devil-dog. Miller runs from one grisly situation to another. Every person he meets is eventually savaged to death by robo-Rottweiler. In flashback, we see how Miller got himself into this mess. Both he and girlfriend Irene Montala played a game of "infiltration" where foolhardy young people sneak into immigration control zones as a dare. Montala was caught and raped, then slain by the dog, while cowardly Miller ran for it, was captured and then escaped. To make amends, Miller, one year later, is now on his way back to the zone to discover what became of his girl, unaware that she is dead. To titillate the audience, Miller searches for Montala in a brothel before the dog makes an unwelcome appearance among all the half-naked women, causing havoc. Finally Miller unearths his girlfriend's chewed-up body on a beach. "You said you would die for me," the corpse whispers so him. To redeem his tortured soul, Miller has one last fight with his canine pursuer. Both end up dead in a conflagration, and the last shot shows three skeletons lying in the sand as dawn breaks. The Rottweiler, steel teeth gleaming from a disfigured face, eyes glowing like blue coals, makes 1983's *Cujo* look like a puppy-dog. The scenes of him tearing his victims to shreds are not for the faint-hearted. It's just a pity that overall the movie is lackluster, due to a weak central performance and an uninspired storyline. The frightful carnage caused by the dog (slavering over entrails and ripping off limbs) and the arid mountain scenery is enough justification to catch this disappointing Spanish horror flick, although little else is.

Sabretooth
International Film Group 2002; 90 minutes; Director: James D.R. Hickcox; Rating: ☠☠

Scientists using DNA extracted from fossilized rocks clone a saber-toothed tiger. A truck transporting the beast to a mountain laboratory for observation crashes, the creature escaping from its container into the forest where it goes on a rampage.

Poor effects work and flat direction mar this retread of countless "monster-at-large-in-the-woods" flicks. On this occasion, Vanessa Angel and John Rhys-Davies are the mismatched scientists on the saber-tooth's track, aided and abetted by Angel's ex, hunter David Keith, desperate to kill the "kitty-cat with an attitude problem." Not only has the big gray feline got its yellow beady eyes on them but it also has its eyes on a group of four hikers on a field trip, led by Jenna Gering. It's a well-trodden route the picture heads down as Rhys-Davies, Angel's female assistant and three of the hikers are finished off by those lethal fangs and claws. Keith, following a skirmish in an abandoned mine with the monster, manages to impale it on a stake after the devious Angel (who wanted the saber-tooth left alone for her own nefarious purposes) has been dragged away and mauled to death. The end sees Keith, Gering and Josh Holloway-Trent hobbling off on the path to the nearest habitation, leaving a trail of butchered bodies in their wake. CGI-wise, the huge cat is unconvincing as a ferocious predator. Furry and cuddly is a more apt description of this cartoon-looking creation, although the head, exhibiting long curved teeth and worked by ani-

matronics, is far more feasible in design. The opening pre-credits sequence of a laboratory cleaner inadvertently locking himself inside the room that houses the monster's cage, only to be torn to bloody shreds, is a decent scene-setter that the rest of the film fails to surpass or even equal.

Savage Planet
Hand 'n' Hand Films 2007; 85 minutes; Director: Paul Lynch; Rating: ☠

In the environmentally ravaged future, a group of scientists travel 20,000 light years through a time portal to a new planet, Oxygen, to try to salvage the human race.

And what do they find when they get there? A very un-alien-type landscape resembling an English meadow in high summer populated by tribes of oversized brown bears bent on eating them. Oh, and a green viscous substance that can repair horribly damaged flesh wounds (and even severed limbs). The feuding team (why *do* these teams always bicker?) is made into mincemeat by the badly superimposed grizzlies (or a giant model furry claw) while trying to locate a piece of equipment that will enable them to return to Earth (a piece of equipment that wouldn't have looked out of place in an old *Buck Rogers* serial). Audiences have to either suspend disbelief and watch to the bitter end or give up on this puerile rubbish. The end, if we do decide to sit it out through director Lynch's artistically bankrupt picture, has the surviving hero (Sean Patrick Flanery) and heroine (Reagan Pasternack), having escaped the alien bears, make the trip back to Earth with the green healing goo and somehow saving the planet from further harmful pollution. A cheap exercise with hardly any redeeming features to its name, saddled with hopeless dialogue, *Savage Planet* is an insult to any self-respecting sci-fi fan's intelligence. It's no real surprise that this mind-numbing grade Z turkey has rarely been seen outside of the United States, although it *is* available worldwide on DVD if one's foolish enough to want to buy it!

Scorcher
Cinetel Films/Reel One Entertainment 2002; 91 minutes; Director: James Seale; Rating: ☠☠

The Chinese detonate three atomic bombs deep underground, causing the Pacific tectonic plates to shift, resulting in a series of worldwide catastrophes.

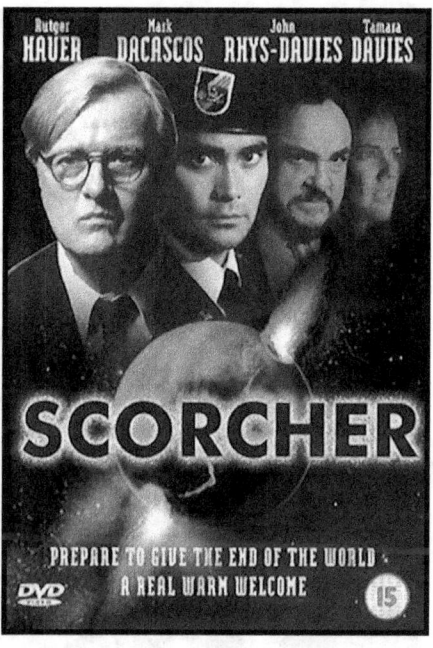

With an opening scene lifted directly from *Dante's Peak*'s opening scene and a plot cobbled together from *Armageddon*, *The Core* and even UFO's *Deep Core*, we are on habitual and very stale territory in *Scorcher* which, after a fairly lively 20 minutes, goes downhill rapidly. So in that first 20 minutes, we are treated to erupting volcanoes, earthquakes, sheets of flame emerging from the polar ice and cities on fire. The dour-faced U.S. president (Rutger Hauer) and his team are informed that if the plates widen to a gap of 44 centimeters, Earth is doomed. The cure to the problem is to trigger two thermo-nuclear devices under Los Angeles that will prevent the fissures from opening any further. Enter colonel Mark Dacascos, scientist Tamara Davies and her father, ill-looking John Rhys-Davies, who, together with a crack army squad, drive into the city (which is being evacuated) to plant the devices some six miles apart for maximum impact. In a couple of sub-plots, Dacascos' daughter, after miraculously surviving a fireball in a road tunnel, is abducted by a bald, disfigured freak but eventually escapes. Finally the mission is almost sabotaged (why is never made clear) by Mark Rolston, who plays a psychotic agent. Not unexpectedly, both bombs are successfully triggered simultaneously in the city's ventilation system, thus saving the planet from extinction (but destroying L.A. in the process). A gung-ho script backed by a bombastic, pompous soundtrack might fool audiences into thinking that they are watching a classy end-of-the-world actioner, but this is pure cinematic camouflage. Woeful acting, dumb dialogue and cardboard effects all contribute in making this a doomsday flick of the lesser kind.

Session 9

USA Films 2001; 100 minutes; Director: Brad Anderson; Rating: ☠☠☠☠

A group of disparate workmen gathers in a vast derelict lunatic asylum to strip the building of asbestos, each member targeted for terror and death by a former psychopathic inmate who could be one of them.

The real star of this neat little shocker, shot direct to digital, is the asylum itself, a real life but now disused Gothic-looking institution in Danvers, MA. Within the edifice's crumbling, rotting interior, the team of laborers begins to

crack up under the spell of the silent, malignant atmosphere. One of them discovers a collection of archive audio tapes relating to a psychotic inmate who suffered from multiple personality disorder, another has a deep fear of the dark (not the sort of place to be working in, then, particularly when the generator packs up!) and a third disappears without a trace, later found tortured to death, a metal spike protruding from his eye. Could this former patient heard on the tapes be one of the crew, released years ago and now carrying out a string of bloody murders for reasons known only to himself, a personal vendetta of sorts? Anderson takes full advantage of those gloomy, labyrinthine corridors, dusty hallways, begrimed walls plastered with fading photographs and dimly lit rooms containing unsettling medical apparatus to crank up the sweaty tension as one man after another is horribly butchered by an unseen assailant. After a taut 70 minutes, the final 30 minutes almost falls apart at the seams and sadly, the denouement is a touch confusing, the ambiguous climactic imagery never really offering an explanation as to what the psycho's motives are, and who the killer is (team leader David Caruso or his close friend, paranoid Peter Mullan, beset with marriage problems?). Nevertheless, *Session 9*, although filmed on a shoestring budget, is directed by Anderson with a keen eye for the institution's morbid surroundings and acted with utter conviction by the small cast. It's just that little bit more unconventional than the normal run of horror fodder.

7eventy 5ive
aka: **Dead Tone**
Codeblack Entertainment 2007; 100 minutes; Directors: Brian Hooks and Deon Taylor; Rating: ☠☠☠

Teenagers attending a party held inside a mansion make a series of prank telephone calls, but the trick backfires when a hooded ax murderer decides to join in the festivities, slaughtering them one by one.

Commencing in grisly spirits 10 years previously when a masked maniac butchers adult party members, leaving several children orphaned, *7eventy 5ive* is a gory take on *Scream*, *Scary Movie*, *Urban Legend* and the rest. Rutger

Hauer's crumpled detective bolsters the movie, the cop not only on the trail of the butcher but frantically trying to locate the surviving kids who are being sought out and sliced up by the selfsame lunatic. Then we move forward a decade (Hauer actually looks 10 years younger!). Students Jonathan Chase, girlfriend Jud Tylor and their college pals drive off to Chase's expensive pad, a rambling country mansion, for a spot of partying. In other words, boozing, smoking pot and having uninterrupted sex all night long while Mom and Dad are away. Bored with the proceedings, black dude Brian Hooks (the film's co-director) convinces everybody to play his own party piece. Ring someone at random and if, after 75 seconds, the caller can convince the party on

the other line that the prankster is a genuine caller, the prankster wins a prize. Unfortunately a caller gets through to the killer featured in that opening scene (don't ask how, just go along with it!) and the maniac turns up, stainless steel ax in hand, carving a bloody path through the partygoers. In the meantime, Hauer and partner Gwendoline Yeo home in on the action. Well-directed, with a score of vicious set pieces to satisfy the bloodlust, the movie is unfortunately lumbered with the most god-awful bunch of pouting, posing teenagers audiences are ever likely to encounter on celluloid. We *know* that teens can be an almighty pain in the butt at times, but do these pictures *have* to portray them as such intolerable, objectionable morons who appear to be living on a different planet from the rest of us? Every single one of them is dead by the final reel and we almost feel like shouting "good riddance" from the rooftops. Yes, there is a hoodwinking conclusion (Wil Horneff, one of the original kids who witnessed the horrific slaughter of his parents, is the killer, but he's not working alone). In true *Halloween* style, the real psycho (Kyle Turley) lives to fight another day. *7eventy 5ive* has enough ketchup to more than satisfy all slasher freaks and, despite those terrible teens, is a notch above for fodder of this type.

Severed
aka: **Severed: Forest of the Dead**
Brightlight Pictures/Submission Films 2005; 93 minutes; Director: Carl Bessai; Rating: ☠☠

211

Sap from genetically modified trees, when in contact with human blood, turns a group of loggers into flesh-craving zombies.

Vivid Day-Glo photography, a claustrophobic forest setting, an environmental group (the Forest Action Committee) challenging corporate greed and giant trees that, when felled, ooze bloody sap bode well for *Severed*. That is up to the point when one of the tree-cutters who has been exposed to the tree's secretions transforms into a pale-faced, raving zombie. Then we're off down the *28 Days Later* route with grainy camera shots of the jerky, virus-infected flesh-eaters homing in on, among others, Sarah Lind (leader of the protesters), Paul Campbell (the chairman's son), Julian Christopher (the hefty chief logger) and J.R. Bourne, the cowardly laboratory technician who is secretively aware of the company's experiments in injecting trees with a hormone (GX11.34) to speed up growth. Can they escape or can't they? That's the plot in a nutshell. The survivors from repeated zombie attacks stumble upon Patrick Gallagher and his rough gang (they include a religious nut who thinks the apocalypse has arrived). By the finish, everyone, apart from Lind, has been zombiefied. Director Bessai ladles on the gore with gusto (the living dead scooping handfuls of gooey viscera and munching on body parts), but audiences can't get away from the fact that since Danny Boyle's 2002 *28 Days Later*, this frenetic style of in-your-face zombie action has been done to death and is starting to wear a bit thin. Acting, direction, cinematography and script all fit the bill, but the second-rate material kills it after a promising opening 15 minutes. This movie is for die-hard zombie fanatics only.

Shark Attack
Nu Image 1999; 92 minutes; Director: Bob Misiorowski; Rating: 💀

Super-intelligent sharks run amok in the African town of Port Amanzi, leading to a loss in fish stock that threatens the locals' livelihoods.

This is a poor man's *Deep Blue Sea*, with marine biologist Casper Van Dien alighting at the port to investigate a spate of shark attacks—12 in three months—and running up against a nutty scientist (Bentley Mitcham) who is medically modifying sharks' DNA to help find a cure for cancer. Jennifer

McShane provides the romantic interest as the sister of a biologist who has been tied up and tossed to the sharks for interfering in the scientist's shady affairs. His rotting arm turns up in one of the predators' bellies. To begin with, there is a plethora of grisly attacks on boats and against Van Dien and McShane in an underwater cage and sunken vessel. Plus a female tourist nearly has her leg severed. The doctor (whose experiments haven't received official approval) is treating child cancer patients in the local hospital with "shark steroids" serum, without much success. After 50 minutes, this middling South African addition to the "animals against man" horror genre dies on its feet, with not even the South African scenery coming

to its rescue. Van Dien's finely chiseled features remain expressionless throughout, despite all the dangers to which he is exposed. The man-eaters are quickly forgotten and all audiences get is a series of badly edited car and boat chases between our hero, McShane and the corrupt police chief's mob, who are backed by the crooked mayor (Ernie Hudson). Oil has been discovered near the harbor and the mayor wants the fisherman out of the way so that he can sell the town to the oil giants. The sharks are a convenient way of getting rid of busybodies. Stilted dialogue and stiff acting, plus some pretty uneven shark effects, all go into making this a very tired movie that will probably send audiences to sleep long before the climax. When the baddies are defeated in a blazing gunfight in Mitcham's laboratory, Hudson is finished off by a Great White and Van Dien gets McShane all to himself.

Shark Attack 2
Nu Image 2000; 93 minutes; Director: David Worth; Rating: ☠☠

A Great White shark, whose DNA has been tampered with, is captured and put on display in Cape Town's Water World amusement park. The shark breaks free and begins a reign of terror along the coast.

A blatant rip-off of *Jaws 3-D* (which itself was pretty dire), Worth's first contribution to the *Shark Attack* franchise is an improvement on the original,

but it's nowhere near as good as the third. While out scuba diving near a sunken wreck, Nikita Ager and her sister are attacked by a giant shark. Ager survives, her sister doesn't. Danny Keogh, the slimy owner of the local amusement park, wants the shark captured, to be the star attraction in his aquarium center. Enter marine biologist Thorsten Kaye who snares the creature but, on opening day, it escapes after biting its trainer in half and joins up with a pack of six genetically altered sharks from the first movie and begins feasting on humans. This is the signal for the usual welter of severed limbs, chunks torn from torsos, surfers feasted upon during a surfing competition and divers and kids finding themselves in serious peril. Thorsten and Ager (who wants to kill the shark as revenge for her sister's death) hit it off romantically, and the mutant predators are eventually located hiding out in a large submarine cave near the beach. Following a hunt led by Aussie TV naturist Daniel Alexander, the monsters are blown to bits inside the cave after a mini-sub loaded with explosives is guided into the entrance. One of the predators attacks Alexander, but miraculously he escapes with only a chewed-up arm. To enjoy this picture (and in parts it *is* enjoyable), audiences have to turn a blind eye to the acting (wooden, except for Alexander), the script (cliché-ridden), the variable effects work (slipshod CGI graphics, plastic-looking sharks, a cardboard prop standing in for the dorsal fin and sharks that actually roar) and flagrant plagiarism (every character and plot situation is replicated from *Jaws* and its sequels, including that famous reverse-zoom shot). The Cape Town coastal setting is easy on the eyes, and Worth directs this bloodbath with some dash. However, *Shark Attack 2* is definitely for lovers of unadulterated schlock and definitely *not* for lovers of more meaningful fantasy/horror cinema.

Shark Attack 3: Megalodon
Nu Image 2002; 94 minutes; Director: David Worth; Rating: ☠☠☠

A gigantic 60-foot shark, attracted to electrical currents emanating from deep-sea fiber optic cables, goes on a killing spree off the Mexican coast.

Murky underwater photography, an insipid John Williams-type score, vacuous "we've heard it all before" lines, lifeless performances and gimcrack effects all work against this production. This sub-*Jaws* adventure doesn't appear to have a thing going for it. But incredulously director Worth pulls his fat out of the fire during the final 25 minutes, producing a lively, if outrageous, horror show for fans of the truly dreadful, thus elevating it to the best of the three *Shark Attack* movies. When a large shark's tooth is found embedded in an underwater cable, nice but dim beach patrol officer John Barrowman posts a description of it on the Internet. In response, blonde but dim paleontologist Jennifer McShane (playing a different character from her role in *Shark Attack*) arrives from the San Diego Museum of Natural History, stating that the tooth is from a species of shark thought to be extinct for 20 million years. It isn't too long before boats come under attack, severed limbs cloud the ocean with blood, people are gobbled up and the ruthless head of Apex Communications (who puts profits before people's safety) is scoffing at the suggestion that a predator is homing in on his cables, using them to seek out human prey. After the 20-foot specimen is shot in the mouth by Barrowman while smashing its way through a launch's hull to nibble at McShane, its 60-foot mother (an homage to *Gorgo*?) appears on the scene and, what was up until then a pretty appalling exercise in filmmaking, steps up a few notches as the colossal denizen of the deep rears up out of the water, gulping down boats, humans and dinghies into its cavernous CGI maw. A favorite moment occurs when the nasty Apex chief escapes from his sinking yacht on a water scooter, but he rides straight into the monster's gaping, razor-toothed jaws. Barrowman and grizzled old sea salt Ryan Cutrona finish the monster off with an explosive torpedo fired from a mini-sub in the climax, although the last few seconds hint at another giant shark prowling the deep. If audiences can turn a deaf ear to McShane shrieking "Oh my God!" every few minutes as one person after another is eaten alive, and if they can also ignore the fact that Barrowman's pretty-boy looks remain shaken but not stirred despite the traumas he goes through, audiences could be in for an unexpected guilty pleasure thrill ride with this hare-brained addition to the "giant sharks-on-the-loose" genre.

Shark in Venice

Nu Image 2008; 88 minutes; Director: Danny Lerner; Rating: ☠☠☠

A professor from San Francisco's Oceanographic Institute travels to Venice to investigate the disappearance of his father. Immediately he gets caught up in a search for a legendary hidden treasure, with the Mafia and aggressive sharks prowling the city's canals.

Raiders of the Lost Medici Treasure is a more appropriate title for yet another "killer sharks" flick whose storyline could well have been dreamt up by a junior in high school during dinner break. Stephen Baldwin is suspicious of the apparent cover-up surrounding his father's disappearance (or death) while he was diving in a restricted area for a hoard of lost treasure worth $200 million. Mafia mobsters (who are after the fortune themselves) kidnap Baldwin's girlfriend (Vanessa Johansson), forcing him to divulge the location of the goodies. One of the police officers (Hilda Van Der Meulen) *may* be on the side of the bad guys, and the heavily bearded Mafia boss (Giacomo Gonnela) is dropping baby sharks into the canals where they will mature and act as his watchdogs. Add to this mix a bizarre heavenly choir-type score, pleasing shots of the city and a lengthy sequence involving 8th-century crusaders hunting for King Solomon's treasure. What we end up with is a bit of mishmash, which is enjoyable enough if we can switch off the thought processes for 90 minutes. With the aid of his father's map and notes, Baldwin discovers the riches in a booby-trapped underground medieval chamber that can be reached by swimming through several gloomy underwater galleries where the sharks roam. After Johansson is abducted, held hostage and threatened with a bullet, Baldwin has to show Gonnela's divers where the treasure is, the whole shebang ending in an explosive shoot-out as the police arrive. A Great White gobbles up the Mafia leader, the chamber is blown up and sealed by igniting gunpowder, and Meulen turns out to be on the side of the law after all. Two things bother me though. First, if the Medici treasure has been hidden from man for centuries and is so difficult to locate, how is it that Gonnela's hideout is situated about a two minute dive from the chamber and his cohorts have no problem reaching the spot in that murky water? Second, why send all your men into the water when you know that they are going to be finished off by the sharks? Sleepy-eyed Baldwin is slightly more animated than he was in *SnakeMan,* while Johansson adopts that wide-eyed stare (so commonplace among actresses in these indie features) to compensate for her mediocre acting talents. Far less in the way of gore and mangled body parts appear than in other similar outings, although the shark attacks (a gondolier smashed in two; a couple taken by surprise on a quay; divers lunged at) are executed with vigor. *Shark in Venice* may be highly derivative in characters, plot and dialogue, but the rapid pacing, colorful photography and Venice locations make for easy-on-the-eye, thick-ear hokum.

Shark Swarm
RHI Entertainment/Silverstar 2008; 169 minutes; Director: James A. Contner; Rating: ☠

An unscrupulous property developer arranges for toxic waste to be dumped into the California resort of Full Moon Bay to kill off the local fishing industry, thus bankrupting the community and paving the way for plans to develop the town to his financial advantage. Unfortunately, a by-product of his scheme comes in the shape of a pack of genetically tampered man-hunting sharks that begin to wreak carnage among the populace.

Any movie that has the ability to make Nu Image's *Shark Attack* trilogy appear like modern classics can't have a lot going for it, and *Shark Swarm* doesn't. Pedestrian acting, a dreadful script, disjointed continuity and editing (some scenes terminate abruptly in mid-sentence) and bland-looking CGI sharks undermine the production. Armand Assante is the cretin villain, playing a devious businessman up against righteous fisherman John Schneider, his wife Daryl Hannah and professor brother Roark Critchlow, who all oppose his underhand methods at land development. While all this plotting and conniving is going on, a snorkeler, several divers, a teacher, some fishermen, three students, a lifeguard and a canoeist are being gobbled up by the sharks (not that anyone in the town seems to notice) and snoopy investigator Heather McComb is positive that the bay's polluted waters point to

the disused power plant that is leaking poisonous chemicals into the sea. The main flaw with *Shark Swarm* is one of sheer over-length, with far too much screen time taken up with Schneider, Hannah and company arguing with Assante and his heavies, and not enough "killer shark" action to keep horror fans happy. Also, apart from a briefly seen severed arm and a beachcomber having his hand bitten off, where are all those dismembered body parts to appease the gore freaks? Hannah looks to be a shadow of her former glamorous self, Assante appears uncomfortable as the baddie (and his character practically fizzles out in the film's second half), while F. Murray Abraham, playing a university professor monitoring sea life in the bay, attempts to bring a spot of credibility into the proceedings, with little success. Yes, we have Hannah's daughter making eyes at a blonde surfer and Critchlow homing in on McComb. This, after all, is supposed to be a horror-type feature, not a soap opera. The predictable happy ending sees the townsfolk united once more, Assante eaten alive when the jetty he is standing on collapses from a mass shark attack, and a couple of toy-looking pulse guns defeating the enemy. Fair enough, the film's environmental stance comes over loud and clear, but this is a perfect case where some judicious editing (by at least an hour) could have worked wonders. And that soppy final shot of every couple in the picture cuddling one another is calculated to have audiences reaching for the vomit bucket. Note: In some parts of Europe, there's a 95-minute version of *Shark Swarm* going the rounds, and some TV stations have been known to transmit part one (up to the moment when a group of five divers meet their end), only to forget all about part two!

She Creature
aka: **She Creature: Mermaid Chronicles Part 1**
Creature Features Productions 2001; 91 minutes; Director: Sebastian Gutierrez; Rating: ☠☠☠

Ireland, 1905—a carnival showman and his sidekicks steal a real mermaid from the home of an old sea captain and decide to transport it to America. However, the creature possesses telepathic powers that are exerted to devastating effect on board the ship taking the mermaid across the Atlantic. The vessel, now under her spell, unwittingly coasts toward a fabled island where death awaits.

Although famed 1950s producer Samuel Z. Arkoff was the brains behind this horror-fantasy, it bears no resemblance whatsoever to the producer's 1956 *The She-Creature*, with only the ocean being the common denominator. Reminiscent of a Hammer '60s second-feature in look and design, with a touch of *The Elephant Man* thrown into the opening scenes for good measure, *She Creature* is a little on the slow side, particularly in the overlong shipboard sequences. But the movie is strong on period atmosphere, while bewitching Rya Kihlstedt as the mermaid is both splendidly seductive but creepy at the same time. Rufus Sewell stars as the carnie who, with girlfriend Carla Gugino and colleagues, takes the mermaid (housed in a large tank) from Ireland, unaware of the fact that what he has stolen is a siren-type being who feeds on human flesh. Mermaid folklore is cleverly woven into the plot as the creature artfully lures the ship by force of will in the direction of a mythical island where more hungry mermaids dwell, showing her true colors by transforming into a predatory, scaly monster (the "Queen of the Lair") at the end, a flotilla of mermaids feasting on the stricken sailors. Gugino, pregnant, is allowed to live, the battered vessel later discovered abandoned in the Sargasso Sea. Stan Winston created the flamboyant creature that decimates Sewell, the crew and his cohorts in an unfashionable production that could be right out of the year 1966. However, give *She Creature* full marks for at least being on the eccentric side, and any red-blooded male would swim across miles of ocean for a taste of Kihlstedt's aquatic, provocative loveliness!

Shrooms

Capitol Films 2007; 84 minutes; Director: Paddy Breathnach; Rating: ☠☠

A group of American tourists, led by a hippie Englishman, trek into forests in Ireland to trip out on magic mushrooms. They soon are running for their lives from a knife-wielding, hooded maniac on the loose from an abandoned young offenders institution.

Darkly photographed and confusingly directed, *Shrooms* is a fairly unattractive slasher movie. Five Americans (three girls and two guys) are driven into an area of the forest by Jack Huston, their aim to get spaced-out on mushrooms with hallucinogenic properties. Unfortunately, blonde Lindsay Haun goes whole hog and eats a poisonous (and forbidden) specimen that, when ingested, causes her to first go into a fit and then, for the entire movie's running time, experience visions of her friends being butchered to death by a surviving twin from the institution. One of these twins was abused, tortured and hanged, the other facially mutilated and driven insane. Is he responsible for the spate of murders, or is it the two throwbacks living deep in the woods in an old shack? The convoluted climax takes place in the derelict boys' home, Haun the only one to escape the lunatic's clutches, rescued by the police as the two Irish hillbillies are arrested. But on board an ambulance, Haun has one vision too many. *She* has been the killer all along, the mushroom she ate transforming her into

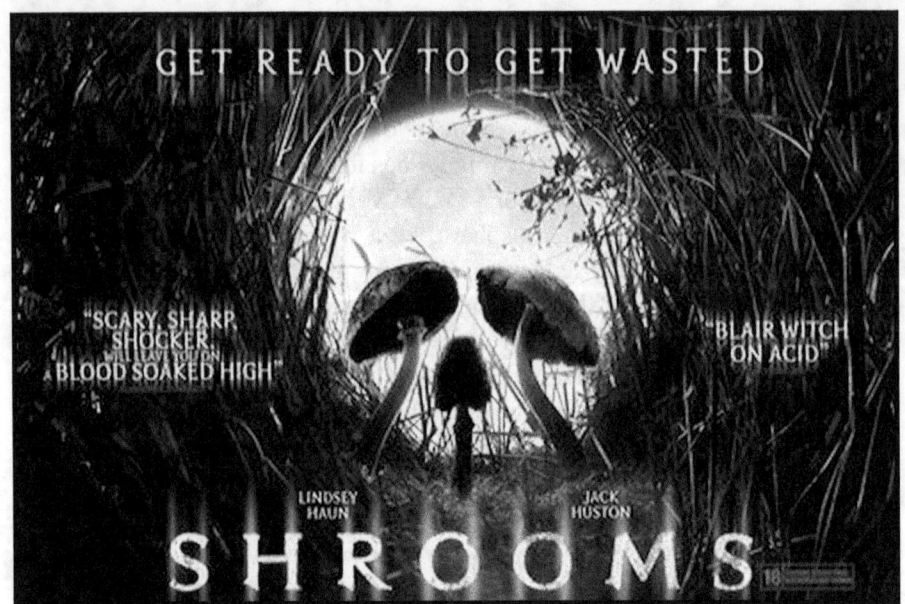

a demented ax murderess, dispatching her five companions. Apart from Haun and Huston, the remainder of the cast exhibit thoroughly immature tendencies so audiences don't get to sympathize with a single one of them. Any suspense generated in the opening 15 minutes rapidly dissipates in a welter of disjointed images designed to shock but failing to do so. One or two atmospheric shots (Haun wading through the borders of a lake, slowly approaching the gloomy institution; a cloaked, hooded figure seen flitting between the pines) don't really make up for the fact that this is just one more teenage horror outing to add to all the others, albeit in a slightly more unusual setting than most. And that talking cow is a big mistake!

Single White Female 2: The Psycho
Third Street Pictures/Destination Films 2005; 91 minutes; Director: Keith Samples; Rating: 💀💀

To get away from her roommate who has bedded her boyfriend, a young career-minded woman moves into another apartment, sharing it with a female exhibiting serious emotional problems.

1992's *Single White Female* was a typical psychodrama of its day, two up-and-coming attractive female leads doing their utmost to breathe life into what was after all a pretty mundane shocker, low on the gore-count to boot. Keith Samples' belated direct-to-DVD sequel doesn't really improve on the first movie, but, on the other hand, it's no better or worse than Barbet Schroeder's effort. Kristen Miller and Brooke Burns are two sassy PR girls both after promotions. When Burns goes behind her rival's back and sleeps with her rival's boyfriend (Todd Babcock) in order to clinch the job of publicizing the opening of his new restaurant, Miller, outraged, takes off and moves into a swish apartment occupied by new roommate, mentally disturbed Allison Lange. Die-hards, without even reading the script, will know what follows. Manipulative Lange colors her hair to look like Miller's, engages in a bit of S&M in a seedy club, murders Burns, accuses a new date of virtually raping her and drugs Babcock's wine, battering him into a coma with a bottle and accusing *him* of near-rape. The manic climax has Lange stabbing a cop, then knifing Miller who knifes her in return before shooting her dead. A couple of psychological reference points are included to add gravitas. Miller witnessed her mother's suicide at the age of seven, and Lange chickened

out of a suicide pact with a school pal, watching the girl bleed to death without lifting a finger to help. And in the final few seconds, the newly promoted Miller, apartment hunting and back with Babcock, sees her mother's face in a bathroom mirror, a razor blade lying close by. Is she as unbalanced as Lange was? Unless a third installment is made, we shall never know. The one genuinely unsettling sequence director Samples summons up is when Miller pokes around under Lange's bed, trying to unlock a suitcase to gain clues to her roommate's troubled behavior. Shot at floor level, Lange's legs appear in the open doorway, looking at Miller unobserved. What a pity these moments of tension are few and far between in what is a smartly made but quite ordinary (and somewhat dated) slasher thriller.

666: The Child

Asylum 2006; 80 minutes; Director: Jake Jackson (Jake Perez); Rating: ☠☠

The sole survivor of a plane crash happens to be a nine-year-old orphan who possesses demonic powers.

The Omen (both versions) revisited! Boo Boo Stewart plays the dark-haired boy adopted by TV reporter Sarah Lieving and her husband, cameraman Adam Vincent. First seen in a hospital killing off a nurse and doctor who have sneaked into a closet for some in-house nookie, the evil kid, ensconced in the family home, then starts to finish off anybody who annoys him. Following an accident with a baseball, a doctor and nurse have their eyes drilled out while trying to diagnose Stewart for possible damage to his head. Vincent's father is slashed to death by a falling ceiling fan. And one of the cameraman's buddies, after coming

across a book of near-pornographic drawings made by the youngster, is chopped up in the workshop by machines that come alive. On top of all this, a nun who tries to warn the couple about their new son, that he was the "Demon Child" responsible for the orphanage burning down, is run over and replaced by a mysterious nanny who is all too aware of Stewart's devilish ways. The gory climax has Vincent shoving a poker into the nanny's mouth as his wife, on an assignment, trips over one of her adopted son's action figures and falls on glass in a hotel bathroom, bleeding to death. Her husband is shot by the police as he is about to shoot Stewart after spotting "666" imprinted on his tongue. Satan's little offspring ends up in the final scene with Lieving's sister, an unsuspecting TV cook who takes the child under her wing. For fans of "satanic brat" flicks, this is a so-so addition, no better or worse than all the others. But if you're *not* a great lover of Damien and Donald (so-named in this film), give this unremarkable horror outing a miss.

666: The Beast
Asylum 2007; 85 minutes; Director: Nick Everhart; Rating: ☠

Now 30 years old, Donald (from *666: The Child*) is married, his wife pregnant and he harbors ambitions to became a leading light in the company he works for.

First thing, how come Donald is now fair and thinning? In the first movie, he sported a mop of thick, jet-black hair. Second, if we're going to have the Chosen One preaching to the masses on top of an office roof, let's *see* those masses, not just three figures in cloaks standing still as audiences hear a background tape of crowds chanting and shouting. There are times when watching this atrocious slice of satanic blather that audiences could be forgiven for thinking that Leslie Nielsen might turn up in one of his skits, that the whole charade is a send-up. But no, the deadpan one doesn't come on set and we are left with Chad Mathews (Donald) being initiated into the firm as junior vice president, while his heavily pregnant wife (Makinna Ridgway) suffers from stigmata-type bleeding, observes ghouls in the streets and witnesses her recently murdered sister visiting her, all the while a concerned priest (Colin Brock) shadows her. Very soon we're deep into *Devil's Advocate* territory, but without the talents of Al Pacino and Keanu Reeves. Mathews murders his boss and promotion-seeking rival, is seduced by the satanic Alma Saraci and, in the clumsily handled finale, Ridgway gives birth in a church surrounded by seven priests all holding crucifixes. Her husband charges in surrounded by flashing blue lights, stabs all seven to death but in turn is knifed by Ridgway. We are then subjected to five whole minutes of sermonizing as Brock explains the significance of the birth to the woman, on how it has been foretold that the child can fight the forces of evil. Lumbered with a ghastly tinkling piano soundtrack, *666: The Beast* is as low an occult thriller as one can possibly get. If only Nielsen had been in the cast to liven matters up!

Slayer
aka: **Predators**
Starz/IDT Entertainment 2006; 88 minutes; Director: Kevin Vanhook; Rating: ☠☠

In the South American jungle, a race of vampires preys on local villagers because their source of food and blood has been depleted by deforestation.

Has Casper Van Dien made a single decent picture since 1997's fabulous *Starship Troopers*? His output from that date has ranged from the passable to the dire, and *Slayer* falls between the two. For aficionados of Bela Lugosi, Christopher Lee and treasured, carefully crafted classics such as *Brides of Dracula* and even *Curse of the Undead*, read no further. Kevin Vanhook's outing has none of the lasting qualities of previous vampire thrillers. This is macho-man vs. bloodsuckers in a jungle setting, and what an odd bunch these bloodsuckers are. Looking more like zombies than vampires, the scruffy, bearded acrobatic creatures leap about in daylight, crucifixes having no effect in repelling them, kick-boxing their way through villagers and commandos alike. Van Dien is horrified to learn that his best pal, black marine Kevin Grevioux, has been turned into one of the undead and is now leader of the pack. It just so happens that Van Dien's ex-wife, blonde entomologist Jennifer O'Dell (kitted out in customary

tight vest and combat trousers), is in the neighborhood, bug-hunting, so the commando and his squad go in search of her, planning to also eliminate the vampire hosts in their cave hideout. We cut from Van Dien cruising down river, to O'Dell going about her business, to the vampires attacking a trading post en masse, to Van Dien and O'Dell, to more vampire attacks, and so on, and so forth. It all gets a bit tedious. Even sexy vampiress Joyce Giraud and the gratuitous bloodletting fail to ignite the screen, with a graphic decapitation, umpteen stakes through hearts, throats slashed and a woman torn in half. Grevioux dies in the end, a lance embedded in his chest, and the *Nosferatu*-type even higher honcho gets his just deserts, a stalactite falling from the cave roof straight through his body. Van Dien then walks off with his ex, presumably to play house in the nearest hotel room. Basically, *Slayer* is bargain-basement fodder suitable only for the younger horror fan. All those of a certain age might well recoil in revulsion at just how tatty these particular vampires are, as, overall, is the movie itself. Oh yes, *Wonder Woman*'s Lynda Carter puts in a brief appearance, playing Van Dien's starchy head of command, suspiciously appearing to carry an unrequited crush on her well-groomed underling.

Slipstream
ApolloProMedia/Film Afrika Worldwide 2005; 89 minutes; Director: David Van Eyssen; Rating: ☠☠

A scientist invents a device that can reverse time by 10 minutes, thus enabling him and those in his vicinity to relive events to their advantage.

English footballer-turned-actor Vinnie Jones shouts, swears, spits and snarls his way through one of the feeblest time travel science fiction flicks in recent years, but at least the thuggish one possesses a certain degree of screen presence. Kooky physicist Sean Astin slurs his lines, which is just as well because most of what he says is gibberish; FBI agent Ivana Milicevic wears a bewildered expression throughout; the other FBI agent, Kevin Otto, is nice but wooden; and Jones' foul-mouthed girlfriend (Victoria Bartlett) would be quite at home fronting any British punk band in the late '70s. Borrowing its central theme from 1993's

Groundhog Day, Astin, under FBI surveillance, trots along to his bank to cash a pay check, reverse time by 10 minutes, cash another pay check, reverse time, cash another—get the idea! In bursts bank robber Jones and his mob to upset the applecart, triggering off 32 minutes of backwards/forwards slow motion trickery as the criminals steal the loot, then they don't, then they do, and so on and so forth. Otto is gunned down, Jones grabs the portable time machine, a hostage situation develops on the freeway, Astin is shot and Bartlett is killed. After much huffing and puffing by the hard-faced crook, resulting in a plane crash, Astin finally, to the relief of all, plugs his device into a laptop and gets it to reverse time by hours, not minutes. We finish the movie at the very beginning and Jones, as animalistic as he is, is smart enough to fathom out that he doesn't want to relive what he has just been through, driving safely away from the bank with his cohorts, all those harmed during the long 89 minutes back on their feet, Astin successfully chatting up the bank cashier, foxy Verity Price. It's noisy, it's unrefined, it's clichéd, it's a one-man Vinnie Jones show. Yes, the guy is no Laurence Olivier, so if we take him out of the equation, what we have here is tedium with a capital "T." Jones, to be honest, is the only reason to tune in.

SnakeMan
aka: **The Snake King**
Nu Image 2005; 96 minutes; Director: Allan A. Goldstein; Rating: ☠☠☠

A gargantuan, five-headed snake guards a scared pool deep in the Amazon jungle whose waters possess the gift of long life.

After a scientific team unearths the body of a Brazilian Indian in a tomb and discovers that he has lived for 300 years, another team, headed by Stephen Baldwin, Larry Day and Jayne Heitmeyer, is sent by pharmaceutical company GenTech into the rainforest to locate the whereabouts of the pool, desiring it because of its commercial possibilities. Very soon, Baldwin and colleagues are being pestered by two warring tribes (one of which worships a snake god) and the monster itself, a gigantic, roaring (not hissing) serpent with five heads that plucks humans from the jungle trails and divides them up piecemeal be-

tween the heads, each swallowing a dismembered body part. Stock situations include the usual "monster viewpoint" shots (in distorted green), Day turning into a psycho, Baldwin bitten by a normal snake but surviving, Heitmeyer saving the life of an Indian child and the greedy corporate boss arriving with his bunch of gun-toting heavies, desperate to find the hidden fountain, regardless of the mighty hydra standing in his path. The climatic showdown occurs in the cave where the pool flows, the boss picked up by the monster, his arms and legs yanked off by four voracious heads. The limbless torso falls to the ground squirting blood and, delivering the *coup de grace*, the creature neatly severs his head from the convulsing body. Heitmeyer emerges from all the mayhem as though she has just stepped out of a beauty parlor, complete with beautifully manicured nails, and Baldwin's impassive features register just the slightest hint of emotion as the blonde actress snuggles up close in the final seconds. Yep, it's certainly not a movie for purists (Ray Harryhausen's seven-headed hydra in *Jason and the Argonauts* knocks spots off this creature), but at least the jungle locations look real enough even if this enormous snake possesses a body that isn't visible to the viewing audience. But from a Nu Image point of view, *SnakeMan* is a bit of a riot if we don't take it all that seriously.

Snakes on a Train

Asylum 2006; 91 minutes; Directors: The Mallachi Brothers; Rating: ☠☠

A young Mexican woman under the influence of a voodoo curse illegally boards a train bound for Los Angeles She hopes once there that her boyfriend's uncle can break the spell that has turned her into a human snake hatchery.

Released to coincide with *Snakes on a Plane*, Asylum's hilariously over-the-top fandango has all the appearances of a '50s Ed Wood horror flick, complete with hard-to-hear audio track (the rattling train swamps most of the dialogue), bland color, wooden acting and nauseous effects. A.J. Castro and Julia Ruiz (see if you can understand a *single* word this woman mumbles) board the train at El Paso on the U.S. border and soon she is vomiting snakes in a green jelly as Castro blows smoke (pot) into her face muttering an incantation to lift the curse, all to no avail. Naturally, the train is home to a bunch of misfits including two teenage girls cornered by a hick, child-molesting cop for trafficking drugs; a nerdy electrical engineer; three surfer dudes; an argumentative couple with their small daughter; and a camp conductor. Moments of gore include the small girl in a toilet gobbled up by a rather large serpent, passengers spewing snakes in a green/red gunk, snakes burrowing into the arms and necks of a couple of Mexican stowaways and Ruiz, suppurating wounds breaking out all over her body, slowly looking more and more like a leper victim. Every daft scene is filmed with frenetic camera action and acted hysterically by all concerned. But, in its amateur-

ish way, *Snakes on a Train* is far more fun to watch than *Snakes on a Plane*, despite its ramshackle approach. The movie saves the best bit for the corker of a climax. Ruiz transforms herself (first fangs, then darkened skin tone) into a huge reptile, eats Castro and crashes through the side of the carriage, growing to the size of Godzilla and soon swallowing the train whole, the surviving passengers leaping to safety. The monster is then thwarted by a magic charm and disappears into the heavens. After downing a few beers, fans will find the film good for a giggle. Devotees of the awful will enjoy the 90 minutes if they take the movie in the context in which it was cooked up.

Snow White: A Tale of Terror

Interscope/Polygram 1997; 100 minutes; Director: Michael Cohn; Rating: ☠☠☠

After her father remarries, a young princess is at the mercy of her evil stepmother who is determined to make the girl suffer for the loss of her stillborn child.

Not commercially screened in Britain but released on cable TV in America, Cohn's lurid take on *Snow White and the Seven Dwarfs* comes across like a Hammer/American International Gothic horror outing from the 1970s and is certainly not suitable for kiddies weaned on the Walt Disney classic. No, this is a dark, bloody fairy tale definitely for adults only. A-listers Sam Neill and Sigourney Weaver play the husband and his new wife, the ex-*Alien* actress producing a truly magnificent performance as Monica Keena's jealous stepmother,

her radiant reflection in a hidden mirror commanding her to commit all manner of vile acts in order to bring about the downfall of both the young girl and Neill's household. Filmed on location in Europe in bold colors, with striking imagery to match, this macabre take on the famous Brothers Grimm story becomes somewhat heavy-going in the second half, rescued by a storming climax when Keena goes head-to-head with Weaver. The girl plunges a knife into the mirror's unholy image, the glass explodes and Weaver ages rapidly, dying horribly under falling beams during a conflagration. The seven dwarfs here are depicted as a motley crew of pug-ugly forest dwellers (and one *is* a dwarf!) working a small mine. At the end Keena is allowed to fall for the rugged charms of Gil Bellows (one of the better-looking workers) and not wimpy doctor David Conrad, her supposed Prince Charming. Personable Neill is always good for the price of a ticket, Weaver is superb (cradling the mummified corpse of her dead infant, eyes gleaming with madness) and the overall look of the movie will please most horror buffs. However, the picture lets audiences down in one or two areas, particularly John Ottman's rather intrusive score, and the movie at times becomes a bit too much to digest in a single helping.

Solar Attack
aka: **Solar Strike**
Cinetel Films/ Reel One Entertainment 2006; 91 minutes; Director: Paul Ziller; Rating: ☠☠☠

A U.S. probe circling the sun is destroyed by a solar flare and soon Earth is under the threat of extinction from a series of mass emissions on a collision course with the planet that could ignite greenhouse gases and burn up the atmosphere.

For the first 50 minutes, *Solar Attack* moves smartly along a familiar path but with a certain amount of bravado. Earth is bombarded by fire-balls emanating from the solar emissions, a space launch is incinerated and a satellite tracking station, immobilized by a wave of flame, has to be taken out of the sky over Detroit, pieces of burning metal raining down on the population. Mark Dacascos, working at the SNEL Space Agency, has a hard time convincing his stubborn superior (Kevin Jubinville) and ex-wife Joanne Kelly that the sun is to blame for these calamities. The Russians are behind it all, states Jubinville, and nuclear subs are sent to patrol the northern oceans. So from a promising end-of-the-world disaster scenario, the movie descends into Cold War boredom as U.S. and U.S.S.R. subs have a standoff near Iceland where Dacascos, on board the Russian vessel, wants the captain to fire five missiles into the polar ice cap to quell the fiery inferno in the sky. Yes, it's *Voyage to the Bottom of the Sea* all over again, but without the big-name stars that made Irwin Allen's 1961 actioner such a huge success. After lengthy negotiations with both presidents and the U.S. sub's hot-headed captain launching torpedoes at the Russian submarine, the missiles are fired

and a colossal cloud of ice puts out the life-threatening belt of raging flame. The special effects in those first 50 minutes are first-class. What a shame that this Canadian sci-fi effort drags its heels toward the stereotyped finale. However, considering *Solar Attack*'s resources, as low-budget DVD fare goes, this isn't a lost cause and for the most part is fairly agreeable.

Something Beneath
RHI Ent./Paquin/Peace Arch 2007; 90 minutes; Director: David Winning; Rating: ☠☠

As the Cedar Gate Conference Center opens for business, a black gooey organism lurking beneath the ground embarks on a killing spree.

This mishmash of a science fiction/horror movie commences with a construction worker dying horribly as he lays pipes for the conference center. One year later, black slime oozes from those same pipes. If anyone comes into contact with it, this oily menace causes people to hallucinate, conjuring up deep-rooted phobias before they go haywire and self-destruct. First to perish, in her bathroom, is ghastly, eye-rolling Paris Hilton wannabe Brittany Scobie (thank goodness). Then heroine Natalie Brown takes a fancy to hunky priest Kevin Sorbo, who is about the only

person aware of what's happening. Various members of the cast roam around in the spacious sewers under the center, dying like flies as the vicious slime drips all over them. Brown wears an ancient Indian amulet given to her mother to ward off evil spirits, and this magic charm is tossed into the mouth of the giant Triffid-like phallic monster at the end, as it attempts to swallow her. Lumbered with a semi-jokey script, *X—The Unknown* this isn't, even if the movie's ultimate purpose is to have a dig at topical environmental matters and ecological disasters due to man's tampering with nature. There are one or two effective moments in the gloomy cavernous sewer sets as the creature strikes, but otherwise, this effort is strictly humdrum and even tiresome to watch in places.

Soul Survivors
Original Film/Lost Soul Productions 2001; 85 minutes; Director: Steve Carpenter; Rating: ☠☠

Following a fatal car crash, three friends, who may or may not have died in the accident, haunt a young girl.

Actually, the young girl (Melissa Sagemiller) *nearly* died. She spends two days on her deathbed, living an existence in limbo, being threatened by punk-type ghouls, her weedy boyfriend (is *he* dead, or isn't he?), uncaring hospital staff and drippy Luke Wilson (on leave from all those soppy rom-coms) playing a priest who apparently passed away years ago. Played out to a background of high-decibel rock music, this supernatural caper is aimed squarely at the "teenagers only" market. It packs in the clichés right up until the not-so-surprising ending, where it is revealed that excitable Sagemiller was the only survivor from the accident. She's been on the brink of death ever since, the angel-like priest attempting to save her soul from torment and damnation as her time is not yet up. Panned by the critics, *Soul Survivors* has a few of moments of promise. But as teen horror movies go, the movie is minor-league stuff, not helped by drab color photography and a cobbled-together script. It doesn't offer anything fresh in the way of thrills either.

A Sound of Thunder

Franchise Pictures/ApolloMedia 2005; 103 minutes; Director: Peter Hyams; Rating: ☠☠

In the year 2055, the wealthy can travel back in time to 65 million years B.C., hunting dinosaurs in the ultimate safari.

Adapted from a Ray Bradbury short story, *A Sound of Thunder* was an unmitigated box office disaster, costing millions but crashing dismally, critics unanimously giving it the thumbs down. Warner Bros., the main distributor, quickly withdrew their expensive embarrassment from general release. Even the presence of Oscar-winner Ben Kingsley sporting a shock of white hair (and bearing a striking similarity to Jeff Morrow's Exeter in *This Island Earth*) couldn't rescue this disaster. For anyone having the money, Kingsley's lucrative Time Safari business can transport them through a time portal in futuristic combat gear to shoot a T-Rex. The one proviso is *not* to step off the path that winds through that fake-looking jungle overlooked by an equally fake-looking volcano. Audiences would think that CGI dinosaur graphics have progressed in leaps and bounds since the days of Spielberg's *Jurassic Park*, but judging by the monster on display here, that's not so. Needless to say, a careless punter *does* step off the path, squashing a butterfly underfoot, thus breaking the link in the time continuum. The ramifications are disastrous. Earth's future is fouled up to the point of regressive extinction. Rank vegetation creeps over buildings, huge primeval trees sprout through the sidewalks, insects multiply in their millions and shock waves sweep through cities as time itself spins out of control. Hundreds of mutated monsters resembling reptilian baboons run amok. Edward Burns and Catherine McCormack, after escaping giant bats and a huge eel in a flooded subway tunnel, eventually put things right by returning to the Jurassic age through the portal and reversing the "squashed butterfly" process. Warner Bros. may well have been behind it all, but *A Sound of Thunder* has all the characteristics of an indie movie from beginning to end, in direction, acting, script, look and effects. If handled with more flair and imagination (perhaps by Asylum, Cinetel Films or Nu Image?), the film could have been a winner. Unfortunately, even the Chicago of the future *looks* like something concocted in a computer. Now if Charles H. Schneer, Ray Harryhausen or even Spielberg had been given this promising scenario to work on...

Space Fury

Greystone International 1999; 80 minutes; Director: Eli Necakov; Rating: ☠

Two American astronauts dock their space shuttle with international space station Tesla. Someone has been brainwashed by a terrorist organization to bring the station crashing down on Los Angeles, thus starting a Third World War.

Space Fury is as dull as ditchwater, the kind of Cold War/sci-fi B feature that audiences would be forced to suffer through in the 1960s, waiting for the better feature to begin. What's more, the incomparable Michael Paré gets top billing, so need we go any further? When Paré first walks on set, audiences can almost see the strings working him, becoming the human equivalent of a *Thunderbirds* puppet, and his style doesn't improve when he reverts to the "psycho-on-the-loose" in the final 20 minutes. Paré and space celebrity Tony Curtis Blondell have flown to Tesla in order to carry out some kind of scientific research. Back on Earth, a murdered prostitute found on the streets of Moscow could be one of Paré's victims (but why is never explained), and a terrorist group bent on putting a spoke into world peace negotiations could also be behind the astronaut's erratic behavior. Shuffling backwards and forwards between the space station, Star City Command Center and a summit meeting of top ranking officials, *Space Fury* encapsulates in its clapped-out framework shootings, fistfights, espionage, space technology and a *Manchurian Candidate*-type thread, failing to raise the interest level on all counts. The special effects look artificial, and the conclusion seems predictable (crazed Paré trapped on the blazing station while Blondell and Lisa Bingley escape in the shuttle). The acting is third-rate throughout. Never has 80 minutes dragged so much than in this low-budget space turkey.

Spiders

Nu Image 2000; 94 minutes; Director: Gary Jones; Rating: ☠☠☠☠☠

Because of alien DNA experimentation, mutated funnel-web spiders go on a rampage when space shuttle Solaris, housing the creatures, is hit by a meteor shower and crash-lands in the desert near a military installation.

Spiders in horror films go back a very long way, almost to the dawn of the talkies, so it comes as something as a surprise that Nu Image's contribution to the genre is a fantastic piece of entertainment, eclipsing many other, higher-budgeted "insect mutation" movies. Fair enough, it's saddled with dumb-ass dialogue and stock situations from dozens of similar "giant arachnid" efforts, but it delivers the goods. Disfigured astronauts play host to the monsters with plenty of gruesome scenes of spiders crawling out of mouths and torsos. *Spiders* features realistic CGI/animatronics effects, taut direction, decent music by Bill Wandel and a final, riotous climax that throws in an enormous spider scuttling through the crowds in Los Angeles, leaving a trail of wrecked buildings,

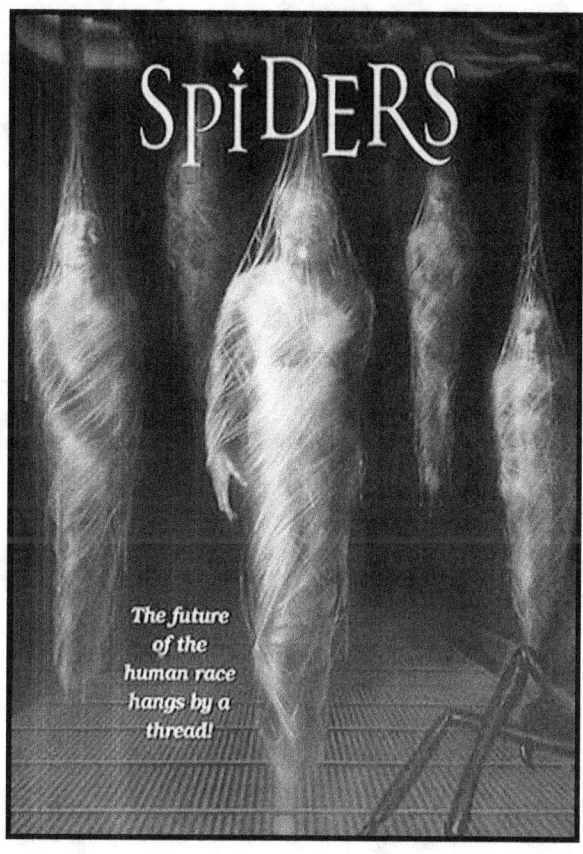

The future of the human race hangs by a thread!

chewed-up humans and crashed cars in its wake. Much of the preceding action takes place in a vast underground military complex as spirited college reporter and UFO fanatic Lana Parrilla and her two male cohorts (Nick Swarts and Oliver MacReady) break in after the space shuttle and its deadly cargo has plummeted to Earth. Certifiable FBI agent Mark Phelan (why are these FBI chiefs *always* depicted as being such hard-faced, trigger-happy bozos?) stalks the trio. The FBI's secret comes to light after innumerable hair-raising (and grisly) encounters with the huge spiders. Phelan and his men want to create a species of spider by alien methods (Project Mother-in-Law) that is totally invulnerable, a killing machine to be used in warfare. Eventually escaping the compound with friendly agent Josh Green, Swarts and MacReady already dead from spider bites, Parrilla hurries back to college for her news scoop and the scene is then set for that mind-blowing finale as a spider surfaces hideously from the odious Phelan's back, grows to the size of a bus, smashes through the college roof and stalks the streets in downtown L.A., causing mass panic. Ultimately Parrilla destroys the giant monster while suspended from a helicopter, firing a rocket launcher at the thing as it perches on the side of a building. Comparisons will be made with 2002's *Eight Legged Freaks,* but *Spiders* wins the contest hands down. *Freaks* lapses into infantilism and becomes tiresome (and far too many spiders were on display). Though fairly tongue-in-cheek, *Spiders* adopts a slightly more serious approach, emerging as a compulsive indie classic.

Spiders 2
Nu Image 2001; 96 minutes; Director: Sam Firstenberg; Rating: ☠☠☠☠

A NEW STRAIN OF TERROR IS HATCHING

Sailing to Honolulu, a young couple is washed overboard during a storm and rescued by the crew of a cargo boat that houses a sinister secret.

A sequel in name only, *Spiders 2* is a fast-paced monster caper full of leering villains, a dishy heroine, her wishy-washy husband and a batch of giant, colorful, monstrous spiders. Richard Moll breeds the spiders in the lower holds of the distinctly non-seaworthy vessel. The madman has been kidnapping occupants of other boats and keeping their bodies comatose in his laboratory, to be used as hosts for a breed of arachnid that, when combined with human DNA, will become a new species of formidable beast. For whatever purpose is never really made clear (to eradicate illnesses in man?), but that doesn't matter. It's babelicious Stephanie Niznik and hubby Greg Cromer up against not only Moll and his monsters but also batty captain Richard Quinn, the latter developing the hots for Niznik big-time. Cromer, drugged up to the eyeballs with one injection after another, is hauled off to the lab where a large mother spider implants an egg into his chest. Niznik proves a dab hand in the karate stakes by fending off the lecherous Quinn, incinerating one humongous creature and rescuing Cromer as dozens of the spiders break out of the lab and go on a rampage all over the floating deathtrap. The effects are wizard, mostly executed by the use of very large models, and a profusion of gory set pieces (spiders erupting out of ribcages, men being spiked on leg spurs) occur to satisfy those with a taste for such things. It all ends happily ever after. One of the spiders carries Moll off, Quinn dies gruesomely and a Coast Guard helicopter saves Niznik and Cromer (having been administered an antidote to kill the egg inside his body) after an aerial tussle with the biggest spider of the lot. Containing a better-than-average script, decent acting and smart direction, not to mention a tasty nude shot of Niznik in the shower, *Spiders 2* is swift-moving horror fodder that won't disappoint fans of the "giant bug" genre.

Swarm
aka: **Destination: Infestation**
Johnson Prod./Ignite/Granada 2007; 89 minutes; Director: George Mendeluk; Rating: 🐜

An army of flesh-eating, genetically mutated ants menaces the passengers on a flight from South America to Atlanta.

Off the record, *Swarm* could have been entitled *Ants on a Plane*, a poor man's *Snakes on a Plane,* already a bad enough movie without audiences having to endure a copycat version featuring ants instead of snakes. The stereotyped cast includes a gawky daughter forever rolling her eyes at her widowed mother; a college jerk complaining about lack of booze; an unhappy young married couple; and Antonio Sabato, Jr., the mandatory hunk who saves the day. These are among the less-than-captivating passengers who, 30,000 feet up, are attacked by swarms of Black Bullet ants that use an overweight tourist as a host, spewing out of his body in the thousands after *he* has unceremoniously vomited all over a fellow traveler. Gilsig just happens to be a doctor/biologist who knows all about these tiny killers, teaming up with Sabato to locate the nest and purge it with a liquid Borax solution. The two fall into each other's arms for a bit of lip action despite all the turmoil that takes place. But what is the point of featuring a life-threatening opponent that is simply exterminated by a fire extinguisher? Umpteen shots of the ants scuttling over hydraulic cables, wires, fuel pipes and ventilation grills, repeated to the point of boredom, don't add up to much in the way of suspense. And the dialogue is dreadful, for example—the Miami traffic control: "What's the emergency?" Captain: "Ants." Traffic control: "You try and diffuse the situation by using a jar of peanut butter." Denied airspace by the po-faced authorities for fear of worldwide contamination, the plane is forced to land on an abandoned military airstrip. The survivors disembark and Gilsig fires a pistol into a pool of gasoline, blowing up the plane with its cargo of ants, although a few are seen in the final shot scuttling around in the bushes. Woodenly directed and terribly acted, *Swarm* is an unappetizing blend of sci-fi and disaster movie that falls flat on its cheapjack face and is instantly forgettable fare, even for the less discriminating punter.

30,000 Leagues Under the Sea
Asylum 2007; 90 minutes; Director: Gabriel Bologna; Rating: ☠☠

A gigantic squid drags nuclear submarine USS Scotia into the depths of the Mariana Trench and the sub is deposited near a huge undersea volcano. When naval vessel Abraham Lincoln and mini-sub Argonaut 3 come to the rescue, they encounter Captain Nemo and the Nautilus.

It may declare in the credits "Based on the Jules Verne novel *20,000 Leagues Under the Sea*, but there are not a great many of Verne's visionary ideas present in Asylum's soggy underwater actioner. Megalomaniac Nemo (Sean Lawlor) is after two things—the stack of warheads on the stricken sub and the Oxygenator device on the mini-sub, a machine that can transform water into air. Using these missiles, the captain plans to wipe out his fellow man. With the Oxygenator, he plans to make habitable the lost city of Atlantis so that he and his floating

city (which is what the Nautilus resembles) can live in peace. It goes without saying that Lorenzo Lamas, commander of the Argonaut 3, has on board his ex-wife (Natalie Stone) commanding *him*, and that they and the other three crewmembers are seized and taken aboard the Nautilus for a guided tour, not to mention having to listen to the ravings of Lawlor. The underwater sequences are quite imaginative, Nemo controlling the giant squids that, on his orders, drag any threat against his kingdom down into the depths (such as another sub that gets too close to the Nautilus for comfort). But director Bologna's persistent and clumsy use of full-face close-ups in the interior scenes irritates, as does Lawlor's overripe Nemo, a combination of James Mason, Vincent Price and Dennis Hopper. The rest of the acting is just as dire. And the scientific world would surely love to know how Stone can defy the laws of physics by managing to swim outside the sub to free the snagged mini-sub propellers at a depth of several thousand feet *and* survive intact without donning a diving suit! Lawlor's madcap scheming comes unstuck in the end. The USS Scotia and its crew, with Lamas and his team on board, make it to the surface as the Argonaut 3 smashes into the Nautilus. The Oxygenator (or Bubble Box, as it is called) sets off a chain reaction with the warheads, and Nemo and his futuristic ship and dreams all go up in one almighty explosion amid the sunken ruins of Atlantis, leaving Lamas and Stone (who has filched Nemo's blueprints for the Nautilus) canoodling, even though they're divorced. Great fare for the children's matinee, perhaps, but distinctly low-grade fare for the discerning fantasy fan.

The Three Faces of Terror
Apocalypse 2004; 85 minutes; Director: Sergio Stivaletti; Rating: ☠☠☠☠

A mysterious doctor gives three strangers traveling together on train macabre foretastes of their own futures.

For any horror fan, it's not too difficult to work out the points of reference director Stivaletti uses in this Italian anthology. We see here pieces of Mario Bava's *Black Sabbath, Dr. Terror's House of Horrors* and other similar movies of the 1960s and 1970s. Three train passengers are hypnotized by staring into a golden ball, and three tales unfold. The first concerns an ornate ring taken from an Etruscan tomb. When the treasure hunter slips it on his finger, he finds that he cannot remove it and metamorphoses into a savage wolf man. The second tale is about a model who visits a clinic to have her features transformed by plastic surgery into those of a famous TV actress. The third tells of two men and a woman who camp by a forbidden lake that is home to a flesh-eating tentacled monster. As the stories conclude, we revisit the characters, showing each individual in the carriage suffering a terrible death. The ambiguous ending has the train stopping at a ghostly station, whereupon the trio, emerging from the carriage, become microscopic entities in a marble on a boy's desk hovering above the Earth, a child drawing pictures relating to the three stories. *Danger: Diabolik* himself, John Phillip Law, not only plays the doctor but also is the trio's nemesis in each of the tales. An atmospheric and unusual horror anthology with a very 1960s feel about it (ruined by atrocious dubbing, but that *was* the '60s!), containing an idiosyncratic score, a memorably frightening wolf man, an insane surgeon and a truly impressive lake monster. It all adds up to a rarely seen effort that is well worth tracking down.

Total Force

Cinequanon Pictures International 1997; 93 minutes; Director: Steve W. Kaman; Rating: ☠

A mad scientist invents a space satellite called the Neurolator that transmits a beam to a person's brain cells, transforming them into indestructible zombie-like soldiers that, after their fighting skills are no longer needed, self-destruct.

It's not often I agree with Internet reviews of movies, but whoever wrote in large letters "TOTAL TRASH" against this one has hit the nail on the head. Was the director intoxicated when he was shooting this on his handicam? Is *Total Force* a spoof of '50s and '60s sci-fi movies? For fans of the latter, they *may*, among all the idiocies on display, spot references to *Creature with the Atom Brain* and even in the way it is presented—solemn voice-over narration, infantile dialogue, uncoordinated zooms, tilts, swoops and pans, comic book acting—*The Beast of Yucca Flats*. Come to think of it, Coleman Francis' legendary 1961 clunker is a work of enduring beauty compared to this farrago, the cinematic equivalent of having one's teeth pulled. Richard Lynch plays the crazy scientist (uncannily resembling Alberto Lupo midway through his man-into-monster transformation in *Seddok, Son of Satan*) whose experimental device has one serious drawback—the recipients of the ray don't self-destruct, they simply pass their amended brainwaves onto someone else, like a virus. Very soon, a lab technician is infected. He in turn passes the force onto a bunch of partying bozos in his house and they stumble around jerkily like zombies, flattening anyone who tries to stop them. After a double-crosser offers $1 million to a terrorist group to steal the device, the authorities decide to terminate the project. Lynch goes mad, threatening to level Los Angeles with the Neurolator if *he* doesn't get paid $1 million. This culminates in Frank Stallone and his Special Forces team storming the scientist's complex and having a prolonged gun battle with the terrorists *and* a bunch of Neurolator-controlled super-beings led by a foxy female in an evening dress. It all sounds ridiculous in the extreme and it is. The direction is abominable, not helped by the insertion of garish stock footage of military/space hardware, the overall look giving new meaning to the word amateurish. Apparently there was a follow-up to this slice of outright nonsense released in 1998, *Absolute Force*, which should be avoided like the plague. *Total Force*? More like *Total Farce*!

Troglodyte
aka: **The Sea Beast**
Cinetel Films/Insight Film Studios 2008; 91 minutes; Director: Paul Ziller; Rating: ☠☠☠

A Canadian fishing community comes under attack from an amphibious monster and its legion of offspring.

Troglodyte (a misleading title on European DVD releases…this creature is certainly no cave dweller) is a less-deliberately paced version of *Loch Ness Terror*, also directed by Ziller, packed full of routine monster incidents, a hybrid of many other Cinetel Films creature-features. Nothing new appears in the way of plot, but we are treated to delightful outdoor locations, adequate acting and an imaginative assailant, one in a long line emerging from a Canadian lake! As with RHI's *Eye of the Beast*, the fish population in a Canadian lake is in sharp decline, so female scientist Camille Sullivan gets busy collecting water samples to test for pollution, even though grumpy old sea salt Brent Stait claims he saw a monstrous creature in the lake, and, according to him, it's this creature that's responsible for the missing fish. When fisherman Brandon Jay McLaren is gobbled up on a jetty, his severed arm floating to the water's surface, it's apparent to one and all that Stait's fanciful stories may be true. Ziller then takes us swiftly down the well-worn indie gore-laden monster trail without any preamble. Teens Daniel Wisler, Miriam McDonald and Christie Laing get stuck on an island, under attack from baby (but still ferocious) creatures that spit green corrosive venom at their prey. Boat's captain Corin Nemac and Sullivan go looking for the youngsters and Sheriff Gary Hudson and his posse hunt for the monsters in surrounding woodlands. Taking a cheeky leaf out of *Predator*'s book, these amphibians (boasting sinuous, ribbon-like tongues that ensnare their victims) can mask themselves in a cloak of invisibility, appearing as semi-transparent forms in the treetops. When visible, they resemble giant prehistoric fish possessing rows of needle-sharp fangs, hopping around on arms and legs. The climax takes place on board the beached decaying hulk of a derelict ship, Nemac blowing the vessel and its cargo of creatures and eggs to smithereens by igniting oxyacetylene cylinders. Distorted shots seen through the creatures' eyes are plentiful in this agile little monster flick that, like most other features from this company's stables, might have been worthy of a cinema run a few years back.

Turistas

Stone Village Pictures 2006; 94 minutes; Director: John Stockwell; Rating: ☠☠

A doctor specializing in organ removals from living bodies preys upon eight backpacking youngsters on holiday at a remote Brazilian resort.

Two things lift this loud, brash but ineffective semi-exploitation movie from one-star status to two—a stunningly staged coach crash at the beginning, the vehicle sliding over the edge of a road as the passengers make their escape. And some superb underwater cave sequences stand apart. Otherwise, all is strictly routine as Josh Duhamel, sister Olivia Wilde and friends head to a beach and lark around in the surf, flirt with the locals, get drunk and wake up robbed of their belongings with two of the group killed, at the mercy of unethical doctor Miguel Lunardi, who takes from the rich and gives to the poor—organ donations, that is! Led away from the area by kindly, sympathetic Brazilian Agles Steib, the party has to negotiate a series of partly flooded caves before reaching a house (supposedly a refuge, but in fact something more sinister) in the middle of the jungle. Lunardi turns up in a helicopter with a posse of assistants and guards, drugs all six and performs one very grisly operation (the only bit of graphic gore on display). The others, with the help of Steib, break free from their bonds, Lunardi gets beaten over the head with a rock and only three make it in the end. Dark, muddled jungle photography, in which it's impossible to make out who's doing what to whom, doesn't help. Neither does the unintelligent cast who simply go through the shrieking "let's get the hell out of here" motions. A major disappointment all round, *Turistas* quickly falls into the I-have-seen-it-all-before bracket and, despite all the pumped-up publicity at the time (it failed to get a major U.K. release) and picturesque locations, patently fails to deliver.

Tyrannosaurus Azteca
aka: **Aztec Rex**
Rigel Ent./North Shore Films 2007; 84 minutes; Director: Brian Trenchard-Smith; Rating: ☠☠☠

By offering their gods hearts torn from living bodies, Mexican savages summon their protector, a Tyrannosaurus Rex, to attack the invading Spanish conquistadors in 1521.

Listen, this is a fun movie! Any fantasy buff worth his salt can pick holes in almost every conceivable area of its 84-minute running time, but what's the point? So what if Spanish leader Cortes (Ian Ziering) has Hollywood blue eyes and speaks with an American twang (as do the rest of the cast); that the Aztec altar, with its T-Rex mosaic, is about the size of your average kiddie playhouse; that the jungles of Central America are, in fact, gloriously shot Hawaiian locations; that skimpily attired, highly desirable Indian stunner Dichen Lachman (what a figure!) sounds like a typical 21st-century TV starlet; that the script also contains many 21st-century colloquialisms; that Ziering's all-conquering troop comprises half-a-dozen men, up against half-a-dozen Indians; and that the dinosaur's feet hardly ever touch the ground. The tale goes that the marauding Spaniards meet hostile savages (and a missionary) who call upon T-Rex to do the dirty business and eliminate the invaders. Chief's daughter Lachman, engaged (against her wishes) to marry devious warrior Kalani Queypo, runs off with good Spaniard Marco Sanchez, while Ziering pinches the temple riches and heads off in the direction of the ocean with his squabbling group. Sandwiched between all this, a male Tyrannosaurus is lured into a pit and killed by the soldiers; a female comes looking for her mate, but she is shot in the eye. Sanchez dispatches the enraged beast on the Aztec altar as it gobbles up the body of Queypo, a lighted arrow shot into a gunpowder keg stripping the flesh from the beast's head. Okay, the CGI Tyrannosaurus may not be in the *Jurassic Park* class, but at least it gets to chomping up humans with relish, lumbering about with bloodstained jaws and chewed limbs dropping from its slavering mouth. One of the great scenes occurs when one soldier, realizing that the monster has ripped off his leg, holds up a crucifix in defiance as the beast hovers over him, but his severed arm is still clutching the cross, discovered later by Sanchez. Audiences didn't get to see any of *that* in Spielberg's two *Jurassic Park* movies. In the end, Ziering boards a Spanish vessel *without* the gold and Sanchez, married to Lachman, has turned native, electing to stay behind. Echoes of Mel Gibson's ultra-violent *Apocalypto* are built into the scenario to keep smiles on our faces, and who can blame Sanchez for wanting to spend the rest of his days sampling the pleasures to be had from the exotic Lachman. The final credits proclaim that, "No dinosaurs were harmed in the making of this film." That just about sums up the spirit of this lively, far-fetched but enjoyable fantasy that audiences could never, in a million years, take seriously.

Undead
Spierig Films 2003; 104 minutes; Directors: Michael and Peter Spierig; Rating: ☠☠☠☠

A meteorite shower over the tiny fishing village of Berkeley in Queensland, Australia, carries a deadly virus that turns humans into flesh-eating zombies.

Stay with this bizarre zombie flick for the first brainless 10 minutes and enjoy a feast of lousy acting, cartoon characters, gore-splatter effects, bad taste galore, non-stop profanities and a script that will make audiences hoot with laughter (sometimes unintentionally). The whole shebang finishes in a flourish with a *Close Encounters of the Third Kind*-type finale. Berkeley's local beauty queen (doe-eyed Felicity Mason), gun-toting wild man Mungo McKay and an assorted bunch of oddballs find themselves holed up in McKay's shack, under siege from mobs of zombies after rocks have rained down on the community, infecting all those that have been hit by the missiles. Cue the ravenous creatures (one of whom helps itself to a woman's brains) to be mowed down, decapitated and limbs torn off as the group tries to escape via an underground bunker. To add to all the mayhem, acid rain falls from the sky, mysterious clouds loom over the landscape, cloaked figures with glowing heads appear and first insects, then humans, are beamed skyward in tunnels of light. Choice snippets of dialogue include Mason's rival, Lisa Cunningham, spitting the following verbiage: "You may be the f—g beauty queen but I've got the voice of a friggin' angel," the dumber-than-dumb cop coming up with the old cliché: "We have ourselves a situation," as the zombies close in and McKay stating to Mason with deadpan delivery: "Are you a fighter, Fish Queen, or are you zombie food?" So grossly over-the-top that we wonder if the Spierig Brothers were taking the p—s out of all those Sam Raimi and George Romero zombie classics. *Undead* suddenly turns serious in its last 20 minutes as a gigantic circular alien craft arrives on the scene, "cleanses" the zombies so that they return to a normal human state, zooms off into the starry heavens and breaks up into a dozen separate ships, the world's media watching in awe. The very last shot depicts a tooled-up Mason keeping watch over thousands of humans infected by another outbreak of the virus (including McKay), all contained within a vast enclosure, the benevolent aliens never having returned to cleanse *them*. Wacky and off-the-wall, this cult Aussie freak-show is an unholy mixture of horror, comedy and sci-fi thrills, revitalizing to some extent the wearily familiar (and now quite stale) cycle of zombie actioners. It will have you laughing one minute and grimacing with revulsion the next. They don't come any weirder than *Undead*!

Under the Radar
Macquarie Film Corporation 2004; 95 minutes; Director: Evan Clarry; Rating: ☠☠☠

A surfer, a girl on the run and two men suffering from severe disabilities meet up with a group of sadistic, double-crossing gangsters who will stop at nothing to lay their hands on a stash of drugs.

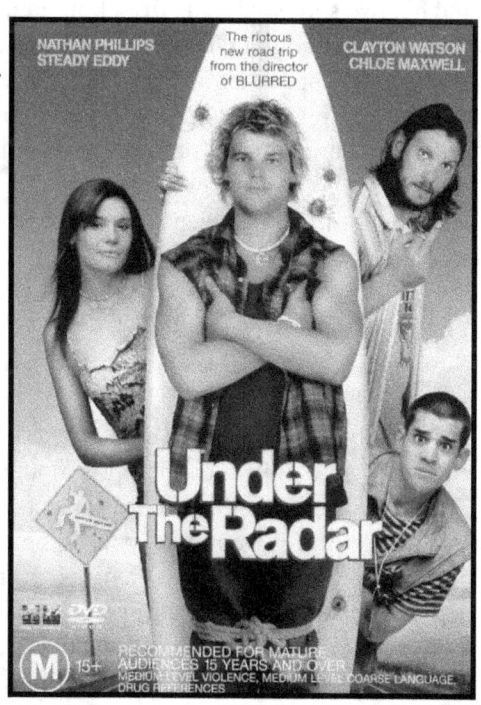

Commence in *Reservoir Dogs* fashion, mix in a *Pulp Fiction* scenario, add a dash of *Memento* and blend it all with some *Hostel*-type savagery, not forgetting a few comical elements to lighten the load. What have we got? Well, the ultimate in quirkiness, a bumbling road-to-hell Australian movie shot by a bunch of amateurs that somehow, against all the odds, works. It starts with the pursuit and capture of amnesiac Clayton Watson and surfer-dude Nathan Phillips, both tied up in a shack and brutally interrogated (orally and physically) by reptilian Robert Menzies. But Menzies suddenly dies of a heart attack, as the picture flashes backwards and forwards, explaining how these two (plus two others) found themselves in this life-threatening predicament. The authorities send Phillips to McCormack House, which specializes in the care of the severely disabled, as punishment for roughing up a Downs Syndrome kid on a beach. The surfer is subsequently allowed by the head of the house to take Watson and Steady Eddy (afflicted with cerebral palsy) to the coast for a surfing lesson. En route, they pick up Chloe Maxwell, drive onto private property and spot a couple of men disposing of some unknown object in a stream (it turns out to be a corpse). Chased by the two gun-happy thugs, we are now at the point where we came in. Night falls, and three black-clad psychos in a black van enter the scene, they being members of a rival gang looking for a hoard of drugs. The psychotic boss (Damien Garvey) is mighty angry because Maxwell, his supposed girlfriend, ran out on him and teamed up with another crook whose body, along with his associates (all with their throats cut), lies in the surrounding scrub. In a previous scene, the gangly Eddy finishes one of the gang members off with a harpoon through the throat. It's all set for a fearsome finale after Garvey and his mob terrorize Phillips and company, planning to tie up all four hostages and set them on fire. Garvey's van blows up and sends his flaming body through a window, a falling beam crushing him to death, while his two cohorts burn alive in agony. Queensland's glorious coastal scenery is encapsulated in the final scene, showing the surfer and his two screwball pals frolicking in the surf while the delectable Maxwell sunbathes. Although Phillips has the lead role, it is Watson who sparkles as the young man whose memory ceased to function properly when his parents were killed in a car accident in 1993, every incident since that date written down in a diary to remind himself of what he is doing each 15 minutes of every day. All credit must go to this low-budget sub-Tarantino enterprise that veers (uncomfortably at times) between overt violence and laughs, but ultimately emerges an offbeat winner.

The Unsaid
New Legend Media/Minds Eye Pictures 2001; 108 minutes; Director: Jim McLoughlin; Rating: ☠☠☠☠

A therapist whose son committed suicide interviews a young man traumatized by the violent death of his mother. But is the youth's outwardly calm exterior hiding something more sinister internally?

The Unsaid is a complex psychological thriller that centers on the age-old destructive curse of many a family—guilt. Andy Garcia feels guilty after his depressed teenage son gases himself inside a car. Youngster Vincent Kartheiser feels guilty after witnessing his father beating his mother to death. Garcia's headstrong daughter (Linda Cardellini) feels guilty over her unreasonable hatred toward her father. Three years after his son's suicide, Garcia, on the prompting of ex-pupil Teri Polo, meets Kartheiser in a home for wayward boys. Gently at first, he attempts to open up the boy's mind, hoping to delve into his disturbed psyche, to discover what makes him so withdrawn. In doing so, he triggers an alarming change in the youth who, sexually repelled by female contact, reverts into savagery if he is touched, murdering a girl who does just that at a rave party and erupting into uncontrolled violence near the end, almost killing ex-student Polo. Garcia, by this stage, has transferred any feelings he nursed over his dead son to substitute offspring Kartheiser (even playing handball with the kid).

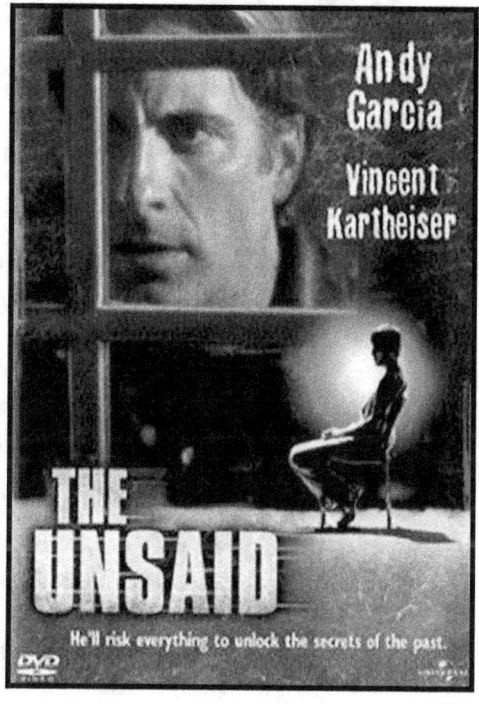

Hitchcock would have reveled in this psychoanalyst case study material years back. After all, he did it with *Spellbound* and *Marnie,* and look how these movies turned out. Director McLoughlin allows the events to unfold without resorting to horror histrionics. Rumpled-looking Garcia delivers a fine performance as the angst-ridden therapist, but it is slight, baby-faced Kartheiser who carries the day, a teenage Norman Bates in the making, placid and doe-eyed one minute, frighteningly animalistic the next. Marred somewhat by an out-of-place schmaltzy soundtrack, *The Unsaid* is a rewarding, if talkative, excursion into several people's troubled personalities, a modest psychodrama that quietly delivers the goods.

Unspeakable
Pav Films 2002; 108 minutes; Director: Thomas J. Wright; Rating: ☠

A criminologist tries to delve inside the mind of a charismatic serial killer using an experimental device termed "The Brain Polyscanner," but she finds herself bending under his all-powerful will.

Unspeakable is a classic example of one of those "non-films" mentioned in the *Simply Not Good Enough* introductory chapter and beggars the question—what was the point of it all? Was the movie adopting an anti-capital punishment stance, as witness the lengthy electric chair sequences? Was it concerned with the age-old battle of good versus evil? Was it simply a serial killer movie that, somewhere along the line, came off the rails? A complete lack of narrative

thrust, couldn't-care-less acting, Dennis Hopper turning in one of his trademark basket case performances and numerous plot themes never fully expanded upon doom the unwatchable movie from the start. After Mexican laborer Marco Rodriguez is arrested for the murder of a female cop on border patrol (her body minus the brain topples out of his car), crime doctor Dina Meyer is convinced, by using her revolutionary lie-detecting machine that can throw up images from the mind, that he is innocent. Foul-mouthed Hopper, the warden, disagrees and the man is sent to the electric chair. At the same time, prolific killer Pavan Grover is brought to Hopper's security prison-cum-hospital and Meyer decides to use the device on him, with disastrous results. Dark and handsome Grover (he has his own adoring three-woman fan club) has slain dozens of people who have sinned, and his dominant will can influence those around him. Grover forces a guard to blow his head off with a rifle, and Hopper bashes his head against glass, then rips his face to shreds, under Grover's influence. After a couple of gruesome (and farcical) attempts, Grover is finally fried in the chair but resurfaces, chasing Meyer around an abandoned warehouse with less-than-honorable intentions before she shoots him dead. Those loose plot ends include a carnivorous worm that is transmitted from Grover's head to Hopper's brain (perhaps adding a touch of creature action to boost the interest?), Meyer feeling guilty about her aborted daughter following a fling with the state governor, talk of Grover being the Antichrist and Lance Henriksen (as Meyer's boss) standing on the sidelines, his overall contribution a big fat zero. *The Silence of the Lambs* and *The Green Mile* are both obvious influences in a picture that needed a ton of cement to weld all the cracks and unrelated scenes and bring just a suggestion of cohesiveness to the proceedings. "Why did they bother" is the remark most fans will mutter after sitting through this substandard serial killer flick.

Vacancy
Screen Gems/Lieberman Company 2007; 85 minutes; Director: Nimrod Antal; Rating: ☠☠

A couple whose car breaks down on a lonely highway spends the night in a motel and find themselves the new "stars" of a snuff movie produced by the sadistic manager.

Since Hitchcock's *Psycho*, horror filmmakers have come up with umpteen variations on the motel-from-hell theme, ranging from the good to the atrocious, none measuring up to the master's legendary 1960 shocker. Is *Vacancy* any different, or worse, than the rest? Unfortunately, no. Bickering estranged couple Luke Wilson and Kate Beckinsale decide to spend the night at the Pinewood Motel, run by bespectacled Frank Whaley, after their car develops engine trouble. Settling down in the filthy surroundings of Room #4, a loud banging and knocking is heard from the adjoining room. When Wilson slips a tape into the video player, it shows various people tortured and murdered in this very same

room. Cameras are spotted hidden behind grills, windows are boarded up and a trapdoor in the bathroom allows strangers access to each room. Twenty-odd minutes into the movie, seasoned horror buffs will know exactly where *Vacancy* is headed. The couple is earmarked to feature in Whaley's next snuff production and has to escape from the motel and the masked killers employed to do the job. Director Antal orchestrates the set pieces for maximum tension as the pair scramble through a myriad of dimly lit passages, trying to telephone the police and repeatedly fending off Whaley's henchmen who are out to silence them. After Wilson is stabbed (but survives), Beckinsale hides in the ceiling and finally confronts the misogynistic manager in his office, shooting him dead following a violent tussle. She then calls the cops, cradling Wilson in her arms. It's a refreshing change to see Wilson casting off those namby-pamby roles he so loves to play in rom-coms. At least he gets to act a bit dirty in this flick. Beckinsale doesn't do much other than pout or scream, and Whaley is no Anthony Perkins, but then, who could ever be? The Saul Bass-inspired opening credits are a joy (a nod in the direction of *Psycho*, perhaps?) and at least the musical score isn't the usual deafening racket prevalent in most modern-day releases. But *Vacancy* is still seen-it-all-before fare whichever way we look at it, satisfactory in parts, derivative in others.

Visitors

Bayside Pictures/AFC 2003; 91 minutes; Director: Richard Franklin; Rating: ☠☠☠

Becalmed off the Australian coast, a young woman on a solo round-the-world voyage is prone to hallucinations, most involving her deceased parents.

Australia seems to have cornered the market in nautical mystery-cum-horror dramas (*Dead Calm*, *Open Water*), and *Visitors* is a worthy addition to the genre, featuring a bravura performance from 25-year-old Radha Mitchell as the yachtswoman confronting her innermost demons and, in the end, defeating them. This is a movie in which audiences can read into it what they will. Does Mitchell still feel guilty over the accident that paralyzed her father (Ray Barrett), even though she was only 12 at the time? What about her manic-depressive mother (Susannah York) who slashes her wrists with a razor blade? Then there's her cheating boyfriend (Dominic Purcell), carrying on behind her back with the head of the yacht sponsor company. Intercut with the highly emotive plans for the trip, she confronts the spirits of both parents, she hears footfalls, she makes love to a fantasy figure (Che Timmins), she encounters a group of modern-day pirates and she battles a colony of flesh-crawling spider crabs that scuttles over her deck. Isolation, cabin fever and the woman's nocturnal fears rise to the surface to almost mentally destroy her. Mitchell talks to the boat's cat in order to preserve her sanity. Mitchell's mother's accusing spirit terrorizes Mitchell that, in the climactic head-to-head, mother's spirit vanishes in a flood of such brilliance when her daughter declares her love for her. Sailing into the harbor thronging with TV news teams, Mitchell sends back Purcell's engagement ring in a waterproof container, turns about and heads out for new pastures. Psychological conundrums don't come more perplexing than this and audiences need to watch *Visitors* a couple of times to grasp all what's being said. The climax, sad to say, is a shade flat, but blonde Mitchell (from *Pitch Black*) handles the plot complexities without resorting to over-dramatics. Franklin's assured direction keeps the interest going. Yes, it's another winner from those moviemakers Down Under!

Vlad

Quantum/Basra 2003; 98 minutes; Director: Michael D. Sellers; Rating: ☠☠

Four students set off into the Carpathian Mountains, each preparing a thesis on Vlad the Impaler. They ultimately meet up with the real thing.

Earnest approaching dull is the best description of this lukewarm vampire tale that delves at great lengths into the legend of Vlad Drakul, forgetting along the way that this is supposed to be a horror film, not a history lesson. Billy Zane (looking as though he wished he was starring in any picture other than this one) is the students' foreign mentor, aware that one of them (it's Romanian Monica Davidescu) has in his/her possession Vlad's original medallion dating from 1447. A secret sect wants this treasure for world domination because of its supernatural powers, but the student plans to take it back to the Impaler's tomb to lay him to rest. Everything is tossed (not too constructively) into the mix once the foursome finds itself trekking through the misty woods. The resurrected Drakul (Francesco Quinn) murders Zane, and Davidescu has visions of Vlad as he was centuries ago. The students soon team up with a Van Helsing-type priest. A reincarnation of the vampire's wife (Ivana Hasperger) materializes in the woods and takes a shine to English student Nicholas Irons. Vlad abducts Kam Heskin, making her his new bride after she undergoes a blood ritual in his castle before brother Paul Popowich and Davidescu locate the vampire's tomb. Upon placing the necklace in the tomb, the Impaler crumbles into a skeleton. The final scene is of Hasperger and Irons (who was killed by the vampire) reunited in England at the time of King Arthur, he being a knight, she being the damsel in distress, thus fulfilling one of his private fantasies. One or two moments show Quinn's features contorting into those of a wolf, but overall, the movie lacks Gothic atmosphere, a strong central performance (Quinn, dark-haired and clad in black, tries hard to appear menacing but fails) and blood. All this makes the film hard going, even for lovers of vampire fodder. Hammer would have come up with a real feast here considering the material available.

Voodoo Lagoon

Matador Pictures 2006; 91 minutes; Director: Nick Cohen; Rating: ☠☠☠

Seven teenagers holidaying on a remote tropical island face torture and death at the hands of a bloodthirsty voodoo priest.

Hands up everyone. Are voodoo films frightening? Let's face it, in the long history of horror, not that many are. Classic voodoo features are few and far between, so why not juice things up a little with a dose of *Hostel*-type misery instead of all that native mumbo-jumbo? Perhaps more human suffering and less mysticism is most needed. That appears to be what this little-seen horror movie is stating loudly and clearly as yet one more in a long line of insufferable, party-on teens land on the island to the sound of heavy rock music, play a midnight game of "what are your worst fears?" and are subsequently abducted singly by craggy metal mask-wearing John Noble. With his two assistants, he drags his victims to a tree-house chamber and proceeds to inflict upon them a variety of tortures suited to their deep-rooted fears (one girl is covered in spiders; another smothered by sand; one guy has nails driven into his scrotum; another is lowered into a tank full of rats and devoured alive). Erika Haynatz, who works in the hotel, has designs on 16-year-old virgin Lincoln Lewis, wishing to make him a voodoo initiate. Noble sends out evil thought waves, causing maximum disruption among the worried group. To be honest, the film, although displaying imaginative touches here and there, is an absolute jumble of lurid images and crackpot ideas, most of which defy all logic. We are led to believe that blonde Lara Cox is Noble's daughter, in cahoots with her father who wandered destitute over the island years back and was taught the black arts by a voodoo expert. Haynatz's character oddly disappears 50 minutes into the action. After Cox has forced boyfriend Ashley Hamilton to set fire to himself on a yacht, the virginal, tousled-haired Lewis winds up the villain of the piece, having ripped out Noble's heart and taken over as voodoo boss, with Cox as his sidekick. Given a bigger budget, this could have been an off-the-wall winner. As it stands, fans of the unusual should seek it out and relish a voodoo flick that tries its best to be just a little different from all that have gone before.

War of the Worlds
Asylum 2005; 93 minutes; Director: David Michael Latt; Rating: ☠☠☠☠☠

An astronomer returning from vacation in his woodland retreat is caught up in a tidal wave of terror as extraterrestrial beings invade Earth.

Well, if George Pal could update H.G. Wells' classic novel in 1953 and Steven Spielberg spend $130 million on doing the same in 2005, why cannot independent outfit Asylum do the same on a measly $1 million budget? But on the kind of bucks that Tom Cruise probably earned tenfold in Spielberg's movie, Asylum has produced a low-budget winner that gives Paramount's flick a run for its money, remaining more faithful to the spirit of Wells' tome than certainly Spielberg managed in his over-hyped blockbuster. Yes, C. Thomas Howell as the astronomer who treks across country to locate his wife and son in the ruins of Washington hasn't Cruise's looks or box office clout, but he brings far more conviction to the role of the "hero" than the angst-ridden superstar ever did. As in the other versions, we commence in grand manner with cylinders raining from the skies, unleashing giant war machines resembling armor-plated crabs that incinerate everything with death rays, spike humans using their pointed legs and  tear people apart with pincers. Howell teams up with a soldier in an effort to find his brother (he does, the man dying, possessing only half his torso) and then a priest (Rhett Giles), who is fast losing faith in the Almighty because of all the death and destruction taking place around them. After a lengthy interlude in which Howell and Giles hide out in a ruined house near a crashed cylinder, the priest has the flesh stripped from his body by one of the aliens. Howell stabs the octopus-like creature with a hypodermic containing an experimental rabies serum and eventually locates his family in a devastated Washington, the invaders rapidly dying from the combined effects of the rabies and Earth's natural bacteria. Much like Roger Corman's post-apocalyptic thriller *Day the World Ended*, *War of the Worlds* focuses on small groups of survivors coping with the catastrophe rather than a series of expensive, slam-bang showpieces. When the effects do kick in, they're minimal but adequate. Some impressive effects sequences include black machines striding over towns, ray guns blazing; humans cocooned in green webs, ripped apart by the inquisitive aliens; a green gas swirling down the streets; and fried corpses lying in the rubble. Jake Busey appears as an over-enthusiastic military thug, and in the opening couple of minutes, Howell's wife (Tinaire Van Wyk-Loots) gets to display all in a nude shower scene intended solely to ensure audiences remain watching! But we will continue watching anyhow because of even more thoughtful and darker imagery (gritty color photography; a wordy, believable screenplay; disheveled Howell munching on raw carrots dug from the ground; sounds of sirens and explosions; the war machines moving stealthily through the night). Asylum, amazingly, has pulled it off and done more than enough justice to many of the ideas incorporated in Wells' Victorian science fiction masterpiece.

War of the Worlds 2: The Next Wave
Asylum 2008; 90 minutes; Director: C. Thomas Howell; Rating: ☠☠

Two years after the first Martian invasion, Earth is attacked by a second invading wave. But this time, a group of resistance fighters decide to do something about it.

As all cinephiles are aware, it's quite a task, even in big-budget sci-fi spectaculars, to produce a sequel that is as good as, if not better, than the original. And Asylum's follow-up to their 2005 version of Wells' classic is no exception. Howell's direction is rudimentary but adequate, the newly designed Martian fighting machines (biomechanical "walkers") are arrestingly different, and the acting (including Howell himself) is passable. However, the gaping holes in the plot and continuity do not bear close scrutiny. Frequent shots of Howell, Christopher Reid and others on board a Martian vessel, then stepping out into a street, then going back on board, then exiting on that road again, only muddy the waters. The ship's interior, festooned in what looks like red drapes (the craft is supposedly a living entity), reminds one of *Dr. Who* at its tackiest. And how come a fleet of fighters can fly beyond Earth's atmosphere, enter a wormhole (or "time hole") to reach Mars, engage in a skirmish with the Martian war machines, and then fly home without the crews suffering from all manner of intergalactic health problems (such as, for instance, breathing on Mars!)? No actual Martians are ever seen and mankind is saved when contaminated human blood is injected into the mother ship's "brain." A barrage of meaningless scientific jargon spouted by Kim Little in the Free Forces base and lab is just that, meaningless. Howell's real-life son Dashiell crops up as his screen son, disappears for much of the running time but reappears near the end. Give credit where credit's due. Haggard, unshaven Howell is fittingly morose in the main role, and the picture has a bleak end-of-the-world air about it. One or two grand sequences occur showing the walkers zapping humans from high above the rooftops, but the rushed ending cuts corners, as though everyone involved had run short of inventiveness. This is a crying shame when we consider that Asylum's 2005 movie equaled (and in many instances bettered) Spielberg's blockbuster of the same year.

Whisper
Gold Circle Films/Deacon Ent. 2007; 94 minutes; Director: Stewart Hendler; Rating: 👤👤

A couple, released from prison and destitute, becomes involved in the kidnapping of an eight-year-old boy from a wealthy family. However, they take on more than they bargained for when the lad turns out to be the spawn of the Devil.

Never given a theatrical run by Universal, *Whisper* is bereft of any spark of originality, content to rehash *The Omen* in plot, characters and supernatural situations to a point where, mentally, audiences switch off. Young Blake Woodruff plays the demon child, abducted by Josh Holloway and girlfriend Sarah Wayne Callies, in collusion with ex-partners Joel Edgerton and Michael Rooker, all acting on behalf of a mysterious "Mr. Jones." Holed up in a mountain cabin while negotiations with the police take place over the matter of ransom money, Woodruff soon exerts his devilish influence by thought whispers, conjuring up big black vicious dogs, compelling strangers to commit murder and tying the group up in knots as they begin to realize just what they have in their midst. The Devil's spawn draws a wall mural depicting those implicated in the abduction, but the figures are blacked out as they die. The trouble with the movie is that we can guess what's coming before it actually does. Edgerton falls beneath a frozen lake, Rooker suffers a heart attack, Callies shoots a cop and Holloway accidentally shoots Callies,

all on the telepathic orders of Woodruff who, in his own words, is an angel "casting for souls." The New England winter snowcapes are harshly beautiful without adding to the supposed diabolical suspense. Similarly, all those aerial shots achieve little more than admirable scenery. Okay, the surprise that Mr. Jones is in fact the child's mother (Teryl Rothery) who wanted to offload her troublesome offspring (apparently, the kiddie murdered his father and nanny), is just that, unexpected. But that is the *only* surprise as the picture heavy-handedly limps toward its predictable climax. Holloway, cornered by four snarling dogs, hurls an ax at the child (thus killing him?) and leaves the ransom money with Father Christmas as he wanders the dark, wintry streets alone. Woodruff, easily the most watchable cast member, shines as the far-from-innocent little monster in a picture that, despite the obvious low budget, is equal to 2006's expensive remake of *The Omen*. But that isn't really enough recommendation to watch, is it?

Wilderness

Ecosse Films 2006; 93 minutes; Director: Michael J. Bassett; Rating: ☠☠☠

Six brutal youths from a young offenders institution are sent to a remote island off the British coast as part of a rehabilitation program. Once on the island, a mad psychopath picks them off, one by one.

The first part of *Wilderness* has the same harsh, abrasive, in-your-face quality that hallmarked 1979's *Scum*. Within the bleak walls of Moorgate Young Offenders Institute, a timid youngster, unable to stand up to unending bullying, slashes his wrists in despair and is found dead in a pool of blood. In reprisal, the six youths sharing the same ward as the victim are sent packing to a wooded island under Sean Pertwee's strict supervision, to experience some much-needed discipline. But when Pertwee is savaged to death by a pack of dogs, the youths plus Alex Reid and her two female offenders find themselves on the run from a killer who is determined that none of them shall leave the island alive. Halfway through, the psycho's identity is easily guessable. It's unbalanced Stephen Don, the father of the lad who committed suicide. Enraged at the injustice surrounding

his son's death, he wants to severely punish all those who were responsible for tormenting the lad and anyone else who happens to get in his way, carving "I bullied Davie" on the corpses. It's a shame that the gritty Pertwee is done away with pretty quickly because his hard-nosed style of acting is the best thing in this picture. For the rest, some disturbingly gruesome and overlong death scenes (including Pertwee's) flood the screen that might upset more sensitive viewers. Non-stop swearing and general coarseness exhibited by the young cast is the norm, each character meeting a grisly fate except for Toby Kebbell and Lenora Crichlow. Following a bloody fight with an ax and knives, Kebbell fires a bolt from a crossbow into Don's face, and he and Crichlow head out to the open sea in a motorized dinghy to start a new life. A savage interpretation of *The Most Dangerous Game* designed for the modern-day horror enthusiast, *Wilderness* drags its feet toward the end, although it's still well done slasher fare. And at least these ungodly teens are a bit more down-to-earth than most!

Wind Chill
Blueprint Pictures/Section 8 Prods. 2007; 91 minutes; Director: Gregory Jacobs; Rating: ☠☠☠☠

A young student hitches a ride to her parents' home two days before Christmas, but en route, the car crashes near a bridge on a lonely stretch of road inhabited by the ghosts of people who have died there in strange and violent circumstances.

What a great pity (and a crime) *Wind Chill* was given the cold shoulder by Britain's major cinema chains, for it is a superior, methodically paced ghost movie that bravely eschews slam-bang gruesome effects. The movie is content instead to concentrate on a slow build-up of terror and suspense, with a neat twist in the tail, something hard to find these days. Emily Blunt is the young college student uncomfortably sharing a car with pale-looking driver Ashton Holmes, motoring through a bleak snowy landscape toward Delaware. Shortly after stopping for fuel at a curiously dilapidated gas station, Holmes, for some unaccountable reason, takes a shortcut and swerves to avoid an oncoming vehicle in the

dark, ploughing into a snowdrift where they become stuck in the freezing cold. As night descends, ill-defined figures make their presence felt and the pair find themselves singled out by long-dead ghouls caught up in a ghostly time loop, caused by psychotic cop Martin Donovan. This maniac slaughtered innocents by the dozen in the area years ago before crashing his police vehicle and burning to death. Cutting down on the normal ear-blasting soundtrack, director Jacobs quietly focuses our attention on the couple trapped in the car, on their growing relationship from mutual mistrust to mutual solace, throwing in several shocks along the way. The clever screenplay shrewdly works into the framework hints as to what is behind Holmes' vague manner. For audiences paying attention (particularly during the gas station sequence), it won't take long to grasp the crux of the matter. That is, from Blunt's very first meeting with her escort, it was crystal clear that Holmes was in fact one of the dead, a tormented soul burdened with reliving past events. The two main leads are fine in their respective roles, although it's perfectly obvious to any red-blooded male that sexy Blunt could eat pasty-faced Holmes for breakfast. And "Jingle Bell Rock" will never sound the same again after one sits through this picture! Full marks go to a modern-day supernatural feature that caters to the more selective viewer without recourse to blood, guts, loudness and profanity.

Wing Commander
Carousel Pictures/No Prisoners Productions 1999; 100 minutes; Director: Chris Roberts; Rating: 💀

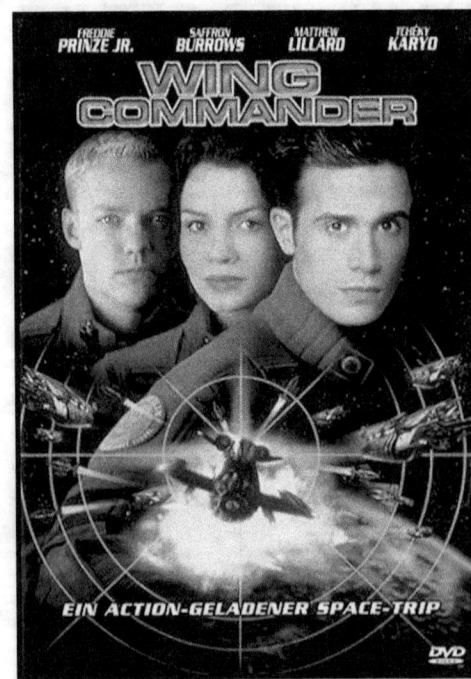

In the year 2654, Earth is under threat from the Kilrathi, an alien race amassing an armada of war machines that are hidden in the asteroid belt. But one young pilot possessing remarkable fighting skills arrives on the scene to upset their plans.

Star Wars, *The Empire Strikes Back*, *Star Trek*, *Battlestar: Galactica*, even *Starship Troopers*—these are the templates. Produced on a fraction of the budget expended on the foregoing, *Wing Commander* blatantly copies almost every space opera committed to celluloid over the past two decades and still manages to end up a crushing bore. Despite reasonable CGI effects, realistic-looking hardware and the presence of two heavyweight British actors (David Warner and David Suchet), the film falls on its face. In what basically amounts to a 100-minute video arcade game on the big screen (it was never shown commercially in England), top gun buddies Freddie Prinze, Jr. and Matthew Lillard take up employment on Tigerclaw, a massive destroyer commanded by grim-faced Suchet that is monitoring the Kilrathi battle fleet. Everyone is suspicious of Prinze, Jr. because he's "half pilgrim, half human," although the connotations behind being a "pilgrim" are never given a full explanation. Following the destruction of the Pegasus space station and the theft of the Pegasus Navcom (this device contains valuable information regarding Earth's own battle plans), equally grim-faced Admiral Warner has instructed the young pilot to deliver an encoded message to Suchet that gives the precise coordinates of the Kilrathi war fleet and a particular jump-off point in space whereby they can attack Earth at a moment's notice. From the moment Prinze Jr. and Lillard set foot on Tigerclaw, we are in the thick of numerous (and repetitive) dogfights. It all ends on a happy note. The cat-faced Kilrathi are annihilated, Earth is saved and ice maiden Saffron Burrows finally thaws, gazing into the boyish face of the young wing commander with undisguised passion. Audiences will gain much more pleasure by slotting in a DVD of any low-budget '50s or '60s sci-fi schlocker than from this uninspiring effort. The acting is poor, the soundtrack (by David Arnold and Kevin Kiner) too loud and too grandiose, the script cluttered with incomprehensible space jargon and, sin of all sins, not enough is made of the ferocious bewhiskered aliens themselves (audiences only get to see them fully 85 minutes into the picture). Heavy going and totally forgettable, *Wing Commander* might have been a novel cinematic viewing experience in 1977, but not now. This is one place audiences will *not* want to boldly go where no man has gone before.

Wyvern
Cinetel Films/Insight Film Studios 2009; 90 minutes; Director: Steven R. Monroe; Rating: ☠☠☠☠☠

In Alaska, a melting glacier unleashes a mythical, giant winged monster known as the Wyvern on the local populace.

Sober. Restrained. Subtle. Not words you would normally associate with a modern-day monster movie, yet *Wyvern* has all of those attributes. Plus many others, including strikingly photographed wooded Canadian locations, astute dialogue, telling performances from the small cast, a lack of thumping music, superb effects and a fabulous monster as the icing on the cake. Nothing much happens in the sleepy backwoods Alaskan town of Beaver Mills until the legendary Wyvern appears, fresh from a thawed glacier and hungry for human flesh. Director Monroe introduces us to the characters pretty swiftly to make way for the monster mayhem. We have Nick Chinlund, the hunky workman; Erin Karpluk, the dishy owner of the town's solitary diner, who fancies Chinlund;

Sheriff John Shaw; Colonel Don S. Davis; radio broadcaster Tinsel Korey; trapper Barry Corbin; and chubby Elaine Miles, the deputy sheriff. The local doctor is the first person to encounter the swooping creature, followed by Corbin and Davis and then the whole community as Festival Day comes under attack from the monster. The creature homes in on the barbecue-loving residents, leaving a trail of mangled corpses in its wake. Of course, none of this is exactly new. From the first sighting of a huge yellow eye peering out from fragmenting ice (reminding this reviewer of the opening shot in Universal's *The Deadly Mantis*) to the eye-catching Wyvern nosing its colorful snout into buildings and vehicles, we are treading very familiar waters indeed and it's to the filmmakers' credit that they have produced a captivating, low-budget creature-feature that involves its audience from beginning to end. Hell, we even care for the people who go up against the flying reptilian terror. How often can we say that nowadays? The poor old doc has his left arm ripped off, is dumped in the monster's nest with three eggs, then picked up again and deposited unceremoniously in the town center as bait. No wonder this poor guy doesn't make it to the final reel! On its rampage, the Wyvern smashes up cars on the main highway and even grabs hold of a helicopter, sending it spinning to the ground. Chinlund eventually defeats the Wyvern by luring it to a cliff edge in his new rig, one egg strapped to the back. As the thing alights on the truck to protect the egg, Chinlund jumps out to safety, the rig hurtling over the edge and both vehicle and monster are destroyed in a fireball. For a refreshing change, no other creature appears to upset the applecart, and Karpluk gets her man. Dedicated to Don. S. Davis who died shortly after completion of filming, *Wyvern* is a smashing little monster movie that doesn't let fans of the genre down one tiny bit.

Zombie Nation
Heidenheim Films 2004; 81 minutes; Director: Ulli Lommel; Rating: ☠

A psychotic cop tortures and murders five women, but they refuse to stay dead, and rise from the grave as zombies to gain their revenge.

The spirit of Edward D. Wood, Jr. most definitely lives on in director Lommel's hilariously awful zombie flick. Zombie films, by their very nature, aren't known for displaying much cinematic virtuosity, but none have quite plumbed the depths that *Zombie Nation* so admirably achieves. We can describe it in one single word, "Crap," or perhaps write a thesis on its less-than-finer points. Filmed on what appears to be one set which covers for a police precinct, warehouse, furniture store and a bedroom, the simplistic storyline has wooden police officer Gunther Ziegler cruising the streets, pulling women over for non-existent traffic violations, driving them to a deserted warehouse, molesting and killing them and then burying their bodies in woodland and desert locations. Seems that, as a kid, Ziegler lived in an insane asylum, after being abused by his wicked mother who repeatedly subjected him to ears, eyes and throat examinations before he was beaten with a stick. No small wonder that he's now screwed up. His partner (Brandon Dean) smells a rat, but Phil Lander replaces him and wonders why Ziegler spends so much time in that warehouse. However, the deranged cop's bosses appear to know all about his misdeeds. Unfortunately for him, Ziegler's fifth victim (Martina Bottesch) has been involved in a voodoo ritual presided over by several priestesses. When Ziegler dumps her corpse in the sea, she returns panda-eyed from her watery grave, teaming up with the other victims (Szilvi Naray-Davey, Karen Maxwell, Naidra Dawn Thomson, Victoria Ullmann) who finally eat Ziegler alive. A list of cinematic absurdities includes five zombie women, sporting shades, all fully-fledged cops at the end;

Ziegler becoming a zombie, staggering from the ocean; director Lommel, playing a doctor, examining Ziegler's teeth, uttering that immortal line from *Marathon Man*, "Is it safe?"; the zombified babes being told to eat cheeseburgers if they feel hungry; the priestesses clothed in Arabian Nights attire; Bottesch chewing on a ripped-out driver's tongue with relish; and more than enough cleavage to satisfy all *Playboy* fans. Remember, this was the man who brought us *The Raven* (2006), an equally deplorable exercise in moviemaking. *Zombie Nation* is no better, although in a perverse kind of way, it may leave a big grin on the audience's face if they can manage to weather its 81-minute running time.

If you enjoyed this book, check out our other Midnight Marquee titles. E-mail, call or write for a free catalog.

Midnight Marquee
9721 Britinay Lane
Baltimore, MD 21234
410-665-1198
mmarquee@aol.com
www.midmar.com

www.ingramcontent.com/pod-product-compliance
Lightning Source LLC
Chambersburg PA
CBHW071307110526
44591CB00010B/809